that Changed
the World

Child, if betide thou shalt thrive and thee [prosper],
Think thou was a-fostred upon thy modres knee;
Even have synde in thyn herte of tho thynges three –
Wan thou comest, whan thou art, and what shal come of thee

Middle English lyric

25 Royal Babies

that Changed the World

A History, 1066 to the Present

AMY LICENCE

AMBERLEY

for Rufus and Robin

First published 2013
This edition first published 2015

Amberley Publishing
The Hill, Stroud
Gloucestershire, GL5 4EP

www.amberley-books.com

British Library Cataloguing in Publication Data.
A catalogue record for this book is available from the British Library.

ISBN 978 1 4456 4649 7 (paperback)
ISBN 978 1 4456 1780 0 (ebook)

Typesetting and Origination by Amberley Publishing.
Printed in the UK.

Contents

Introduction

In 1555, the Spanish Ambassador at the court of Mary I, Simon Renard, wrote that 'the entire future turns on the accouchement of the queen'. He was referring to Mary's eagerly anticipated labour, nine months after the wedding that had united her to the man of her dreams, the young, handsome Catholic, Philip II. The queen had displayed all the expected signs of pregnancy, from morning sickness, cravings and the cessation of her menstrual cycle to the gradual swelling of her belly and apparent foetal movement. In April she retreated to her rooms at Hampton Court, which had been equipped with religious relics, blankets, cushions, wine, spices, medicinal herbs, thick tapestries and a cradle, as well as the retinue of women who would support and comfort her through the coming ordeal. Others were on standby to nurse, wash and rock her child.

Mary had high hopes for the future. She would bear a son, the fourth generation of the Tudor line. He would be raised a Catholic and restore England to the old ways of his mother's childhood, before the Reformation had destroyed the monasteries and burned the icons of the saints. No doubt he would inherit the sturdy build, athleticism and red-gold hair of his grandfather and the handsome looks of his father. His perfection would be the earthly manifestation of God's blessing upon Mary's marriage and reign. It would be confirmation that the difficult years of waiting; the illness, illegitimacy and submission, had all been part of His plan. Daily prayers were said for her safe delivery. All she needed now was a baby.

But no baby came. Mary I never bore a child. The pregnancy of 1555 was a false alarm, a phantom, which left her humiliated and distressed, although it did not prevent her from making exactly the same mistake two years later. It was hardly Mary's fault; the majority of her doctors confidently assured her she would soon be a mother and those who may have entertained doubts expressed them in private. When she died, heartbroken, in 1558, the throne passed to her sister. As a monarch, Mary's gynaecological failure was a scandal on a scale that few of her lowliest subjects ever experienced. Instead of the blessing the queen had hoped would validate her succession, her fertility was called into question, as it was considered commensurate with her ability to rule. It invited criticism and speculation, even insubordination, among those who interpreted it as divine disapproval or who railed against Catholicism or the novelty of female rule. A queen's duty was to be ruled by her husband and provide him with heirs. As a wife, she had failed in that primary duty; as a woman, she had rendered herself obsolete.

Sixteenth-century attitudes towards motherhood were inflexible and did not make allowances for gynaecological difficulties. Infertility, miscarriage, stillbirth and birth defects were attributed to injudicious maternal behaviour, which could encompass diet, activity levels, sexual practices, the calendar, inappropriate thoughts and wilful disobedience. Wives who proved unable to bear live children were marginalised, as Mary's own mother, Catherine of Aragon, had discovered in the 1520s and 1530s. Not even her position as an anointed queen had been able to override the incapacity of her bodily functions. A queen's ability, or inability, to reproduce would define her power and determine her country's future. This was not unique to Mary's era. Throughout history, the fertility, pregnancies and labours of queens have shaped national politics as well as their own personal relationships. Despite the differences in their circumstances, the experience of childbirth creates a maternal connection, an unbroken chain of accouchements through time, which can offer an alternative narrative of English history in contrast to that of the lives of great men. In fact, the Spanish Ambassador's comment about the future turning on a royal accouchement is pertinent to the last thousand years.

This is the story of twenty-five births. Or rather, it is twenty-five separate stories that have many elements in common but differ in their outcome, location and context. They have been selected for a range of reasons, out of the many pregnancies and deliveries undergone by women in the immediate royal circle over a millennium of British history. Quite simply, something about each of these babies has interested me, as a historian, author and mother, inspiring me to write about them. The arrivals of those others, who did not make it into this book, are just as worthy of being told but have been excluded simply as a result of the physical constraints of time and space, which necessitate a limited number. And there was a vast field to choose from. With one notable exception, all queens of childbearing age actively tried to conceive children, in the understanding that their tenure of the throne and their own personal survival could depend upon it. Elizabeth I was unique among them in disengaging her fertility from her sovereignty and choosing to rule without a husband. This unprecedented choice went so against the grain of expectation that it is still giving rise to speculation about her identity and sexuality today. These twenty-five births unite women across time, due to their shared emotions of fear and pain, love and hope, while remaining uniquely personal records of the process by which a woman has become a mother and a new life has been created.

In recounting these examples, it has often been necessary to consider the courtship, marriage and personalities of the infants' parents, as well as exploring antenatal and post-partum care, so far as it was given. Royal fathers have not been overlooked. To state the obvious, the ability of a queen to conceive was dependent upon her husband. Not just in terms of his physical health and performance, as may have been the case with Henry VIII, but in a man's historic ability to determine the nature of the marriage and the frequency of intercourse. In the early years of the nineteenth century, Queen Caroline was so despised by her husband, George IV, that he reputedly only slept with her three times, although this proved sufficient for her to conceive a daughter. Caroline's unsatisfied maternal instincts led her to adopt a number of poor children but this resulted in damaging social scandal. Although deeply in love with her husband, Albert, Queen Victoria's comment that 'all marriage is such a lottery' applies equally to physical compatibility and joint fertility.

Expectations have always been high when it comes to royal babies. From the eleventh century through to the twenty-first, these important infants have arrived under a wide variety of circumstances. While some were born in times of peace, others were delivered during episodes of civil warfare or national depression. A few became the casualties of political conflict, such as Edward of Westminster and Edward V, who both lived and died in the turbulent fifteenth century. Some were born great, as the eldest children of reigning monarchs, some achieved greatness through battle or political change, while others had greatness thrust upon them, as in the cases of younger sons Edward II, Henry VIII and Charles I. One had been destined to rule but saw that opportunity snatched away: the son of James II and Mary of Modena arrived after his parents had already lost five children, but his birth proved the catalyst for the revolution that removed his father from the throne. Rates of fertility among reigning queens also differed vastly, from those who failed to produce a single live child, such as Mary II, to the fecund Queen Charlotte, who bore George III fifteen babies over a period of twenty-one years. Others had no difficulty conceiving but sadly lost those they had borne, like Anne, whose tragic catalogue of stillbirths, miscarriages and rates of infant mortality eventually saw the Stuart throne ceded to the Hanoverians.

Royal blood was not a safeguard against the high rates of infant mortality that remained constant through this period. Some babies were lost at birth or claimed by illness in their early years; they would have been kings or queens but never made it, like the twelfth-century William, Count of Poitiers, or Prince George, who would have ruled instead of Queen Victoria. Their stories allow for a little tantalising speculation about 'what could have been'. With such a subject, it is inevitable that not all the accounts are happy ones; infant and maternal mortality were unavoidable even in the richest palaces in the land, even given all possible assistance that contemporary medicine and surgery had to offer. To only tell the stories that resulted in happy outcomes would be to give a false picture of childbirth in its historical context and the nature of royal inheritance. This book will put some of the lost heirs to the throne back on the family tree.

Rates of survival were as much determined by the times in which babies were born as by the effects of injury and illness. The study of such a wide period of history, from the arrival of the Normans, through the Middle Ages, Renaissance, Enlightenment and into the modern era, encompasses huge developments in medicine and the changing fashions in pedagogy. Some royal births were attended by the twelfth-century surgeon or the fashionable male accouchers of the eighteenth century, while some queens between these times excluded men entirely from the birth chamber. The personal circumstances of each mother are also a window into their political moment. The future Edward V was born in sanctuary, amid chaos and privation, while the luxurious chambers of Mary of Modena saw almost two thousand gather to witness her son's arrival. While Mary's child brought her kingdom to its knees, others, like Arthur and Amelia, were considered to be heralds of happier times. Therefore, the story of these babies' arrivals is also something of a history of midwifery and the narrative of Britain itself.

Not all these babies' arrivals were welcomed by their future subjects. The responses of the populace were determined by political and economic factors, with the most significant of these being the development of the media. Until early modern times, the news of a royal arrival would have been disseminated fairly slowly across the nation, by letter and word of mouth. Those in London would have learned of the birth by the firing of gunshot, before being treated to free wine, blazing bonfires and the ringing of bells. In many cases, there was already an established prejudice regarding the newcomer, shaped by the people's views of its parents. As Henry VIII's discarded wife Catherine of Aragon had been popular, the pregnancy of her replacement, Anne Boleyn, did little to relieve her poor reputation among her husband's subjects. The development of printing also facilitated communication in an unprecedented way. William Caxton had first set up a printing press in London in 1476 but, by the seventeenth century, a proliferation of small presses flooded the market with pamphlets, chapbooks and newspapers, making the spread of information more immediate. Not all of this was favourable to the monarchy. The ballads written in their honour sat alongside seditious material which was difficult to regulate, particularly once words were replaced by images. The satirical cartoons of the Georgian era allowed criticisms of the royal family to spread further, among the illiterate, but by the nineteenth century, the tide had turned again. Mass-market magazines and newspapers upheld Princess Charlotte and Queen Victoria as examples of an aspirational standard of domesticity. This era's proliferation of commemorative items, such as coins, ribbons, ceramics, spoons, fans, postcards and poems, established a custom that continues to the present day, with the recent range of royal wedding and Diamond Jubilee items. Developments in cinema, radio and television gave twentieth-century audiences unprecedented access to the private lives of their kings and queens, with millions watching and waiting as the details of pregnancies and births were related. This intense media speculation has made the lives of Elizabeth II and her offspring accessible in lurid detail, for better and worse, resulting in the breaches of privacy that have necessitated injunctions being brought against the most intrusive of the paparazzi. Nowhere is this more poignantly illustrated than in the marital career of

Princess Diana, from the first photographs taken of a shy nursery nurse to her tragic death in a Paris underpass.

The arrival of Charles and Diana's grandchild, in July 2013, was reported in the most accessible and instant of any media forum: the internet. In common with the births of the other twenty-four babies recounted in this book, Prince George's arrival excited interest, speculation and questions about the future of the monarchy. One of those questions has even prompted a change in the law of succession. In April 2013, Parliament approved a new law determining inheritance of the English throne. For three centuries, the rules of primogeniture have meant that male children automatically took precedence over females, relegating them to the status of marital bargains. The Succession to the Crown Bill removed this archaic clause, ensuring a succession unconstrained by gender.

1

Matilda, 1102

The people called her Godiva. It was an old English name, a reminder that she was a direct descendant of Edmund Ironside, the great-niece of Edward the Confessor of the Anglo-Saxon ruling house of Wessex. Some said it with affection, others as a term of derision. She knew there were barons who had disapproved when the Conqueror's son had chosen her as a bride, yet Henry I had desired her above all others. She had already changed her name once to please them, from the English Edith, which her parents gave her, to Matilda, which was more suitable for a wife of the new dynasty. Godric and Godiva, they whispered, as she and her husband passed by, with his sympathy for the old English ways and her Wessex blood. Yet names alone could not hurt; after all, she was the anointed queen. She had been crowned by Archbishop Anselm on the steps of the new Westminster Abbey and a few weeks later, at Christmas, she had taken her place beside her husband for a formal crown-wearing. That had silenced the wagging tongues for a while. Now she was expecting a child, in whose veins would flow the blood of the old kings and that of the new Normans. She was twenty-one, young and strong. She had felt the child quicken and her belly continued to expand; the physicians watched her closely and declared that all was well. This royal heir would one day unite all opposition. It would symbolise the new kingdom of England.

There were still old men who remembered the invasion of the Normans in 1066, who spoke in horror of the terrible slaughter that had taken place on a mild October day at Senlac Hill in Sussex. It had happened before her birth, but on long winter nights in the glow of the great hearth, she listened as they drank deep and talked of the slaughter. A fleet of ships had landed on the grey shingle of the south coast and disgorged thousands of men, dressed in heavy chain mail, their crossbows slung across their shoulders, hungry for blood. The English had stood strong, shoulder to shoulder, with the enemy arrows bouncing off their wall of shields. It had even seemed at one point that the Conqueror himself had fallen, when his horse was shot from under him; but in the half light, the old scarred men told how William had risen from the ground and thrown off his helmet to show his face. That was when their courage had begun to fail and their brothers were cut down around them. Harold, the English king, had been killed, struck in the eye by an arrow, so they said. When news of his defeat had spread, the Witan, an ancient folk meeting of wise men, declared his fifteen-year-old grandson, Edgar, to be king. But the Normans had marched on London and the boy had never been crowned; he had fled with his mother and sisters to the Scottish court, to the protection of Malcolm III. There, Edgar's sister had become Malcolm's bride and had borne a daughter, whom they named Edith, or Matilda, now Godiva.

It had not been an easy path to the throne. Matilda was Scottish by birth, arriving at Dunfermline in 1180. The Conqueror's wife had attended her christening, where the baby was reputed to have pulled at her headdress, and this was taken to be an omen that she would one day be queen. At the age of six she had been sent south, to be raised by her aunt Christina in the Abbey of Romsey, near Southampton, which was renowned as a seat of learning for children of the nobility. Situated on the edge of marshland, the Vikings had razed the original building to the ground but it was rebuilt in the year 1000, when Matilda's ancestors had ruled the land. She was an intelligent, devout and literary girl and, in spite of her parents' intention to make her a glorious marriage, Christina forced her to wear the 'chafing and fearful' black hood of a nun and go 'in fear' of her rod, although she would claim this was to protect her niece from the 'lust of the Normans'.[1] It had not worked: now Matilda was married to one. After Romsey, she had finished her education at Wilton Abbey in Wiltshire, where her father was reputed to have visited her and torn the veil from her face in anger. In 1093, at the age of thirteen, she was engaged to Count Alan Rufus, Lord of Richmond, a much older man, who had been born around 1040 and probably fought at the Battle of Hastings. He abandoned her on the death of her parents that same year, after which William de Warenne, 2nd Earl of Surrey, may also have been a suitor. Soon, though, a more formidable young man emerged, who was determined to make Matilda his wife.

The young Matilda left Wilton in 1093, aged thirteen, and the contemporary chronicles lost sight of her for the next seven years. It is possible that she may have been at the court of the Conqueror's eldest son, William Rufus, at Westminster and Winchester, although the lack of a queen meant there was no female establishment to shelter her. Given her education so far, it seems more likely that she entered another religious establishment of some kind or the household of a relative, which allowed her to attend state occasions. The court of the bachelor William II is reputed to have been dissolute and eccentric; he was not popular and held his conquered people in scorn. William of

Malmesbury described him as being short and pot-bellied, with red face, yellow hair and different-coloured eyes. In contrast, his vigorous and amorous younger brother, Henry, was described by the same author as being of 'middle stature' with black hair 'set back upon the forehead; his eyes mildly bright; his chest brawny; his body fleshy'. Approaching his thirtieth birthday, Henry appears to have been attracted to Matilda during these missing years, with Orderic Vitalis claiming he had 'long adored her' and William of Malmesbury confirming that Henry had 'long been attached' to her.[2] Matilda was no great beauty but, according to Malmesbury, she was 'not bad looking' and Marbod, Bishop of Rennes, praised her for not following the fashion of binding her breasts to appear slimmer or painting her face. Marbod wrote that 'no woman equal[ed]' Matilda 'in beauty of body or face', yet her modesty led her to hide 'her body, nevertheless, in a veil of loose clothing' and that she had 'fluent, honeyed speech'.[3]

These indications suggest it may have been a love match but if so, affection had followed the path of wisdom. Matilda was a judicious choice for Henry, a symbol of the continuity of the country's past, which Henry's reign would promote, as well as the personification of learning and literacy that he valued. Once credited with claiming that an 'illiterate king was a crowned ass', Henry was the first of the Norman kings to have English as his native tongue and was known as 'beauclerc' or fine scholar. Peter of Blois claimed that he was a 'young man of extreme beauty', very 'astute' and 'much better fitted' to reign than his brothers.[4] Henry was the youngest son of the Conqueror, but the first to be born after the battle of 1066 and the only one to arrive on English soil. The chronicle of John of Worcester related how he restored the law of Edward (the Confessor), removed 'evil customs' and restored peace.[5] When his unpopular brother, William Rufus, had been killed in an accident during a hunting expedition in the New Forest, Henry had hurried to Winchester and seized the crown. He was anointed in Westminster Abbey on 5 August.

It had not been easy for the couple to marry. Questions had been raised over Matilda's past and possible intention for the Church and Archbishop Anselm of Canterbury even urged her to return to her convent. However, after consulting the couple, he summoned a convocation of bishops to Salisbury, to investigate the legitimacy of their proposed union and Christina was summoned from Romsey to give evidence. Anselm was clearly impressed by Matilda, with whom he later corresponded, calling her his 'glorious queen, revered lady and dearest daughter',[6] and ruled that her education had been intended to prepare her for marriage rather than religious vows. While Christina repeated her claim that she had acted to defend her niece against abduction, Matilda described how she had stamped the hated black veil underfoot as soon as her aunt's back was turned: she used it to 'vent [her] rage and the hatred of it which boiled up in [her]'. According to the chronicler Eadmer, Matilda then swore she was free to marry, which is exactly what she did, a few days later, on 11 November 1100. Eadmer described how Anselm relayed the findings of the convocation of bishops to the crowd and invited objections. None came. Instead, the assembled witnesses called out for the marriage to be solemnised. The compiler of the Anglo-Saxon Chronicle echoed popular feeling when he wrote that she was of the 'rightful royal family of England'. In 1102, that indigenous line was to continue through Matilda and Henry's unborn child.

Yet this may not have been their first child. The exact

details of a possible previous pregnancy are unclear. It has been suggested that Matilda conceived almost immediately after the wedding and underwent labour during the summer of 1101. This is datable by the invasion of Henry's elder brother, Robert Curthose, which the Abingdon Chronicle equates with her lying-in period in July or August. The royal physician Faricius was reputedly summoned to her bedside and some sources list the arrival of a female child, Euphemia, who was either premature, stillborn or died shortly afterwards. It was recorded by Wace that Curthose called off his siege of Winchester because she was in labour there and that her difficult delivery required consultation from the best physicians in the land. John of Worcester has Curthose landing at Portsmouth around the feast of St Peter ad Vincula, on 1 August, but, frustratingly, makes no reference to the queen's pregnancies. However, the numbers do not add up. There is no doubt that Matilda bore a live daughter in 1102, whom she named after herself, but the traditional birthdate of 7 or 8 February and the arrival of an elder, stillborn sibling the previous summer are not compatible. To have arrived full term early in February, Matilda would need to have been conceived at the start of May 1101. Either the second daughter arrived later, in July 1102, or else confusion has resulted in a single pregnancy being recorded as two. If Matilda became pregnant for the first time in May 1101, it is possible she experienced complications during her first trimester and threatened to miscarry that summer, although she then went on to carry the child to term. This may have given rise to rumours that she had in fact miscarried, which were then ascribed to the period before her surviving child arrived. Just to complicate matters further, Gervase of Canterbury, in his Itinerary of Henry I, lists just one birthdate of 31 July 1101.[7]

Whatever confusion has arisen over the queen's deliveries, it is certain that she bore one live daughter, probably in February 1102. Matilda was attended by the most skilled 'leech' of the day, an Italian doctor named Faricius, whom Henry had appointed Abbot of Abingdon. Even though he was a Benedictine monk, he earned enough money from practising medicine that he was able to restore and extend the abbey buildings and treble its library, which included his own writings. William of Malmesbury notes that Faricius was learned, courteous and elegant, although his 'foreign tongue' could put him at a disadvantage, while his eulogy, written by Peter Moraunt, a monk at Malmesbury in 1140, claimed he was 'skilled in all laws which medicine teaches, he won favour from Kings for his healing gifts'. In his care of Matilda he was assisted by his fellow countryman, friend and doctor, Grimbald, who slept in the corner of Henry's bedroom and interpreted his dreams, according to John of Worcester. Doctor Grimbald is described as using urology, one of the newest fashions in Norman medical practice, where the colour of urine in glass vessels was used for diagnosis.[8] Both doctors were already known to the royal couple and were on hand through the autumn of 1101, being showered with gifts issued from London and Abingdon, suggesting continual attendance upon the queen.[9] She established herself at the royal manor of Sutton Courtenay, rather than at Winchester or London, in order to be near the abbey where Faricius was based. The manor house, 2 miles south of Abingdon in Oxfordshire, was listed as Sudtone in the Domesday Book of 1086 and was probably simply Sutton in Matilda's day, as the Courtenay family did not arrive there until 1170.

Matilda's choice of doctors pre-dates the trend for all-female delivery rooms that would emerge later in the medieval period. One twelfth-century medical text would recommend that they did not look the mother in the face, as women 'were accustomed to be shamed by that during and after birth'.[10] It is not surprising that her attendants were monks, as they were among the few people with access to the medical texts of the day as well as the body of knowledge and practice of the monastic infirmary. In comparison with modern knowledge, eleventh-century gynaecological understanding was primitive but a number of herbal texts and charms were available in English and Latin, combining Graeco-Roman, Hebrew, Greek, Arabic and Celtic traditions. Two contemporary versions have survived of an early Latin herbal, thought to have been translated into Anglo-Saxon for Alfred the Great, in which the medicinal uses of herbs are described, although these are often used as charms as much as they are made into potions and salves. Norman doctors were usually referred to as 'leeches' and their manuscripts of remedies were 'leechbooks', the most famous being the ninth-century *Medicinale Anglorum*, also known as *Bald's Leechbook*. Listing the uses of over 500 plants, the unknown author refers to two other doctors, Dun and Oxa, who had previously made him prescriptions from their 'wyrtyerd' or herb gardens. The most commonly occurring were marigolds, sunflowers, peonies, violets and gilly-flowers or wallflowers but these were often mingled with charms, invocations and Christian prayers. One contemporary remedy book, the *Lacnunga*,[11] states that mandrake roots had human limbs and that diseases were caused by flying venom and the malice of elves.[12]

The contemporary texts also contained prayers, charms and remedies for fertility and pregnancy. Even if the child Matilda bore in 1102 was the result of her first pregnancy, she had conceived fairly quickly into the marriage and would not have needed the henbane boiled in milk that the *Leechbook* recommended, or the coriander seeds bound against her left thigh, supposed to aid fertility. She may, though, especially if she had lost a first child, have followed its advice to not eat 'salt or sweet, nor drink beer, nor eat swine's flesh, nor aught fat, nor drink to drunkenness, nor fare by the way, nor ride too much on horse, lest the bairn come from her before the right time'.[13] The *Lacnunga* contained a 'recipe' for the preparation of a textual amulet on parchment, offering help in childbirth, which was written on strips of paper to be worn as a girdle about the waist. Sheets of battered tin were also inscribed with charms and runes to help women conceive while an amulet of virgin parchment bound around the thigh, above the right knee, was reputed to help with delivery.[14] As Matilda prepared for her delivery, storing up provisions and other necessaries, she may also have taken a bath or drunk the water springs dedicated to the saints. In his Life of Merlin, Geoffrey of Monmouth wrote that the hot springs of Bath were beneficial in many aspects of women's health.[15] On the advice of her leeches, Matilda may have combined Pagan cures with the holy water and Mass of Christianity. Delivering a child was a dangerous and potentially lethal business, as Matilda may already have discovered. When her labour pains began, Faricius and Grimbald would have administered to her physical and spiritual needs although her status as a queen may have relegated them to the position of observers, while experienced women handled her body as she gave birth.

Most sources agree that Matilda's daughter arrived early in February 1102. As the anticipated heir, the child uniting the old and new England, she must have hoped for a son to secure the future of the dynasty. The queen would have relied on whatever soothing effects plants and prayer could offer in the absence of pain relief, and probably remained fairly mobile and active until the end. She was more likely to have delivered kneeling or squatting, rather than lying on her back, in order to let gravity assist as much as possible. When the baby arrived, it was carefully checked and washed, then the cord was cut and tied. Outside her chamber, Henry would have been waiting to hear the news; perhaps he heard the child's first cries or else a servant hurried to inform him that mother and daughter had survived the ordeal. For Matilda, however, it was not over yet. The *Leechbook* contains remedies to assist in the delivery of the placenta; perhaps her doctors boiled old lard in water and her ladies used it to wash her vulva. They may have boiled up a mixture of ale, hollyhock or brooklime on the fire and encouraged her to drink it, as it was essential that the afterbirth be expelled in full. In the case of excessive bleeding, she would have been given burdock boiled in milk to eat and the juice to sip. The queen was young and strong; she was fortunate that there had been no complications that could not be overcome. She recovered from the birth and may have christened her daughter Adelaide, although the girl came to be known by the same name her mother had adopted, Matilda. In the veins of the infant flowed Norman and Wessex blood but the royal couple hoped that she would soon be joined by a brother, who would prove to be a great future king.

That autumn, the queen conceived again. In August 1103, she was probably at Winchester for the delivery of her son, William Adelin, whose birth appeared to guarantee that his sister's life would be one of domesticity and maternity. Another daughter, Elizabeth, was born in the later summer of 1104 but died young. For reasons unknown, their mother Matilda did not bear another live child, although their father Henry fathered at least twenty-two illegitimate babies by at least seven mistresses. Matilda played a significant role in politics, leading the king's council while he was in Normandy, issuing charters and using her own seal. A document of 1111 bears the rare surviving seal of a queen consort.[16] When Matilda died in 1118, Henry was in France. Their son William acted as regent of England in her place; however, this 'pampered Prince',[17] known as 'rex designates', would never sit on the English throne. At the age of seventeen, he drowned in the tragic sinking of the *White Ship*. Matilda had been married to Henry V, Holy Roman Emperor, then Geoffrey V of Anjou, but on her father's death returned to claim the throne, calling herself 'Lady of the English'. Her cousin, Stephen of Blois, challenged her right, as a woman, to rule even though her father had named her his heir and the resulting anarchy lasted almost twenty years. Matilda outlived Stephen and saw her eldest son ascend the throne of England as Henry II.

2

William, 1153

The twelfth-century treatise *The Art of Courtly Love* describes an imaginary French court steeped in chivalry and the romantic notions of the Provençal troubadours. In it, young men fall in love with beautiful, unattainable women and pine away in secret, longing for one kind look or word. Others set their 'princesse lointaine' (distant princess) on a pedestal and summon up the courage to declare themselves, only to be scorned or derided. Some ruin themselves attempting to complete almost impossible labours designed to prove their devotion. Courtly Love was a platonic, chaste ideal, conjuring up images of doe-eyed beauties in the neatly manicured walled gardens that can be found in medieval manuscripts and the stories of lovers told by Chaucer, Malory, de Troyes, Gower and Dante. It was a passion rife with paradoxes; a strange balance between the spiritual and the erotic, noble yet illicit, elevating and humbling.

Using a series of imaginary dialogues, the tract describes the nature of this formalised, abstracted love, this social and literary convention that existed outside the dynastic conventions of the day. The author Andreas Capellanus refers to thirty-one 'cases' of disputes between lovers, which high-born ladies would discuss and resolve as a kind of jury of romance. While the women consider love an ennobling emotion, when they are asked whether it can exist between a married couple, they reply that this is unlikely, as true love was private, difficult and unconsummated, thus 'can have no place between husband and wife'. Spouses were allowed to feel 'immoderate affection' for each other but romantic desire was ruled out of the relationship. The mysterious location of Capellanus's description has been identified as the Poitiers court of the twice-married Eleanor of Aquitaine; the author even refers to 'Queen Eleanor', resolving some of the lovers' disputes personally. Eleanor herself was the granddaughter of the 'first' troubadour poet and crusader, William IX of Aquitaine, whose poems in Provençal and Occitan are the earliest of the genre to survive. By the time Capellanus was writing his treaty, she had been Queen of France and England but, as her fictional ruling on the nature of marital love might imply, the course of her marriages had not run smoothly.

In March 1152, Eleanor was aged around thirty. Her birthdate has been estimated as between 1122 and 1124, based on the date of her first marriage. Her parents, William X of Aquitaine and Aenor de Châtellerault, had been married for a year and at their Poitou court she received an education in languages, literature, music and the arts. It was said that she was to poets what the dawn was to birds. Those poets and chroniclers of the day were in agreement about her beauty; Bernard de Ventadour, reputedly in love with her, praised her 'lovely eyes and noble countenance', while the collection of German songs *Carmina Burana* presented her as a priceless object of desire: 'that price were not too high, to have England's Queen lie close in my arms'.[1] She had been married at the age of fifteen to Louis VII of France, travelled with him on crusades and bore him two daughters. Her actions during the Second Crusade, recruiting women at the reputed tomb of St Mary Magdalene, marked her out as an Amazon, although claims that she dressed as one may have been exaggerated. A series of disasters on their campaign led to Louis and Eleanor returning home to France in separate ships, defeated on the religious and personal fronts. Amid slanderous accusations that she was conducting an affair with her uncle and fears that she would never deliver the desired son, Eleanor's marriage was annulled in March 1152, on the grounds that she and Louis were closely related in blood, being third cousins. According to the standards outlined by Capellanus, this was more of a loss in political than romantic terms. However, when she took a second husband only eight weeks later, Eleanor broke all the rules.

The ex-Queen of France had chosen to wed Louis's eighteen-year-old enemy, Henry Plantagenet, Duke of Normandy and son of Empress Matilda, who was related to her even more closely than her first husband had been. He had already been considered as a husband for Eleanor's elder daughter Marie, then aged seven, although it had been dismissed because of that very blood relation which was now overlooked. Perhaps Eleanor had already been considering Henry as a husband or lover and found an excuse to prevent the union so she could have the young man for herself. Their marriage, on 18 May 1152, had probably already been arranged before she was officially free and may have been based in physical attraction; their life together was certainly passionate and tempestuous. The young Henry's appearance was described by the Bishop of Oxford as 'square and substantial', slightly over average height with a round head 'after the Norman type' and reddish hair, cropped short. He had a fiery, lion-like face, prominent jaw, square chin, grey prominent eyes, 'a short bull neck, broad, square chest, the arms of a boxer and the legs of a horseman'.[2] Contemporary accounts agree that he was restless, always on the move, cared little for appearances and never sat down. Henry already had one illegitimate son, born in the same year as his marriage, and Eleanor had already proved that she was capable of delivering healthy children, even if they were female. That November 1152, six months after their wedding day, Eleanor was at Angers when she discovered that she was pregnant with her first child by Henry. He, though, was absorbed in the fight to regain his mother's inheritance.

The Anarchy, the name given to the civil conflict between Empress Matilda and her cousin Stephen of Blois, had been raging since the death of Henry I in 1135. Now, Louis VII united with Henry's rebellious younger brother, Geoffrey, to attack Aquitaine and King Stephen of England seized the opportunity to lay siege to castles in England that were loyal to Matilda and her son. The French attack fell apart when Louis was taken ill, so Henry crossed the Channel early in 1153, leaving his pregnant wife behind. Alone with her ladies, unsure when she would see Henry again, or what the outcome of the conflicts would be, Eleanor would have felt her child quicken that spring. As Henry sailed in terrible weather, supported only by a small troop of mercenaries, his wife must have wondered what the future held for their firstborn.

Eleanor had survived pregnancy before. With two daughters already by Louis, she knew the potential dangers of delivery but it would no longer have held, for her, the fear of the unknown. She may have been familiar with the cures recorded in the contemporary *Treatments for Women*, written by an Italian woman named Trota, recalled by history as Trotula or Chaucer's 'Dame Trot'. She was likely to have been a general practitioner who also produced *Practica*, a compilation of herbal remedies, but these were unusual in deriving from the Mediterranean, rather than from the Arabic or Graeco-Roman tradition, and were, perhaps, closer to Eleanor's Aquitanian roots. The advice given for a woman in the early stages of pregnancy was that she must not set her mind on anything she could not have, as this could occasion miscarriage. However, if she suffered from pica and desired clay, coals or chalk, she should be given beans cooked with sugar to satisfy the irrational craving. It was thought that during the first trimester, coughing, diarrhoea and dysentery could cause the foetus to be lost but that once it was 'infused' with a soul 'it adheres a little more firmly and does not slip out so quickly'.[3] Approaching the time of birth she should bathe often, to soften herself up, eat light and easily digestible food such as poultry, quince and pomegranate, and rub her belly with olive oil or the oils of violets.[4] If her feet swelled they should be rubbed with rose oil and vinegar and if she suffered from wind, a mixture of wild celery, mint, cloves, watercress, madder root, iris and sugar should be bound together with honey and consumed with wine.[5]

If she was following similar ideas to Trota's, Eleanor would have been 'led slowly about the house' as her contractions started. Gravity and motion would have assisted her delivery. She may have drunk salt water, rose water or asses' milk, or had ground summer savoury tied to her belly.[6] She may have worn a snakeskin girdle, held a magnet in her right hand, drunk ivory shavings, worn coral around her neck or consumed a potion made from 'the white stuff found in the excrement of a hawk'.[7] Later, she may endure being 'subfumigated from below', with smoke wafted into her vagina from burning fish eyes, horse hooves or cat's dung. The womb was thought to respond to sweet scents and loathe foul ones![8] Alternatively, strange mystical combinations of letters and symbols could be carved in cheese or butter for her to consume: *Treatments for Women* recommends 'sator arepo tenet opera rotas', a well-known palindromic charm, which reads the same vertically and horizontally. It can loosely be translated as 'as you sow, so shall you reap', reminding women of the original sin they committed in order to conceive. Known as a cryptogram, it dates from the Roman period and also appears as a charm for childbirth in thirteenth-century manuscripts from the Aurillac region of Auvergne, of southern central France, not too far away from Eleanor's homeland.[9] Perhaps Eleanor or her ladies used this magical formula in the middle of August 1153, as she was labouring to deliver her child.

On 17 August, Eleanor's child arrived. It was a healthy boy, whom she named William, or Guillaume, the traditional name of the dukes of Aquitaine, used by her father and grandfather. Henry was still in England. That July, he had confronted Stephen when their armies faced each other on either side of the River Thames. A peace had been reached but while Eleanor laboured, she was unaware of the strange turn of events that took place next on English soil. The very same day that she delivered William, Stephen's son and heir, Eustace, then twenty-four, died suddenly at Bury St Edmunds, reputedly of food poisoning or by choking on a dish of eels or lampreys. To the superstitious twelfth-century mind, there was a neat symmetry to this. Suddenly, the expectations of Eleanor's little boy altered. That November, Stephen and Henry signed the Treaty of Winchester, by which the king acknowledged his younger kinsman as his adopted heir, overlooking his own surviving son. Messengers hurried across the Channel. Recovering in Normandy, Eleanor learned that there was a good chance her husband, and by extension their son, would one day be King of England, while Henry received news that his boy was thriving. From shortly after his arrival then, baby William, already Count of Poitiers, was considered the future heir to the throne and he would need to be educated and trained accordingly.

Even though Stephen and Henry sealed their compact with a kiss in Winchester Cathedral, there were still factions that opposed the new succession and, amid rumoured assassination plots against him, Henry returned for a brief spell to Normandy. There, he was reunited with his wife and saw his young son for the first time. Eleanor had already completed the recommended period of post-partum recovery and had been churched, so marital relations were soon resumed. In common with the practices of the day, her son would have been handed to a wet nurse of healthy appearance and good character; Agatha, one of the women the queen employed, was later rewarded with the grant of lands and a manor. Agatha certainly nursed Eleanor's last son, John, while in 1157, Richard was suckled by a woman named Hodierna, who was the mother of Alexander of Neckham, Abbot of Cirencester.[10] Breastfeeding by noblewomen was uncommon; one famous account of Ida, or Yde, of Boulogne tells how her crying child was fed by a waiting woman while she was in Mass. On coming out and witnessing this, Ida shook her son so violently that he vomited up the milk, upon which, she continued to suckle him herself.[11] If this story is true, Ida was an exception. Without the protective effects of breastfeeding, Eleanor's fertility soon returned and that May, nine months after delivering William, she fell pregnant again. However, the future they had envisioned as a result of the Winchester Treaty was to arrive sooner rather than later. On 25 October 1154, King Stephen died of stomach complaints while staying at Dover Priory. Henry, Eleanor and their young son William were now the new royal family of England and needed to leave their Normandy home and take up residence in Westminster.

Bad weather delayed their departure until early December, by which time Eleanor was seven months pregnant. Then, they crossed the Channel safely and headed for London, arriving at the new Norman Palace and Abbey of Westminster, with its impressive Thames-side location and Great Hall, built by William Rufus. At the time of William's birth, King Stephen had added a new wing to the palace, with a series of royal apartments stretching down to the river. On their arrival though, the family found that these had been vandalised: another indicator that they were not necessarily welcome. The new king's reputation was already well known and while some of Stephen's supporters were slow to accept the new regime, they were in the minority; the Anglo-Saxon Chronicle records that 'no man durst do other than good' for fear of Henry and that he was 'received with great worship' wherever he went.[12] Many were pleased to see an end to the disorder that had characterised Stephen's reign. Eleanor must have had concerns about the kingdom her young son was to inherit. Henry of Huntingdon elaborated on the Anarchy as a time of 'universal turmoil and desolation', of terrible famine and deserted cities. England was a 'scene of calamity and sorrow, misery and oppression', with 'malicious minds' bent on causing trouble and bloodshed.[13] A strong ruler would be needed to bring the country back into line.

Henry and Eleanor were crowned in Westminster Abbey on 19 December. They passed Christmas in the palace, restoring it to cater for their new establishment and the little luxuries that Eleanor had been used to in her role as Queen of France. The household details of Henry's reign, recorded in the Little Black Book of the Exchequer and the Little Red

Book give food allowances for 40 people to eat the 'royal' diet while 150 were provided with food of middling quality and 120 were given basic fare. Eleanor's costs included payments for her favourite Rhenish wines, gold plates, incense for her chapel, furnishings for her private rooms, with their tiled floors and glazed windows, decorated with oriental carpets, cushions and silk hangings.[14] That February Eleanor bore a second son, named Henry, and in September of the following year a third, the future Richard the Lionheart. Besides Westminster, one of the most luxurious royal castles was Wallingford, which had played a significant role during the Anarchy, as a site of sieges and treaties. Gervase of Canterbury records how it was strongly fortified and held by troops 'in the flower of youth'.[15] Situated along the River Thames, it was a pleasant alternative to Westminster and it was here, during the spring of 1156, that young William, aged two, went to stay with his retinue of nurses.

Eleanor's first son never became William III, King of England. In April he suffered from a seizure and died. No other details are known; whether he was a regular sufferer of fits or if it was occasioned by a recent illness. His death as a toddler was typical of the losses suffered by mothers of the time, sudden and unexplained, with 'seizures' and fits explained by a variety of medical and superstitious causes. He was buried at Reading Abbey, with his great-grandfather Henry I. Eleanor already had two sons, so the succession was secure; she would go on to bear five more children, including an additional two boys. Initially, the death of little William did not appear to have huge dynastic implications. However, the remainder of his father's reign would be characterised by infighting between the brothers. Henry followed the Capetian practice by crowning his eldest surviving son, Henry, with whom he fell out soon after. Eleanor's marriage also turned sour and she sided with her boys against her husband, who had an infamous liaison with Rosamund Clifford, during which he considered getting a divorce. Arrested in France after supporting her son Henry's revolt, the queen spent sixteen years in prison before being released on her husband's death. She went on to rule England as regent while her favourite son, Richard, was on crusades in the Holy Lands. She also lived to see the succession of her fifth son, the disastrous King John, in 1199. If her firstborn son, William, has survived, and proved a strong king, the turmoil of his ambitious and quarrelsome brothers may have been avoided, as would the civil war of John's reign.

3

Eleanor, 1215

The castle at Gloucester was strong and well appointed, located within the gardens of St Peter's Abbey and overlooking the winding River Severn. From its windows, Queen Isabella could see the land rising greenly towards the hilly border with Wales in the west, making the country appear peaceful enough. Appearances, however, were deceptive. As she waited for the arrival of her sixth child, she could not be certain exactly who was in charge of the kingdom or what her future would be. Somewhere across the miles, men were locked in combat and the air resounded with the clash of swords on shields or bone. The last twelve months had been filled with conflict, as she and her husband, King John, fought to regain lost French territories and to subdue civil uprisings at home. According to the chroniclers of the day, the marriage was less than harmonious too. Now she was alone, as John faced his rebellious barons, and guards stood on duty outside her door. Were they there to protect her, or to prevent her from leaving?

Her child had been conceived the previous summer. They had been fighting to regain the Angevin lands in Normandy, which had been held successfully by John's father, Henry II. Their loss had left the country vulnerable to invasion so it was vital that these territories be recaptured. John had spent years amassing ships, funds and, after a long dispute, finally received the backing of the Pope. However, he lacked the backing of his own people. As they were about to leave England, many of the barons had refused to fight or to send men, so the army had largely composed of last-minute mercenaries. After an encouraging start, the king had been angered to find the Angevin nobles, on whom he should have been able to rely, as reluctant to support him as their English counterparts. The campaign had failed and John had been forced to sign a humiliating truce with Philip II of France but, when he and Isabella returned to England, they found further danger still lay ahead. The barons' lack of co-operation had deepened into dissatisfaction. Within weeks, full-scale civil war was brewing, threatening to unseat John from his throne and, ultimately, resulting in the production of one of the most influential documents ever created, the Magna Carta. That January, he held a council to facilitate peace negotiations but, by April, the barons had organised themselves into a formidable opposition. Heavily pregnant, Isabella could do little to help. Nature would soon bring her to a halt. She must put aside her fears over the country's struggles and deliver her child.

Isabella of Angoulême is one of England's most controversial medieval queens, yet her story is infrequently told and clouded by contemporary rumours. The circumstances in which she became queen, the nature of her marriage and motherhood are as contentious as her husband has proved unpopular over the intervening centuries. John had been born around 1166, making him old enough to be his young wife's father, although this was standard practice for the time and would not have raised any objections. More scandalous, though, was the end of his first marriage and the way he manoeuvred Isabella, barely out of her childhood, into his bed. While some of the worst accounts of their behaviour can be set in the context of a wider anti-John discourse, the king's actions certainly set tongues wagging.

The initial problem was that John already had a wife. When he was ten years old, he had been betrothed to Isabel of Gloucester, the great-granddaughter of Henry I, through an illegitimate line. She was only three at the time but had been made her father's sole heir, allowing John to assume rights over her lands and properties when they married in 1189. Despite the ceremony going ahead at Marlborough Castle, the Archbishop of Canterbury, Baldwin of Ford, then declared the union invalid as they were closely related as half-second cousins. John appealed to the Pope, who lifted the ban Baldwin had placed on John claiming his wife's inheritance, but, in a bizarre twist, forbade the couple from sleeping together. Whether or not they complied with this, no children were born to them and soon after the death of his brother, Richard the 'Lionheart', in April 1199, John sought an annulment. With so many older brothers, it had never seemed likely that he would sit on the English throne but, by outliving them all, he was suddenly in the position of needing to provide the country with an heir. The marriage was dissolved a few weeks after he became king, when his thoughts turned to finding a new wife.

John had already entered into negotiations for the hand of a Portuguese princess, when the succession question forced his hand in France. English law had supported his claim to the throne as the only surviving son of Henry II, while Angevin custom upheld the right of his brother Geoffrey's son, Arthur. No one had opposed John's Westminster coronation in May 1199 but, across the Channel, a double threat had arisen, threatening to tear his empire in two. King Philip was on the verge of invading Normandy, while Arthur and his ally, Hugh de Lusignan, were besieging

John's mother, Eleanor of Aquitaine, then in residence at Mirebeau Castle in the mid-west of France. Marching to liberate her, John may have had another motive entirely. Hugh de Lusignan was betrothed to Isabella, heiress of the Count of Angoulême, although the marriage itself had been delayed to take account of the bride's extreme youth. After he had captured the castle and released his mother, John killed his nephew Arthur and stole Hugh's fiancée. On 24 August 1200, John and Isabella were married at Bordeaux. Then they departed for England, where they were crowned jointly at Westminster in October.

Isabella's exact age has given historians cause for speculation. The contemporary chronicler Ralph of Coggeshall recorded upon her arrival in the country that she looked about twelve, the age at which canon law fixed the issue of consent.[1] Her parents had been married sometime between 1184 and 1191, so although she is usually recorded as aged twelve, she may actually have been slightly older or even younger. Described by many as one of the most beautiful women of the time, she may have genuinely attracted John, who was already notorious for choosing his mistresses from among the ranks of aristocratic and court wives, thereby causing further contention. Reports that the couple spent the Christmas season of 1201 at Caen, feasting and lying in bed until late, did little to dispel beliefs that Isabella's hold over John was sexual. It is interesting that she did not conceive her first child until January 1207 though, suggesting that marital relations may have begun before the onset of her puberty, supporting the theory that this had been the cause of de Lusignan's delay. Until that point, she had spent much of her time lodged with John's first wife Isabel at Winchester, reinforcing a sort of child-like dependence that implies she was still young or required looking after or watching. She bore Henry in October 1207, and conceived her next two children rapidly afterwards, with Richard born in January 1209 and Joan in July 1210. After an interval of four years, she gave birth to another daughter, Isabella, before falling pregnant again in late spring or early summer 1214, with the child she was about to bear at Gloucester.

However, Isabella's status as queen gave rise to some controversy. Much of it appears to be part of a wider anti-John rhetoric and underlines the way that unpopular women were subject to attacks on their sexuality and integrity. Early comments highlighted her physical appeal, as she supposedly detained John in bed and kept him from his duties. There was also the couple's reputed vanity, fuelled by their appearing in the ornamented clothes and furs their position demanded. Quickly and predictably, the sexual slurs encompassed other lovers. While the gifts John made to his favourite mistresses and their offspring were recorded in the royal accounts, Isabella was supposed to be above reproach in her personal conduct, to ensure the legitimacy of the future heirs to the throne. Of these unsubstantiated rumours, the worst claimed she was involved in an incestuous relationship with her half-brother, Pierre de Joigny, whose presence in England she requested during her first pregnancy. There were even reports of an illegitimate son born to the pair, as, in 1233, an Irish chronicler recorded the death of a 'Piers the Fair', reputed by local legend to be the 'son of the English Queen'. Isabella's childbearing history only allows for one possible window for the conception and delivery of an illegitimate child, assuming her five others were fathered by John. An interval of four years between the births of her third child, Joan, and the arrival of her next daughter, Isabella, would allow for the creation of the mysterious Piers. This is not impossible, if it is considered in conjunction with the accounts of the queen's incarceration, although there is no concrete evidence for an additional pregnancy or that any of her offspring were fathered by anyone other than her husband.

The queen's final baby, Eleanor, was born at Gloucester. Her mother had arrived there late in December 1214 after spending an anxious Christmas at nearby Worcester. The thirteenth-century chronicle Flores Historianum relates how John only allowed for the Nativity to be observed for a single day before he hurried away to deal with matters in London. Isabella went on to the safety of Gloucester, where she stayed until May 1215. As it is likely that she did not travel very late into her pregnancy and had allowed for a period of lying-in and, equally, did not move on again until she had physically recovered, the baby would have arrived between January and April. A record of Eleanor's first marriage in April 1224 stated that she had already reached her ninth birthday, confirming this time frame. This means she was conceived between April and July 1214 in France. After their return to England that October, John was busy with the rebels' demands while his queen's movements about the country were overseen by a bodyguard, Terric the Teuton. John wrote to him at the end of the month, as he accompanied the pregnant Isabella north, asking him to 'keep your charges well' and inform him of their 'state'.[2] This has been interpreted by some historians as sinister, supporting theories of the queen's incarceration for various crimes but, in her state of pregnancy, with the national mood so volatile, it was probably a precautionary measure. Presumably, John had not forgotten the rumours that had circulated two years earlier that Isabella had been raped and their son Richard murdered. Roger of London relates that the queen had been found guilty of witchcraft, adultery and incest, with John ordering her lovers to be strangled in her own bed and that she was locked away from around 1209. The Canterbury Chronicle says she was 'enclosed' or 'confined', which may have related to her lying-in during childbirth, although she was apparently in 'custody' after her first child arrived at Corfe Castle in 1207.

Isabella has also been accused of being a callous mother. After John's death, she returned to Angoulême, leaving her children behind in England, and rarely had contact with them after her marriage to the son of her former fiancé Hugh de Lusignan. It was common practice for the children of the aristocracy to be raised by wet nurses, in their own establishments, typically having little contact with their parents. This was often necessitated by the frequent movements of the royal household and the political and administrative demands placed on their parents. However, the tide was beginning to turn in favour of more involved parenting or, at least, the closer establishment of familial relations. Children were considered a blessing; one early herbal contained a charm for a woman who was unable to rear her own children, which presumably held greater meaning for them then than the modern translation suggests: 'Everywhere I carried for me the famous kindred doughty one, with this famous meat doughty one, so I will have it for me.'[3] This runs counter to Isabella's lack of involvement with her offspring and suggests that some parents of the day approached their role with something closer to our modern sensibilities. In 1240, Franciscan monk Bartholomeus Anglicus wrote *On the Properties of Things*, an encyclopaedic-style work partly aimed at students, which lays out a more active and involved role for parents, in this case, a father, who 'gyveth to his children, clothyng, meate and drynke, as theyr age requyreth and purchaseth londes and herytage for his children ... the more a father lovyth hys chylde, the more busyly he teacheth and chastiseth hym'. This work may not have been known in England until the 1290s, from when a Latin copy in Oxford dates, but it reflected a changing trend in pedagogical thought.[4]

Eleanor, though, was not to enjoy a relationship with her father. He was at Winchester in 1215 when his barons rebelled, attacking a string of castles before going on to seize the capital. In June he met them at Runnymede, by the Thames near Windsor, and was forced to sign the Magna Carta, which set out their rights. A year later he launched a counter-attack, but while marching south to confront the rebels he contracted dysentery and died at Newark in October 1216. Isabella left her children behind in England when she returned to Angouleme the following year and it appears the two-year-old Eleanor never saw her again. John was succeeded by his eldest son, the nine-year-old Henry III, who is depicted as a swaddled baby lying in a cradle carved with geometric patterns in the margins of Matthew Paris's *Historia Angolorum*.[5]

Alone among the children of John and Isabella, Eleanor's arrival came at a time of national chaos. Even her closest sibling, Isabella, who arrived early in 1214, was born before the disappointing failures in France that year and the uprising of the barons. As a fifth child, and a daughter, Eleanor could expect little more than to be advantageously married as soon as she was out of her childhood. She was raised under the care of her brother's regent, William Marshall, Earl of Pembroke, and betrothed to his eldest son, William, who was about twenty-five years her senior. When they were married on 23 April 1224 Eleanor was only nine, and, following the groom's death in 1231, she swore an oath of chastity before the Archbishop of Canterbury. When she was twenty-two, she broke her vow when she secretly married Simon de Montfort and went on to bear him seven children. Her husband and eldest son were killed when mounting a challenge to the throne at the Battle of Evesham in 1265, after which Eleanor fled to France, where she lived out her final decade in a nunnery.

4

Edward, 1284

It was April, a season described by Bartholomeus Anglicus as 'the time of gladnesse and of love; for in Sprynging time all thynge semeth gladde'. In the Welsh countryside, the 'erthe wexeth grene', trees burst into bud, 'medowes bring forth flowers' and the world was coming back to life: 'al thynge that semed deed in wynter and widdered, ben renewed'. The sun shone weakly down across the Menai Straits, between Caernarfon and the Isle of Anglesey, and seabirds flew up from the Irish Sea, with their hungry cries and wide, white wings.

But Eleanor could hear another noise, less harmonious, more grating. Over the past weeks, the queen had grown accustomed to the hammering of chisels against stone. The walls of her temporary bedroom were thick canvas pulled over a timber frame, hardly soundproof as the building work carried on around them. Resting her hand on her swollen belly, she wondered whether perhaps she would have been better delivering her child in the safety and comfort of another of the royal castles, but Eleanor never really regretted accompanying her husband on his travels. After all, at almost forty-three, she had already borne fifteen children and knew what to expect. She had been with him on the Crusades, delivering his babies in Palestine and Acre, in the Holy Lands. The English had been at war with the

Welsh and Edward was consolidating his recent victory by building a series of castles in order to defend his realm. This latest one, at Caernarfon, promised to be the most impressive of all, with its huge blocks of stone cut from the Anglesey quarries and timber shipped from Liverpool. As the spring days wore on and the walls grew taller, Eleanor began to feel her time was approaching.

Eleanor had been born in Castile, Spain, in 1241. She was named after her great-great grandmother, the English queen Eleanor of Aquitaine. Her marriage to Edward I had been arranged as part of a settlement over disputed lands by King Henry III of England and her half-brother. The ceremony had taken place when she was thirteen at the Cistercian monastery of Las Huelgas, founded by her grandparents, who were also laid to rest there. Her teenage husband was only two years her elder and his nickname of 'Longshanks' reflected his unusual height. His youth had proved to be a troubled one, amid rumours of insubordinate behaviour, as he struggled to decide with whom to ally. In addition, he had faced a second rebellion of the barons, although he managed to secure victory at the Battle of Evesham against Eleanor of Gloucester's second husband, Simon de Montfort. He had been absent from England on Crusade when his father died and was proclaimed king in his absence. According to Matthew of Westminster, London welcomed Edward on his return, with the streets hung with tapestry and arras, while the aldermen threw handfuls of gold and silver coins out of their windows in order to show their joy at the new king's safe return;[1] three weeks later, Eleanor had been crowned alongside her husband in Westminster Cathedral, excited at what the future would hold for her as Queen of England. The marriage also went from strength to strength: some sources suggest that genuine love developed between them over time. The pair appeared devoted to each other and Edward was unusual among medieval kings for not taking mistresses or fathering illegitimate children. Eleanor's string of pregnancies pointed to their physical closeness and, unlike previous royal parents, they appear to have taken a genuine interest in their children given the dictates of their roles.

It is difficult to untangle the exact details of Eleanor's previous pregnancies. Records of births would not be formally kept until the sixteenth century, with the introduction of parish registers. Of particular confusion are reports that she bore a stillborn daughter seven months after her marriage, when she would have been aged fourteen. If this pregnancy went to full term, the child must have been conceived in August 1254, before the wedding that November, which is not impossible. What is of surprise though, is that her next recorded conception did not take place until 1263. Then, she became pregnant with a girl, whom she named Katherine, whose arrival was first recorded in mid-June 1264 and who died that September. Katherine's birth must have taken place well before April though, to allow for the queen's next conception. The nine-year interval is unusual but it was often the case that the late onset of puberty delayed childbirth until a few years into the marriage, so perhaps the records of this first child are mistaken, or else confused with the second, Katherine. There is the possibility that the first, early, experience temporarily damaged her fertility or that other children were conceived and lost in between, although her later births are mentioned by many of the era's chroniclers.

Eleanor and Edward experienced a high rate of infant mortality, which was not uncommon at the time. By the time of her final pregnancy, at Caernarfon, they had already lost nine children. Two unnamed daughters, Katherine, Joan,

John, Henry, Juliana, Berengaria and one son had already died and, that August, she was also to lose her eleven-year-old Prince Alphonso. Over a period of twenty years, she conceived regularly. Where data about her deliveries survives, the average interval between her bearing one child and conceiving the next was eight months, although sometimes it was less than six. In one case, she gave birth to a short-lived daughter, possibly named Juliana, in Palestine, in April 1272 while on the Ninth Crusade, and fell pregnant again that July, with Joan, who was born at Acre the following April. Soon after this, an assassin attempted to kill Edward and, although he survived, this left him with a festering wound. About six months later, news arrived in the Holy Land of the death of his father, Henry III. The wound delayed their departure, but Eleanor was pregnant again by the time they left, delivering Alphonso in Bayonne, in France.

There had been a little advance in the study of pregnancy in the decades before Eleanor's Caernarfon labour, although one key figure many have been personally known to her. Perhaps the most famous doctor of the age was Peter of Spain, who had been appointed Professor of Medicine at the University of Siena and, by the 1260s, was a close associate of Teobaldo Visconti, who became Pope Gregory X in 1471. Visconti was in Acre, fighting with Edward at the time of his appointment and Peter of Spain was his personal physician. Peter himself went on to become Pope John XXI. His medical advice, based on the lectures he gave between 1246 and 1272, was aimed primarily at the poor, where he advocated that women use pepper, rue, sage and mint for conception.[2] Herbs had always been used by mothers in all stages of pregnancy. By the time of Eleanor's pregnancies, many of the old Anglo-Saxon herbals had fallen out of favour, although transcriptions of Macer's tenth-century

Latin herbal, in verse form, would continue to be produced all through the thirteenth century. If spring had arrived early, Eleanor may have sent her attendants out into the fields to look for the familiar blue faces of one of the most popular medieval flowers, the periwinkle, which was used to alleviate the cramps pregnant women suffered in their legs and could also help treat haemorrhages. Also well known at the time and later listed by Chaucer was the *Compendium Medicinae* of Gilbert the Englishman, who may have studied at Salerno. Along with herbal remedies, his work included charms, prayers and a section on pregnancy, menstruation and childbirth.

Perhaps the most significant new text of the time, though, was the *De Secretis Mulierum*, or *The Secrets of Women*, written by St Albert the Great, in the second half of the thirteenth century. It combined predictable material on the influence of the planets and gender prediction with chapters on foetal creation and development, fertility and birth. At least eighty-three copies were made of this text,[3] giving it a wide circulation and influence although some textual references, to 'brothers' and 'companions' as well as the author's theological knowledge and practice of hearing confession suggests it was initially created for use in a monastic community.[4] As with the birth of Matilda, religious figures were still the key deliverers of medicine and surgery to the aristocracy and royalty, although this knowledge was by no means their exclusive preserve. This raises the interesting question of male knowledge of the female body: even with the practical experience of attending deliveries, where exactly did authors of such texts get their detailed understanding of the workings of women's bodies, when it came to menstruation, the behaviour of the womb and the intimate symptoms of pregnancy? The *De Secretis*

Mulierum illustrates the way gynaecological knowledge was divided between the genders. The text draws on sources that are primarily philosophical, particularly the metaphysical writings of Avicenna and Averroes: in one section on giving birth, a comment is even made that 'this subject is a medical one, so is omitted here'.[5] In contrast, the female tradition was an oral one, passed down through generations of women based on their attendance at the births of their friends, neighbours and family, in villages and towns across the country. As the queen's delivery approached, she would have gathered such knowledgeable women around her, while also having male doctors to hand, in case the need for intervention and surgery should arise.

Royal business went on as usual during the construction of Caernarfon Castle, which had been begun the year before. Edward and Eleanor were present at the site during the summer of 1283, which makes it probable that their final child was conceived there. It was already a location with an impressive royal provenance, which may suggest one reason for it being chosen for construction and the imminent delivery. The building works were taking place on the site of an old Roman fort, Segontium. According to the *Flores Historianum*, a contemporary chronicle originally written at St Albans and Westminster, the body of the Roman Emperor Maximus was found there late in 1283 and reburied in the local church. Edward was pleased with this imperial connection and may have designed the angular towers and bands of different-coloured sandstone to echo the architecture of Constantinople. The works were overseen by James of Saint George, a Savoyard architect who had undertaken Edward's other building projects and was recorded as being in North Wales from 1278, while Flint, Rhuddlan, Builth and Aberystwyth castles were being constructed. The year after Eleanor's child was born at Caernarfon, James was appointed as Master of the Royal Works in Wales. His wife, Ambrosia, may have been present in Eleanor's retinue, perhaps even in attendance as she prepared for the coming ordeal.

The court had been in residence about a month before Eleanor's labour began. This represented the usual lying-in period and suggests she had a fairly accurate idea of when she had conceived and the date she should expect the child's arrival. Previously, they had been at Rhuddlan Castle, where the last piece of official paperwork was completed on 20 March. The queen was eight months pregnant when the party left, travelling west and arriving at Caernarfon before 6 April, when Edward granted the right to hold a weekly market to a local landowner.[6] He made a further grant five days later, then there is a pause in the paperwork of almost a month before the confirmation of a charter on 6 May. The king had, in fact, left for Rhuddlan Castle and during his absence, Eleanor gave birth. A son arrived safely on 25 April, the feast day of St Mark the Evangelist, which was often considered unlucky.[7] He was named Edward. The *Flores Historianum* stated that at his 'birth many rejoiced, especially the citizens of London', although the anecdote that the king presented the baby to the Welsh people as their native-speaking future ruler appears to date from after the sixteenth century. He does appear to have paid 12 shillings to feed 100 poor people and given a further £9 in alms to the Caernarfon townspeople.[8] Tradition places Edward's birth in a small first-floor room of the Eagle Tower, but the construction had only begun a few weeks before, so it is more likely that he arrived in a temporary timber-framed tent, which would have allowed a degree of privacy. The baby was given a Welsh nurse, Mary Maunsel, and attendants,[9] although later Mary would fall ill and be replaced by Alice Leygrave, 'the king's mother, who suckled him in his youth'.[10] The baby was christened there on 1 May and the Calendar Rolls suggest the queen remained there until the first week of July, so she was probably churched there too. Edward was sent from Wales to Bristol in the autumn, to join his sisters in the royal nursery.

Prince Edward would be Eleanor's last child. At almost forty-three, there is no record of her conceiving again and it is most likely that her menopause began soon afterwards. A combination of good health and luck had allowed her to survive sixteen pregnancies but, after 1284, the court accounts list frequent payments made for medicines for her use. Three years later, a letter from a member of the court referred to her suffering from a 'double quartan fever', most likely to have been malaria. Although not fatal, this may have left her weakened and susceptible to other infections. It was reputedly some sort of fever that claimed her life in November 1290, at the age of forty-nine, when her youngest child and only surviving son, Edward, was six. The king wrote of his wife, 'I loved her dearly during her lifetime ... I shall not cease to love her now that she is dead'[11] and buried her in a handsome tomb in Westminster Abbey. In her memory, he also erected the Eleanor Cross in the hamlet of Charing, outside the City of London, which would lead to the area being known today as Charing Cross. In 1593, playwright George Peele's play of Edward's life described how he had built 'a rich and stately carved cross, whereon her statue shall with glory shine'.[12] Nine years after her death he remarried, to Margaret of France, who bore him three more children, the last of whom was a girl named Eleanor.

Edward of Caernarfon became Edward II on the death of his father, in July 1307. His twenty-year reign has become notorious for the political unrest prompted by his unpopular favourites and the rumours of his supposed bisexuality. He fathered four children with his wife, Isabella of France, as well as an illegitimate son, but according to the Westminster Chronicle, his 'excessive' devotion to Piers Gaveston caused her to be 'neglected and humiliated'. Uniting with Roger Mortimer, she overthrew the king and he was forcibly deposed by Parliament in favour of his fourteen-year-old son. While Edward lived, he would prove to be a continual threat to any new regime and Isabella must have been aware that. Although she and Mortimer now had control, they had gained it by illegal means and challenges could arise to her rule, particularly if the king's cause was espoused by their enemies. Even if it could be proved that Edward had neglected his kingdom, technically, he had done nothing wrong, so he could not be tried. Parliament would have been reluctant to pronounce the death sentence on such slender grounds, or on an anointed king, so his wife and her followers may have resorted to murder. The details of Edward's end are still uncertain; he was imprisoned first in Kenilworth Castle, then at Berkeley Castle in April 1327. Despite some modern historians arguing that he escaped to Italy, he was never seen again. Chronicler and lawyer Adam Murimuth, who had served Edward, gave the cause of his death as suffocation, while the Lichfield Chronicle cited strangulation. The official record of his death cited 'natural causes' although, three years later, Isabella's lover, Roger Mortimer, was accused of his murder. The popular story that he had been impaled on a red-hot poker began to circulate in the 1330s, although it did not become widespread until much later, when all those involved were dead. It seems most likely that he was murdered but the exact method and circumstances may never be known.

5

Edward, 1330

Suspended in mid-air above a tomb in Canterbury Cathedral
are a pair of copper gauntlets, the knuckles studded and
jointed, fingertips pointing down. By contrast, the insides
are lined with doeskin, soft and pliant against the hand.
Beside them hangs an iron jousting helmet lined with
red velvet, surmounted by a leather lion, whose shaggy
mane is still visible, etched out in plaster. There is also a
scabbard, a belt and a jupon, or close-fitting tunic, in red
and blue embroidered with gold. A dark shield of poplar
wood, stuck together with sheets of linen, bears heraldic
charges made from boiled leather. Below them, the solid,
rectangular tomb was made by master mason Henry Yevele
to the specifications of its occupant, with a base of Purbeck
marble, effigy of brass and painted wood tester depicting the
Holy Trinity. The figure reclines, with his fingertips touching
in prayer. He wears a helmet, denuded of the precious
stones that once adorned it, a chain mail hood and armour
featuring the fleur-de-lis. At his feet, a French bulldog grins
up at the tourists leaning in to take photographs. If they
have not already guessed, the '*Ich dien*' (I serve) motto and
repeated three feathers motif mark this grave out as having
belonged to a Prince of Wales, another royal baby who did
not make it to the throne.[1]

Edward of Windsor, the son of Edward II and Isabella of

France, had become king on the abdication of his father in September 1327. By this time, a marriage had already been proposed for him with one of the daughters of William of Hainault, who had played a key part in the invasion by which Isabella and Roger Mortimer had effected their coup. An ambassador visiting Hainault in around 1322 described one young lady of the house as having hair 'betwixt blue-black and brown' with a 'clean-shaped' head and 'high and broad' forehead. Her eyes were 'blackish brown and deep', her nose 'smooth and even', although rather broad and flat at the tip, 'yet it is no snub nose'. Her mouth was wide, with full lips, especially the lower one, with slightly protruding lower teeth, although 'this is but little seen'. She had good proportions – 'naught [was] amiss, so far as any man could see' – and was, in all things, 'pleasant enough'.[2] This is reputed to be a description of the eight-year-old future Queen of England, Philippa, although it might equally have been that of her elder sister Margaret or her slightly younger one, Joanna. Then aged about eleven, Margaret would have been more marriageable, as well as being closer in age to Prince Edward. She went on to marry only two years after this description, to Emperor Louis IV, the 'Barbarian'. According to Froissart's Chronicle, Edward may have seen and chosen Philippa himself, on a visit to Valenciennes, when she burst into tears on his departure; historian Ian Mortimer has recently made a good case that Froissart got this anecdote from the lips of the queen herself.[3]

An agreement had been reached in 1326, when Philippa was aged somewhere between ten and fifteen. It was most likely that she had reached the age of consent, at twelve, although she was not to have her own independent household for another year at least. This may be an indicator of her age, although it is just as likely to have been a political move at the instigation of Isabella, in order to retain control over the young couple. Being second cousins, the pair required a papal dispensation, which was issued by John XXII in September 1327. A proxy marriage was conducted in Hainault on 8 October, after which the bride set out almost at once, reaching London on 22 December. This was not her final destination though, for the vacancy for the Archbishopric of Canterbury meant that the ceremony was to be conducted by the Archbishop of York, William Melton, at York Minster.[4] Edward met his bride at the gates of the city and they rode in, side by side. The wedding took place two days later on 26 January 1328. Philippa gave her husband a collection of illuminated texts on the art of kingship, including *Government of Kings*, as well as a book of statues and music, including the motets that may have been sung at the ceremony. Their first child was not conceived until September 1329, which again may be an indicator of Philippa's youth. By this time, she was aged around fifteen.

There are few written records of what pregnant women wore during the fourteenth century, although a number of images record the loose, long garments that were adopted for comfort. Most commonly, this was a loose surcoat over the top of a kirtle, although some wore single gowns gathered at the neck, such as in the 1342 *Birth of Mary* by Ambrogio Lorenzetti. An image included in a 1320s copy of *The Sermons of Maurice de Sully* depicts a pregnant woman receiving religious instruction. She lies back upon a white bed with a red pillow beneath her head and wears a long, loose gown, which covers her to wrist, neck and toe and billows out around her legs.[5] A slightly later image, in *Le Petite Heures de Jean de Berry*, dating from 1375, shows an expectant mother nearing the end of her confinement, with her standing position exhibiting her large belly to the full. She is clothed in a similar garment, with long sleeves, high neck and material trailing behind her on the floor.[6] In 1330, Philippa's servants made purchases for her of Flemish and Italian cloth and green Italian silk embroidered with griffin's heads, bought from the international fairs at St Ives and Boston. Perhaps new gowns were specially made to accommodate her increasing girth, although some manuscript images show how existing ones could be altered. The need for double layering is made clear in Rogier van der Weyden's 1445 *The Visitation of Mary*, where a pregnant woman's gown is spiral-laced at the side, allowing for it to gape open as her belly grows, exposing the clothing beneath. Philippa would certainly have required at least one new dress for her Coronation, which took place when she was five months pregnant. On 17 February 1330, she was anointed at Westminster Abbey in a move intended to secure the legitimacy of her queenship and, by extent, the inheritance of her child.

The court headed to Woodstock Palace, in Oxford, for Philippa's lying-in. It was originally a royal hunting lodge, built in 1129, with huge walls enclosing a park where lions and leopards were kept. It was reputed to have been the retreat used by Henry II and his mistress Rosamund Clifford but the existence of 'fair Rosamund's bower', scene of the lovers' trysts, and the labyrinthine garden Henry was alleged to have built for her around the lodge, are by no means certain and may owe more to romantic legend. Regardless of its past, Woodstock was a quiet, private location for the queen to pass her final weeks and deliver her first child. The court would have taken their own kitchen staff and sourced local food, abundant in the early summer, but Philippa would have been careful what she consumed.

According to the traditions of the day, eating hare's heads would produce a child with a split or hare lip, while a dish of fish heads would shape the child's mouth into a pout. The consumption of soft cheese was reputed to inhibit the growth of a male foetus's penis, while cherries, strawberries and red wine thrown in the face of an expectant mother would produce a birthmark.[7] In preparation for her ordeal, Philippa would have used culinary and medicinal herbs, in particular rosemary, which featured in Banckes's herbal, a manuscript her mother, the Countess of Hainault, sent her. Stored in the library at Trinity College, Cambridge, the text contains a note from an earlier editor, describing how the herb was unknown in England until the countess sent the plants to her daughter. Rosemary has since been associated with weddings and fertility, being affixed to the bride's hair or held as part of a bouquet and was also used as a love charm and to repel witchcraft.[8]

In the middle of June, Philippa went into labour. She may have invoked the name of St Margaret, the patron saint of childbirth or taken the advice of St Hildegard of Bingen to rub certain stones around her thighs and recite that chant 'come forth a shining person who dwells with God'. It was customary for queens to wear or hold one of the many Catholic relics that were preserved in monastic houses up and down the country. This was usually the Virgin Mary's girdle from Westminster Abbey but, as the court was absent from the capital, it could equally have been another. In 1245, Queen Eleanor, wide of Henry III, had delivered at least one of her children using the girdle of St Ailred from Rievaulx Abbey and there were plenty of others to choose from. Philippa delivered a boy on 15 June, who was carefully checked and washed, while his umbilical cord was burned in the fire. This was thought to have purgative effects, removing the evil influence that the unchurched mother and unbaptised child were prone to. Then, the little boy would have been swaddled and laid to rest in a cradle. This may have been a fairly solid, decorative piece, like that featured in an illustration of the fable of St Ambroise and the Bees, in *The Golden Legend*, a 1348 collection of saints' Lives, which depicts a splendid wooden cradle built like a tiny castle with heavy, round feet and carvings like windows.[9] Another image, this time dating from the 1360s, shows clerics and concubines standing over a red painted cradle, set on rockers, in which a child is tightly swaddled in blue robes.[10] Young Edward would have had his own team of rockers to pacify him as he slept. A painting of 1330, by Geburt Christi showed the infant Jesus wrapped in green swaddling bands, similar to the way Philippa's baby would have been constricted until he reached a year old, when he would be put into looser garments and encouraged to walk. The new prince was named Edward of Woodstock, after the location of his birth, although he would become Prince of Wales just before his thirteenth birthday and later attracted the name of the Black Prince.

The birth of a son urged the young Edward III to take political matters into his own hands. That October, he joined with Sir William Montague in an attack on Nottingham Castle, during which his mother's lover, Roger Mortimer, was arrested and taken to custody in London. Edward then proclaimed that he had taken the government of England into his own hands and Mortimer was hanged the following month. He and Philippa went on to have more children, whose descendants would fight over the crown in the Cousins' Wars, or Wars of the Roses, of the fifteenth century. The eldest, Edward of Woodstock, grew into a renowned military leader, fighting at the Battle of Crécy when he was just sixteen. He fathered a few illegitimate children before being controversially married to his cousin, the widowed Joan of Kent. She had made a secret marriage at the age of twelve before being forcibly rematched by her family; the Pope later overruled this and returned her to her first husband, whom she bore four sons. As Princess of Wales, Joan had another two sons; Edward, who died aged six, and Richard. As a figure of chivalry and a successful leader, defeating the French at Poitiers and Crécy, Edward of Woodstock appeared to have the makings of a popular King of England, much in the style of the future Henry V. However, he never made it to the throne. For the last ten years of his life, he suffered from what was probably amoebic dysentery, contracted while fighting abroad, and died in June 1376. Before he died, he specified the details of his Canterbury tomb, just as Yevele made it; all that was changed was the location. Edward had asked to be buried in the crypt, although his final resting place was the Trinity Chapel, close to the site of Becket's tomb. His father, Edward III, outlived him by a year, after which the prince's surviving son was crowned as Richard II. Edward of Woodstock was not known as the Black Prince during his lifetime. This name is first recorded in the sixteenth century and may refer to the background of his shield, which can still be seen in Canterbury Cathedral.

6

Henry, 1386

In around 1386, poet and polymath Geoffrey Chaucer was working on his collection of pilgrims' stories, *The Canterbury Tales*. Among those he described gathering at the Tabard Inn, Southwark, to walk along the North Downs route to the shrine of Thomas Becket, was a physician. This character was a 'parfit parktisour', spending hours at work on his natural 'magyk', who could speak well on the subjects of physic, surgery and astronomy. His knowledge derived from his reading of the established masters of the profession, Esculapius, Hippocrates, Galen, Avicenna, Gilbert the Englishman, Constantine and others. He was particularly skilled in diagnosing symptoms, attributing the causes of 'every malady' to the four humours that 'engendered' imbalances in the body; he could also save patients from death, 'from the pall', by studying their horoscopes. However, a hint of satire creeps in as Chaucer suggests the mutually beneficial relationship between the physician and his apothecaries, who were ready to supply him with drugs as each of them 'made oother for to wynne'. Dressed in blue and scarlet, lined with taffeta, he was cautious about spending the 'gold he gained from pestilence, for gold in physic is a fine cordial'.[1]

When heiress Mary de Bohun fell pregnant in the winter of 1385, she would probably have not consulted a physician at once. Had she been a princess or queen, Chaucer's physician is exactly the type of man she would have encountered in court circles but, although she would be the wife and mother of kings, Mary herself would never become queen. As a young woman, aged only sixteen or seventeen in 1385, she would have sought advice from her female attendants and, perhaps, her widowed mother, Joan, with whom she had continued to live until 1384 when she came of age. Equally, she may well have had a good understanding of what was happening to her body, as this was not her first pregnancy. Mary had been little more than twelve years old when she married Henry Bolingbroke, the future Henry IV, in 1380. Her brother-in-law, Thomas of Woodstock, had attempted to place her in a nunnery in order to control her inheritance but she was released by John of Gaunt, who married her to his son Henry, or Hal. Aged twelve and thirteen, the couple were considered too young to consummate the match and were kept apart, with Mary returning to live under her mother's roof. Unusually for such a young couple at the time, they defied their parents' orders and slept together, with the result that Mary became pregnant at fourteen. She delivered a son, Edward, at Monmouth Castle, in April 1382, but he died a few days after his birth. This may have prompted her and Henry to put their physical relations on hold, or their parents to be more vigilant, as Mary did not conceive again for over three years. They were permitted to live together at some point in 1484 but it was not until the middle of December 1385 that she conceived a second time.

The early years of Mary's marriage had seen a rising tide of political dissatisfaction. Her husband, Henry, was a grandson of the prolific Edward III, but his father was a fourth son, so it seemed unlikely that his descendants would ever sit on the throne. Instead, the line of descent had passed through Edward III's eldest son, Edward, the Black Prince, whose early death in 1376 had conferred the title on his only son Richard, then just ten years old. Fears arose at the time that Gaunt might attempt to seize the crown for himself and they never really went away. Four years later, the Peasants' Revolt had erupted over the imposition of the poll tax and tensions arose between peasants and landowners. Gaunt's London home, Savoy Palace, 'the fairest manor of England', had been pillaged and demolished by gunpowder. Stowe's London Chronicle recorded that, despite being told to destroy all they found within, some of the rebels found their way to the cellars, 'where they drank so much of sweet wines' that they were unable to escape when shut in 'with wood and stones, that walled up the doors', and perished.[2] French chronicler Jean de Froissart described how the fourteen-year-old king had bravely confronted the rebels, 'demanding' that the 'culpable' were exposed 'under pain of incurring his indignation forever and being considered as traitors'.[3] The rebellion was quelled but more trouble was brewing within Richard's court. The preference he gave to certain unpopular favourites, as well as disagreement over the impending war with France, caused a breach between the king and Gaunt, his uncle. By the time Mary's pregnancy was entering its final trimester, her father-in-law had sailed for Spain, ever hungry for a crown, to pursue his claim to the throne of Castile.

The young couple had made their home at Monmouth Castle and it was there that Mary spent the summer of 1386, waiting for her child to arrive. Situated in south-east Wales, it had once been an important defensive post, overlooking the River Wye and its tributary, the River Monnow. Mary prepared her chamber above the gatehouse, which had a new roof, large windows and was decorated by twelfth-century corbels of carved heads. Her ladies would have been kept busy gathering herbs, distillations of flowers, ointments, linen, candles and firewood, to ensure her comfort during the coming trial. The medieval tract *Hali Meidenhad*, actually written to deter pregnancy, described the symptoms she would have been experiencing:

> Inside your belly, a swelling in your womb which bulges you out like a water-skin, discomfort in your bowels and stitches in your side, and often painful backache; heaviness in every limb, the dragging weight of your two breasts ... your beauty is all destroyed by pallor, there is a bitter taste in your mouth and everything you eat makes you feel sick, and whatever food your stomach disdainfully receives ... it throws up again.[4]

Just like Chaucer's physician, medical practitioners still followed the Galenic belief that the body was dominated by four humours, of which an imbalance would cause illness. This concept would persist for centuries to come but some advances were being made in hygienic procedures that gave patients a better chance of survival. One of the most significant pioneers in the field was John Arderne, who had practised medicine in London and attended troops in battle during the Hundred Years' War. As far as the fourteenth-century practitioners understood cleanliness, he insisted upon it following operations and, at least, the washing of his hands prevented a measure of cross-contamination. Sadly, his ideas were not widely adopted and patients' lives would continue to be lost for centuries as a result of germs being spread by these means. Arderne also wrote a medical manual, *Opera Chirurgica*, illustrated with medicinal plants, showing techniques of treatment, pictures of operations, surgical instruments and remedies. He advocated the use of some plants for their anaesthetic and soothing qualities.[5]

The skills that such physicians could offer mothers in labour were highly prized, as rates of maternal mortality increased with complications such as breech births and unusual presentations. Male doctors were becoming increasingly absent from the birth room, though, which was evolving into an exclusively female zone. Men were summoned to carry out operations, in the event of emergency, although for many women and their children, it was already too late.

Superstitious methods were also employed by expectant mothers. Special 'eagle stones' or 'aetites' were used to assist in childbirth. A 1379 inventory of the possessions of Charles V of France included a 'holy stone', set in gold adorned with pearls, emeralds and rubies, which had been clasped by labouring women to relieve their pains. One oriental tradition ascribes to these stones the ability to emit a low wailing sound at night, in sympathy with suffering mothers and their newly arrived offspring.[6] Gemstones had long been used to relieve aches and pains of all kinds; a huge onyx, which had reputedly adorned the shrine of St Alban, was carried between the houses of aristocratic women to assist them at the time of delivery. The Italian Dame Trota, or Trotula, advised that a lodestone be clasped in the right hand while the mother wore a coral necklace. Somehow these two items were more efficient when used in conjunction.[7] Hildegard of Bingen recommended the use of jasper stones, tied to the thigh through pregnancy, then loosened and held in the hand to assist delivery and repel the Devil. A mother in the fourteenth century would also have put her trust in God, taken Mass and prayed throughout her pregnancy and labour. For Mary, the second time around, she knew what was coming.

In the first-floor room of the tower above Monmouth Castle's gatehouse, Mary's women lit a huge fire. Warmth was considered beneficial to the labouring body, to open and relax the limbs and joints, as well as providing a good temperature for the baby's comfort and water for washing. While the best coverlets were laid on the bed, Mary would probably have delivered her child in a squatting or sitting position, sometimes pulling herself up on sheets or ropes hung from the rafters. A manuscript image of the birth of twins Esau and Jacob, by François Maitre in around 1475, depicts just this, with a mother standing, holding the two ends of a sheet draped around the top of a wooden chair. One woman holds her under the arms, a second is seated behind her, to pull out the child, while a third cares for the older twin.[8] Mindful of her first experience of motherhood, Mary awaited the onset of her labour pains through the first two weeks of September. Wise or experienced women may also have been summoned from the local area, whose knowledge of the female body and the use of medicinal herbs had been passed down through generations of oral tradition. It was not uncommon for a mother to lose a first child, particularly when she had been as young as fourteen, so extra special care may have been taken in 1386. Finally, Mary's waters broke. This probably happened on the night of 15 September, with her son arriving the next day. She called him Henry, after his father. Evidence for the baby's birthdate was only committed to paper retrospectively, after he had become king. This gives his place of birth, the day and time: Monmouth Castle, on 16 September at 11.22 a.m.

Henry was not born to be king. His grandfather was Edward III but, as the son of a third surviving son, he was simply plain Hal of Monmouth. Mary would bear five more children and die while delivering the fifth in 1394, aged about twenty-six. Her father-in-law, John of Gaunt, would die in February 1399. Neither lived long enough to see the political climate completely change and propel Henry onto the throne. Richard II's marriage to Anne of Bohemia had proved childless. Richard was cultured and intelligent, placing poetry and art at the heart of his chivalric court, with both he and John of Gaunt being patrons of Geoffrey Chaucer. From the late 1380s, the period of Henry's birth, the tone of his reign changed, being considered increasingly 'tyrannical' after he moved ruthlessly to execute his enemies and preserve his absolutism. Later historians have suggested that Richard suffered from a range of conditions, from narcissism to full blown schizophrenia. In the summer of 1399, he was overthrown by Henry Bolingbroke and his abdication was accepted by Parliament that September. Richard was imprisoned in Pontefract Castle, where he died early in 1400. The thirteen-year-old Henry of Monmouth became Prince of Wales and, on his father's death in 1413, succeeded to the throne as Henry V.

7

Edward, 1453

With her head bowed, she entered the cathedral. Incense hung in the air, mingling with the dust motes as the light streamed down through the stained glass windows. The shrine of the martyred Archbishop of Canterbury, Thomas à Becket, had been drawing pilgrims for centuries, praying for cures, forgiveness, good health and fortune among a multitude of other things. It had long been popular with royalty too and the young Queen Margaret was hoping that the saint would intercede for her with God and grant her wishes for a child.

The approach to the famous tomb was described in 1512 by Erasmus, guiding supplicants through different areas of the building in a long build-up to their first glimpse of the actual tomb. In the crypt, Becket's skull, with the top sliced off, was encased in silver, with a small space left open allowing pilgrims to kiss his forehead. Beside it hung the hair shirt, girdles and bandages he was accustomed to wear to 'subdue his flesh'. As a queen, Margaret would also have had privileged access to the shrine to the Virgin Mary, concealed from the masses behind iron screens, which guarded its 'burden of riches'. In the sacristy, silken vestments and golden candlesticks flanked Becket's 'pastoral staff', a cane covered in silver. Then, after climbing up more steps, where an array of stained glass images depicted the crowds of previous visitors to the shrine, the final destination came into view.[1]

The shrine's display was pure theatre, designed to create an impact with incense, candles, colour, light and jewels. At first, all that could be seen was a wooden canopy. Before the queen's eyes, this was slowly raised by a complex system of ropes and pulleys, allowing her a glimpse of the stone plinth on which the reliquary was mounted. It was covered in gold plate, studded with gems and adorned with the rich and glittering gifts given by visiting kings, past and present. The ensemble twinkled in the lights of the burning tapers. Erasmus wrote that 'the last valuable portion was of gold but every part glistened, shone and sparkled with rare and very large jewels, some of them larger than a goose's egg'. A prior used a white rod to point out each donation, stating the nature and worth of the gift and the name of the donor.[2] Here, Margaret would have prayed and made her offering, humbly asking that she conceive a child to sit on the throne of England. It was not her first visit. She had been here many times before, as well as to other shrines, all to the same purpose. In seven years of marriage she had not yet fallen pregnant and now, at the age of twenty-two, she was beginning to fear she never would.

In the fifteenth century, the woman was generally held responsible when she failed to conceive. It was seen as a divine punishment for moral transgressions of some sort, so the first place to which a wife hoping to become a mother would turn was the church. While waiting for the saints to intercede, she may also have sought the assistance of doctors, if she could afford their high fees, or else the local women, whose collective knowledge may have suggested certain rituals and herbs. Their cures included a range of ingredients, from the inoffensive ragwort, ewe's milk, pine nuts, pistachios, sugar, chestnuts and tree bark, to the exotic quail and amber. More unpleasantly, they also used rabbit's blood, sheep's urine and winged ants. One early form of pregnancy test included mixing a woman's wine with urine and observing the colour and consistency, or making her drink a mixture of aniseed, honey and rainwater, which should result in mild stomach pains if she was with child.[3] Of course, to state the obvious, if Margaret wanted to fall pregnant, it was essential that her husband sleep with her. This appears not to have happened as much as she would have liked.

Henry had inherited the throne in 1422, before his first birthday. As the only son of Henry V, the legendary victor of Agincourt, it might have been expected that he would continue in that warlike vein but the new Plantagenet soon proved to be quite a different character. Modest and retiring, he favoured an ascetic and abstemious life over that of conquest and politics. According to Henry's advisor, the Carthusian monk John Blakman,[4] the king was pure, truthful and devout; he rejected the immodest fashions of the day and frivolous pastimes in favour of reading the scriptures and worship. Famously, he was scandalised at the sight of naked bathers and desired them to be clothed, disliking the fashion that allowed the female neck to be exposed. His views on sex were equally prudish and rumours circulated court that his confessor had advised him not to have 'his sport' with the queen. Margaret, however, was young, intelligent, energetic and beautiful. They had married in 1445 when she was fifteen and 'already a woman, passionate and proud and strong-willed.'[5] Her arrival in England from France had been heralded as an indicator of peace and promise of future fertility but in terms of temperament, the pair were completely different.

The ceremony was conducted at Titchfield Abbey, in Hampshire, by the Bishop of Salisbury and presumably consummated relatively soon afterwards but the couple's incompatibility became apparent. The exact details of their physical relationship, including the frequency with which Henry visited her bed, are uncertain, although the long delay before the queen conceived, coupled with the anecdotes about Henry's behaviour, suggest it was intermittent. Impotency may have been one side effect of his unstable mental health. No evidence survives to indicate any earlier pregnancies that did not go full term, although if a foetus had been lost before its existence became common knowledge, such information may not have been recorded, or even made public. Yet even fecund couples could experience delays in conception. Cecily Neville, mother of Edward IV and Richard III, had been married at fourteen but did not produce her first recorded child for a decade.

On New Year's Day 1453, after seven and a half unfruitful years of marriage, Margaret made an offering of a 'gold jewelled tablet' bearing the image of the Virgin Mary.[6] Her gift was expensive but it tied her closely with many of her female subjects. Mary was one of the most popular saints for women before and during pregnancy, associated, as she was, with motherhood and loss. Across the country, centuries-old shrines had been dedicated to her, most highly concentrated in East Anglia, with Walsingham as the epicentre. Mary represented the ideal role model for the medieval mother; pure, devout, untainted by sin yet fruitful. She was visible and accessible in many aspects of Catholic life, from church services, feast days and iconic representations, to popular songs, charms, drama and roadside shrines.[7] As winter turned to spring that year, it seemed to Margaret that her prayers had finally been answered. During the days following

Twelfth Night, which had been celebrated at Greenwich, she had finally conceived. She cautiously observed the changes in her body and followed the advice of her doctors, before announcing the happy news. That summer, Cecily Neville wrote to congratulate her, little doubting that it was due to the intercession of the Virgin, 'that Blessed Lady to whom you late prayed ... by whose mediation it pleased our Lord to fulfil your right honourable body of the most precious, the most joyful and most comfortable earthly treasure that might come unto this land'.[8] However, within weeks, Henry's fragile mental state precipitated a national emergency and Margaret found she could not count on his support as her confinement approached.

That summer, the court headed for the Palace of Clarendon, in the centre of the royal forest near Salisbury. Transformed from a hunting lodge by Henry II, it featured tiled pavements, sculptures and paintings of the exploits of crusaders and great kings of the past. It was here that Henry suffered what appears to have been a sudden collapse and became insensible. Days passed but he did not improve, and after weeks of lying motionless, unable to eat, speak or recognise his wife, he was moved back to Westminster. It was a political disaster that intensified the existing quarrel between the houses of York and Lancaster but it was also a personal catastrophe for the queen. There had already been speculation, among those who knew of Henry's abstemious lifestyle, that Margaret had been unfaithful and that her child was actually the son of one of her favourites, Edmund Beaufort, the Duke of Somerset. Now, her reliance upon Beaufort during Henry's incapacity only made matters worse.

To the modern reader, Henry's catatonic state sounds very much like a complete mental breakdown accompanied by clinical depression. It was likely to have been triggered by the territorial losses England had recently suffered in France, which had been part of his inheritance from his father, Henry V. It was a legacy the king had not asked for and found difficult and expensive to maintain. His doctors also recognised the likelihood that his condition may well have had a genetic element. Charles VI of France, who was Henry's maternal grandfather, had suffered from intermittent periods of mental illness, claiming different identities, being unresponsive and believing himself to be made of glass.[9] This had resulted in national turmoil similar to that which now threatened to engulf England. In a deeply superstitious age, where the king's health was held to be a mirror of the health of the nation, strong leadership was required to maintain peace and this illness was a potential disaster. It was imperative that his madness should be cured.

Henry's doctor was Gilbert Keymer, Dean of Salisbury, 'an expert, notable, and proved man in the craft of medicine'[10] who had previously attended the king's uncle Humphrey. He would have been examined, bled, fed a diet adjusted according to the four humours and given all sorts of medicines. Priests were called in to pray for his soul and ask for the relief of his symptoms, bringing with them the relics, texts and holy water of Catholic ritual. Nothing worked. But then, perhaps the cure lay beyond the physician's skill. In the fifteenth century, it was thought madness could be a manifestation of daemonic possession or a symptom of corrupt morality. Henry's piety was well known, so the usual accusations of corruption or lewdness could not be levelled at him, although some would have seen it as the trial of a man unsuited to kingship. While Henry was ill, the country needed a new leader. To Margaret's dismay, Parliament proposed to appoint Richard Plantagenet, Duke of York, as Protector of the Realm. York also had a strong claim to the throne, being descended from the second son of Edward III, whereas the Lancastrian all-male line came through his third son, John of Gaunt. The rivalry between York and Beaufort was already well established by the time of his appointment and, when Parliament tried to summon the duke to attend that October, Margaret's favourite tried to prevent York's appearance. However, by this point, Margaret was approaching her confinement and had to take a step back from politics in order to deliver her child.

Margaret went into labour in the second week of October 1453, at Westminster Palace. Richard II had undertaken an extensive rebuild of the palace in 1394, transforming it into one of the most modern and impressive of the royal properties. Margaret's chambers would have been prepared with necessary bed linen, blankets and clothing, as well as a cradle for the child and swaddling bands. Sequestered away, she would have been brought supplies by her ladies-in-waiting and regularly taken Mass and offered up prayers of thanks and hope. From her apartments, she could look out at the open fields surrounding Lambeth Palace and marshes, as she waited for her contractions to progress. On 13 October, she delivered a healthy son. This was the feast day of St Edward the Confessor, the last Saxon king, who had built Westminster Abbey and whose shrine attracted pilgrims; he was also the patron saint of difficult marriages. Margaret chose to name her son after him.

As Henry lay incapacitated, deep in some sort of coma, he may have heard the screams of his wife, coming from her apartments in the palace, as their child was born. Throughout the autumn the king's condition did not change, nor did he respond to the newborn or recognise him as his own. On New Year's Day, Edward of Westminster was shown to his father for his blessing, but Henry said nothing. He merely looked at him and cast his eyes down again, unable to communicate. When he did finally recover, the following Christmas, he expressed surprise at the existence of the infant, whom he said must have been conceived by the Holy Ghost. Others at Westminster, though, favoured another theory. The rumours of an adulterous liaison between Margaret and one of her favourites, implying Edward's illegitimacy, never really went away. Henry recovered the following year and York lost his position as Protector of the Realm. However, it was not to be the last that Prince Edward would hear from the duke's family.

Soon, full civil war had erupted between the rival Yorkist and Lancastrian claimants to the throne. Richard, Duke of York, was killed late in 1460 but, three months later, his eldest son won a decisive victory at the Battle of Towton and was crowned as Edward IV. The royal family went into exile but, in 1465, Henry VI was captured and Margaret fled abroad with her son. A decade later, after the new king had fallen out with Warwick, Prince Edward of Westminster was married to the earl's younger daughter Anne. An attempt by Warwick to oust the Yorkists proved successful in 1470, with Henry VI released from the Tower and re-crowned, but by the time his wife and son returned from France, Warwick had been killed and Edward IV had gathered a large army in order to retake the realm. The battle they fought at Tewkesbury proved fatal for the seventeen-year-old prince. Edward of Westminster was killed and, the following day, his father was murdered in the Tower. Margaret died in penury in Anjou twelve years later. For a while, it seemed as if the Lancastrian line had been vanquished.

8

Edward, 1470

Elizabeth hadn't planned to give birth in the Sanctuary at Westminster. It was dirty, dark and was known for harbouring criminals, hardly the place for a queen to bring a new prince into the world. Yet, at that moment, it was the only place she and her family were safe. Fickle Dame Fortune had spun her wheel again, casting the Plantagenet royal family down lower than they could have anticipated and raising their enemies dangerously high. In fact, she was scarcely justified in calling herself queen any more, in spite of her lavish Coronation only five years earlier. Then, she had been dressed in scarlet robes lined with ermine, while £280 alone had been spent on cloth of gold for the occasion, as well as the silks for her horses and litter and the gold plate off which she dined in Westminster Abbey.[1] Being served in silence, by noblemen on bended knee, she had felt every inch the queen. Now, with her husband, King Edward, having fled the country, she was uncertain whether she would ever sit on the throne again. The future could prove to be a dangerous place. Only days before, she had been settling into her lavishly prepared apartments at the Tower of London, checking the final arrangements for clean linen and nursery provisions for this new child. It was her fourth by Edward IV, another to add to the three little blonde-haired girls that took after her in looks. Her first husband, Sir John Grey, had given her two sons but he had died fighting for the Lancastrian side, at St Albans, back in 1461. Returning home to her parents, Elizabeth had still been young and attractive. She would later be described by Thomas More as 'both faire, of a good favour, moderate of stature, wel made and very wise'.[2] The young Edward had fallen for her legendary sexual allure and heavily lidded eyes, with even the Italian diplomat Mancini admitting her 'beauty of person and charm of manner'.[3]

There seemed to be little doubt that Elizabeth would marry again but no one could have anticipated just how high she would raise her family, the Wydevilles. Often criticised for being an ambitious commoner, she was not without connections. Her first marriage may have been to an 'obscure knight' but her mother, Jacquetta of Luxembourg, had been the first wife of John of Lancaster, uncle to Henry VI. After the queen, Jacquetta had been the leading lady in the land, taking precedence over all others at court. She outlived her husband and, finding herself widowed, had been prepared to throw her high status away for love. On the way back to England from Rouen, she had secretly married her escort, the handsome Richard Wydeville, Earl Rivers. This breached the terms of her dower settlement, by which she had been granted lands on condition that she did not take another husband without royal permission. When her new marriage became public, the king, Henry VI, banished the pair from court and imposed a heavy fine, although they were eventually forgiven.

Their eldest daughter followed their example by marrying in secret. In 1464, three years after Elizabeth Wydeville was widowed, she attracted the eye of the new Yorkist king, Edward IV, then aged twenty-two, and already well known for his love affairs. Various chroniclers depict their supposed meeting under an oak tree in Whittlebury Forest near her Grafton Regis home, in Northamptonshire, where she waited to petition him for help over the legal wranglings surrounding her late husband's lands. It is possible that she had been known to the king before this, though; her parents certainly were in his favour, receiving an unspecified grant of £100 early in his reign.[4] Like Anne Boleyn over sixty years later, she is reputed to have refused to become his mistress while denying her suitability to be his wife. Whether or not this was a conscious policy to secure his affections or a genuine rejection on moral grounds, is unclear. Elizabeth was a deeply pious woman all through her life and is reputed to have stated she would not spend an eternity of suffering in order to gratify the king's momentary lusts. Her position achieved much the same effect as Anne's would on her grandson, Henry VIII. Thomas More described Elizabeth 'virtuously denying' his appetite, despite 'much wooing and many great promises',[5] while Mancini believed Edward had threatened to kill himself if she refused him.[6] Yet Edward persisted and, as the Gregory chronicler warned his readers to 'take heed what love can do', he won the beautiful widow.[7] They were married in a private ceremony in 1464, probably in the late spring or early summer: the commonly cited date is 1 May. Edward reputedly explained his absence to his court as a hunting trip, consummated the match and returned to his household. Tudor Historian Polydore Vergil explained that the secrecy was due to the bride's 'mean calling'.[8] Perhaps Edward thought he would get away with it.

Within a few months, the actions of his cousin left Edward little choice but to own the match. Richard Neville, Earl of Warwick, had been in the process of negotiating a French marriage with Bona of Savoy, sister-in-law to the

King of France. It was September before Edward confessed
his actions to a horrified Parliament, when it looked as if he
could no longer avoid committing to a French bride. The
news was a blow, as it denied the country an advantageous
foreign alliance, but the main cause of dissension was
Elizabeth herself. Although the new queen's beauty and
virtue was acknowledged, her 'mean calling' was a problem;
she was the first commoner and the first English-born
woman to become queen in three centuries. The incident
sowed seeds of resentment between the king, his cousin
and Parliament; Vergil cited how the nobility 'chafed' at the
'undignified' choice, dictated by 'blynde affection' instead of
reason.[9] Six years on, Warwick's dissatisfaction festered into
open rebellion. Although Edward had expressly forbidden
it, the earl fled to Calais where he married his elder daughter
Isabel to the king's brother and male heir, George, Duke of
Clarence. It was an act of open rebellion and word arrived in
London, in October 1470, that he had returned at the head
of an army to the capital to free the imprisoned Henry VI.
Away from home, in the north of England, Edward had been
forced to flee across the North Sea into exile. His heavily
pregnant wife was left on her own in the capital. She knew
Warwick would not prove a friend to her cause, having
already clashed with members of the Wydeville family and
ordered the beheadings of her father and brother. With her
three small daughters, all under the age of five, she hurried
to safety.

The surroundings in which the queen and princesses found
themselves were far removed from the regal conditions they
were used to. The Westminster Sanctuary comprised a
huge ragstone keep and grounds filled with cramped, dark
tenement buildings and shared latrines. It was barely a
stone's throw from the palace, where the royal apartments

had looked out across gardens to the river; now the view from the window was that of unhealthy marshlands and Thieving Lane, named after the criminals that made their home there. Sixteenth-century chronicler Holinshed describes how Elizabeth arrived 'in great penury and forsaken of all friends', lacking 'such things as mean men's wives had in superfluity'.[10] She was welcomed by Abbot Thomas Milling, who may have offered her the use of his own house until it was safe for her to leave. The heavily pregnant queen had left the Tower just in time. The next day, Warwick's men marched into the capital, took the stronghold and installed Henry VI in her rooms. Confused about his sudden readeption, the gentle Lancastrian nevertheless managed to show compassion to his enemy's wife, sending Lady Scrope to assist her during her labours. Elizabeth's own mother, Jacquetta, recently widowed by Warwick, also joined her there.

Published in 1476, *Celsus De Medicina*[11] contained advice for women in Elizabeth's condition. Predictably, it contained information on the traditional herbs for expectant mothers, delivery and childcare but more exotic herbs now began to appear as ingredients. To 'mollify the womb' the bitter warm seeds of fenugreek were recommended, along with rose oil, egg yolk and saffron. The household ordinances of the Duke of Clarence, Elizabeth's brother-in-law, in 1469, list saffron and rose oil among its spicery provisions but fenugreek is absent. It was probably imported, as it was not known to have been grown in England until the sixteenth century. One pound of expensive saffron cost the duke's household 13*s* 4*d*, in comparison to sugar at 10*d*; pepper, cinnamon and ginger were of comparative price.[12] Equally exotic was pomegranate oil, suggested to help expel the foetus, which was not really known in the country before it was brought by Catherine of Aragon, who adopted it as her symbol in 1501. The presence of these ingredients suggests the text was European in origin, drawing on old Asian and African recipes, although such luxuries would soon have been brought in by the city merchants and were accessible, to the wealthiest, in the grocers' shops along Thames Street. Less likely to have been on sale widely was the lion's fat recommended to aid conception, even if Elizabeth had been in need of it. Ensconced in her sanctuary, she would have missed these luxury items. She would not go hungry though, as London butcher William Gould provided her with weekly supplies of mutton and beef and she had the support and company of her mother, her midwife, Margery Cobbe, and doctor, Dominic de Serigo.

Doctors were valued highly at Edward's court. After the troubles of 1469–71, he would reorganise his household as outlined in the *Liber Niger* or Black Book of the Household.[13] They were permitted to sit in the king's chamber and made an allowance of a loaf, a quarter of wine and a gallon of ale, with suitable clothing, candle wax, wood, rushes and litter. The duties for which they were rewarded included administering medicine, plasters and bleeding patients. The royal apothecary was to have his medicines and ingredients paid for by the jewel house and receive his wages and clothing from the counting house, as well as half a bed for himself and his groom! Edward would amply reward those who had waited on his pregnant wife after his return from exile.

Giving birth in the past was a risky business, even for those of high status provided with all necessary luxuries. Where possible, mothers tried to secure safe, well-provisioned places to deliver their children, even though medical understanding and hygienic standards were lacking. However, the reality was often very different from the ideal, as Elizabeth now discovered, comparing the risks of her present situation to the luxury she had enjoyed at Westminster Palace when bearing her three daughters. After a month in sanctuary, she went into labour in cramped, unhealthy and difficult circumstances, dictated by events beyond her control. She would have been aware that her sister-in-law, Warwick's daughter Isabel, had lost her first child when she went into labour on board ship in the Channel that summer after the rebel fleet was denied entry to Calais. With Warwick now in control of the capital, and her husband abroad, the queen must have been uncertain as to whether Edward would ever return to oust the new Lancastrian regime, or even whether she would see him again. There must also have been considerable doubt as to whether she and her child would survive in the insanitary conditions of their present confinement. However, on this occasion, mother and baby came through the ordeal. On 2 November, Elizabeth gave birth to a son, the heir to the Yorkist dynasty. He was christened in the abbey and named Edward. His gender was of great significance, as there was now a male Yorkist heir to replace the untrustworthy rebel, the Duke of Clarence, in the succession. The Greyfriars Chronicle recorded the occasion with the simple phrase, 'And the Prince born.'

Elizabeth and her children remained in sanctuary for the next six months. Either a wet nurse was found and brought into confinement with them or else Elizabeth broke the queenly tradition of centuries and fed Edward herself; after all, the usual arguments against maternal breastfeeding were hardly applicable in this case. Usually queens resumed their marital and ceremonial duties as soon as they could after their recovery and churching. Shut away, without any idea when or if Edward would return, the survival of the little boy and the dynasty would have depended on him receiving a plentiful supply of milk. If anything were to happen to the king, this tiny infant would reign in his place as Edward V, just as Henry VI had succeeded to the throne before he was out of his cradle. His gender considerably changed the possible outlook for the queen – she was no longer just responsible for arranging good marriages for her girls; now she was the guardian of the future king. When Edward had departed the country in October, he had almost been drowned in terrible weather crossing the Wash. By the spring, he was set to return and re-stake his claim, but his life could still have been lost in battle or by some terrible accident. Perhaps Doctor Serigo brought a suitable wet nurse into the Westminster Sanctuary, with promise of recompense upon the family's restoration; perhaps Elizabeth's straitened circumstances necessitated her feeding her son herself.

Edward did return to claim his kingdom. The *Historie of the Arivall of Edward IV* recounted his arrival in Yorkshire and his march south. Gathering troops, he entered London on 11 April 1471 and was reunited with his wife and children, seeing 'to the Kyngs greatyst joy, a fayre son ... to his herts synguler comforte and gladnes'.[14] Finally, Elizabeth was able to leave her confinement of seven months and spent the night at Baynard's Castle, home of her mother-in-law, Cecily Neville. The following day, Edward set off to meet his enemies. On 14 April, at Barnet, then a village north of London, he defeated and killed Warwick. The following month, he met the exiled Lancastrian forces at Tewkesbury, where the Prince of Wales, Edward of Westminster, lost his life, followed soon after by the death of Henry VI in the Tower. Finally, Edward IV was secure on the throne. He now had a son and more children would follow. Little Edward stayed at Greenwich with his sisters until he was three, after which he was established in a household of his own at Ludlow, under the care of his maternal uncle, Anthony Wydeville, Earl Rivers. The gentle care of children until the age of seven was particularly highlighted by the publication in 1473 of Bartholomeus Metlinger's *Children's Book*,[15] advocating a considered regime. Edward's parents appear to have taken particular care in his upbringing, making provision for his daily routine and visiting him at Ludlow. The time he rose in the morning and went to bed at night were to judged according to his tender years, no swearing or roughness was allowed in his presence and he was allocated time to play and for exercise. His life at Ludlow appears to have been a happy one.

In April 1483, Edward IV died unexpectedly young at the age of forty-one. News arrived at Ludlow that his elder son, the twelve-year-old Edward, was now king and arrangements were made in London for his coronation. Yet the boy would never be crowned. Even before he arrived in the capital, his Wydeville family's well-laid plans had been challenged. On the way east, the party was intercepted by the boy's paternal uncle Richard, Duke of Gloucester, who appeared friendly enough at first. After dining together, he ordered the capture of Anthony and the boy's half-brother Richard Grey. It came as a shock to all, more so when, a week or so later, they were beheaded. Uncertain what to believe, Edward V continued his journey to London, under Gloucester's protection. Once they arrived, he was established in the Tower, where his brother Richard soon joined him. It was the traditional lodging place for kings before their coronation, so the boy dutifully waited to be crowned. The appointed day came and went. Towards the end of June, the pair were declared illegitimate due to a contract of betrothal entered into by their father. Gloucester was then proclaimed King Richard III and the Princes in the Tower were never seen again.

9

Arthur, 1486

There had been a point when it seemed that Elizabeth of York would never sit on the throne. As the eldest daughter of Edward IV, she had been raised in the expectation of a dynastic marriage. As a child of nine, she had been betrothed to the Dauphin of France and had been known at the English court as queen of that country. Traditionally, the match would have been solemnised once she entered her teens, with the elaborate pageants, feasting and jousting designed to mark a royal wedding day. She would have worn cloth of gold and received presents of jewels and treasure before living out her life in one of the sumptuous Valois palaces such as the Château d'Amboise. As a child, she had witnessed the departure of her aunt, Margaret of York, who became the wife of Charles the Bold of Burgundy. But this would not be the case for Elizabeth, as in 1482, Louis XI broke off the agreement and engaged his son to Margaret of Austria the following year. Elizabeth had fled into sanctuary with her mother when the dramatic events of 1483 were played out. Her future husband, Henry, had been an exile in France for fourteen years when he heard rumours that the new king, Elizabeth's uncle, Richard III, was planning to marry her himself. That autumn, he had attempted to invade England for the first time only to arrive amid terrible weather conditions and find the rebels had already been defeated. It was on Christmas Day that year that he had sworn an oath to wed Elizabeth. He was in a position to finally carry out his promise after his second successful invasion in 1485. In January 1486, Elizabeth of York finally became Queen of England. Eight months later, she was ready to give birth.

Henry's Welsh heritage was important to him. He had been born in Pembroke Castle, a descendant of the Tudurs of Penmynydd of Anglesey and the grandson of Owen Tudor, the second husband of Katherine of Valois. Technically, his mother, Margaret Beaufort, had the stronger claim but after the deaths of King Henry VI and his son, Edward of Westminster, Henry became the next Lancastrian male in line. At Bosworth, he had carried the red dragon, Arthur's heraldic device, against a white-and-green background on his banner. His marriage had united the warring houses of Lancaster and York and the son born from that union would reign over a nation that was finally at peace. He would also name the boy after the legendary hero, in 'honour the British race'. Chroniclers described how the people 'rejoiced' in reaction to the child's name, which made foreign princes 'tremble and quake' at the 'terrible and formidable' name.[1] The English people wished them well, hoping to see an heir born. At Bristol, a baker's wife had thrown wheat out of an open window over the newly-wed couple, crying 'welcome and good luck'.[2]

The new prince of the Tudor dynasty would embody the old legends of King Arthur's return. He would not be born at Westminster, like so many of his predecessors but, instead, would arrive in Winchester, the country's ancient capital, reputed to have once been the seat of the famous once and future king. The new ruler, Henry VII, had chosen the city for his firstborn child. Inside the solid thirteenth-century castle hung Edward I's huge replica round table, mistaken by some for the real thing. The legend could also be found in the popular texts of the past and present. Breton minstrels and early Welsh poems such as *Culhwch and Olwen* of 1100 had been drawing on the legend for centuries. The possibility of Arthur's return, or that of his descendent, in times of national trial, was mentioned by William of Malmesbury in the early twelfth century but it was Chrétien de Troyes's new genre of chivalric romance that added the courtly veneer and ritual to existing legends of battles and conquests. William Caxton had printed Thomas Malory's *Le Morte d'Arthur* in 1485, a compilation of well-known fables and stories that established the Arthurian idyll as a golden epoch and formed the basis of most subsequent chronicles for centuries. In the summer of 1486, Queen Elizabeth arrived there, to give birth to her first child. After decades of civil war, the arrival of a son named Arthur at the ancient capital of Winchester would herald a new era of peace.

Winchester was an important city in a religious sense. It lay on one of the major highways of medieval England and contained a centre for pilgrimage, housing around thirty Benedictine monks in 1500, who kept open house for visitors under the new prior, Thomas Silkested. Queen Elizabeth stayed in his lodgings, now renamed the Deanery, at St Swithin's Priory. As one of the richest monasteries in the land, St Swithin's would have had no problem catering for the royal guests: Cathedral rolls show the variety of the monks' diet, which, in 1492, included meals of venison, beef, mutton, calves feet, eggs, dish of marrow and bread; on fast days they had salt fish, rice, figs and raisins. The rolls are full of details for the provision of 'good' beer, cheese, salt, wine, butter and candles; the gardener was to supply apples in season every two days and flowers for Church festivals and the curtarian was responsible for providing for visiting bishops and royalty while the porter was to make up the fire in snowy weather.[3] Elizabeth would have been well provided for by the priory during her stay. Her mother-in-law also played a significant role in ensuring her comfort.

Margaret Beaufort has often been seen as a controlling or interfering character. Some remarks by foreign ambassadors and the order of precedence between the women gave rise to suggestions that she 'oppressed' her young daughter-in-law. However, there is little real evidence to support this and the two women were consistently together. For the inexperienced Elizabeth, about to undergo her first delivery, Margaret's care and organisational abilities are more likely to have been welcoming than controlling. The queen was about halfway through her pregnancy when Margaret drew up her Ordinances outlining the protocol and detail of the lying-in chamber. Once they arrived at Winchester, the detailed instructions would have been carried out. A suitable chamber was selected and hung with heavy arras tapestries, covering the walls, ceiling and windows. The tapestries were carefully chosen for their subject matter, as provoking or disturbing scenes, including hunts and wild or mythological beasts, were thought to startle mothers and provoke miscarriage or influence the character of the child.

Elizabeth would have laboured in a huge temporary pallet bed, 8 feet by 10 in size. It was stuffed with wool and down and covered with crimson satin. There was also a second bed, designed for her use before and after the birth, where she could sleep undisturbed. Two cradles were prepared for the baby. The ceremonial one was 5 feet long and embellished with the royal arms and buckles of silver. Beside it, a smaller cradle of wood, hung with pommels of silver and gilt, with ermine-lined bedding, was reserved for sleep. The room was equipped with piles of thick blankets, fresh chests of linen and double petticoats. Margaret listed yards of fine linen from Rheims and Rennes, imported Tartarin silk, fine lawn and wool, fustian pillows stuffed with down, furred panels, head sheets, a canopy of satin, posts to support the canopy, cushions and mantles all in a red-and-gold colour scheme.[4] Cupboards were stocked with wine, food and spices to revive her during her ordeal, as well as the glittering plate that marked the status of mother and child.

Elizabeth was assisted by Margaret Beaufort and her own mother, Elizabeth Wydeville, as well as Elizabeth's sisters Anne and Cecily, whose youth would have limited their involvement. During the months of her pregnancy, the queen would have been attended by doctors and physicians, such as the Walter Lemster to whom Henry granted £40 a year for life that February[5] but whom would have been excluded from the birth room. The midwife Marjory Cobbe, a favourite of her mother who had delivered the ex-queen's last child in 1480, may also have been in attendance. She would have advised the mother to follow certain folkloric rituals. It was customary for mothers to remove all fastenings rings, buckles, bracelets and laces were thought to mimic a state of strangulation in the body which could be transmitted to the child. Likewise, no one in the chamber would cross their legs, arms or fingers. The labouring woman's abdomen might be rubbed with creams made from a mixture of brandy, distilled marjoram and saffron to aid contractions. During her ordeal, she may well have held the famous Westminster girdle, supposedly made and used by the Virgin Mary, which she would use in later pregnancies.

On the twentieth of September, eight months after her wedding, Elizabeth went into labour. Either her child was born prematurely, as Francis Bacon believed, or he was full-term and conceived before the nuptials. It was not unusual for couples to consummate their union after betrothal but prior to the vows being made. Counting back nine months from Arthur's arrival, we arrive at a date close to Parliament's formal confirmation of the marriage on 10 December 1485. Once it was official, Henry and Elizabeth may have slept together, conceiving almost straight away. It is equally likely that she became pregnant on the wedding night. The baby arrived safely and proved to be the boy that Henry had hoped for. Elizabeth had fulfilled her role and given her husband a son; England had a new prince. Outside, the bells rang and messengers were dispatched across the country to spread the good news. For a few days after the birth, the queen suffered from a fever but she was young and strong and fortunate enough to make a speedy recovery. In gratitude, she would found a chapel in Winchester Cathedral, where Arthur was christened soon after his birth.

Arthur's christening was described in detail in John Stowe's sixteenth-century historical memoranda. It was traditional that his parents were not present and Elizabeth was still recovering from her ordeal but her mother, sisters Cecily and Anne, and her uncles, Edward Wydeville and Thomas Grey, Marquess of Dorset, played prominent roles. The walls of St Swithin's were draped in rich arras and floors spread with carpets and the silver gilt font from Canterbury Cathedral had been borrowed and lined with soft Rennes linen. Cecily carried Arthur, wrapped in a mantle of crimson cloth of gold furred with ermine. After his baptism, with salt, oil and water, the child was passed to his godmother, Elizabeth's mother, who presented him as an offering at the altar, before he was richly endowed with gifts and the party celebrated with wine and spices. Then, the baby was returned to his mother's chamber to be blessed by his parents. Elizabeth would not emerge from her chamber until her churching ceremony, at the beginning of October. She would go on to have six, possibly seven, more children.

It has often been stated that Prince Arthur was reputed to take after his father in appearance, while his younger brother, Henry, born in 1491, was more like Elizabeth's tall, handsome father. Writing in the nineteenth century, historian James Gairdner depicted Arthur as being a sick and weakly child. Yet this was based on concerns expressed over the consummation of his forthcoming marriage at such a young age. The Milanese envoy commented that Arthur, aged eleven, was unusually tall and had 'remarkable beauty and grace'.[6] He promised to be a studious and diligent future King of England, familiar with the best Latin and Greek authors, according to his tutor Bernard André. From his early years, his parents sought a match form him with the powerful alliance of Ferdinand of Aragon and Isabella of Castile. The joint rulers of Spain had four daughters, of which the youngest was Catherine, who was ten months older than Arthur. In October 1501, at the age of fifteen, the princess set sail for England and was married to Arthur in St Paul's Cathedral on 14 November. The young couple set up home in Ludlow Castle, on the Welsh borders, from where they anticipated a glorious future as King and Queen of England. However, Arthur's premature death would leave Catherine a widow and place his younger brother, Henry VIII, on the English throne.

10

Henry, 1511

The queen had chosen a pomegranate as her heraldic device; the round, ripe Spanish pomegranate, slashed to reveal the seeds inside. It was an ancient image of fertility and abundance, found in Renaissance images of the Virgin and child, and contained the promise that she would bear her husband many healthy children. Catherine was petite, plump and pretty, with her long, red-gold hair and gentle features. As the daughter of Ferdinand of Aragon and Isabella of Castile, joint rulers of Spain, she was the perfect match for Henry VIII. At the age of twenty-five, she had seen her fair share of hardship over the past years, but she still retained the good looks that had endeared her to the English people when they had witnessed her arrival as a teenager. Admiring Catherine's regality at her Coronation, Thomas More had written that she would 'be the mother of kings as great as their ancestors'.[1] Now, she was going to provide them with an heir to continue the Tudor dynasty.

It was not her first pregnancy. She had conceived once before, very soon after her wedding day at Greenwich on 11 June 1509, but the child had been lost. The wedding had been a quiet affair, conducted in private and very different from what she might have expected, as befitting a Queen of England. There had been no crowds, no procession or public holidays, just her and Henry, along with their witnesses. They had stood side by side and spoken their vows, promising to love, honour and obey. Perhaps the secrecy of it had been deliberate on his part. Both of them had been aware that this was not her first marriage, nor was it purely a dynastic union. The pair were already well known to each other; in fact, they were related in the first degree. Her first husband had been Arthur, the king's older brother, and recently some had questioned the validity of Henry's marriage to his widowed sister-in-law, even though their father, Henry VII, had been the one to propose it. Then, he had seemed to change his mind and tried to marry his heir elsewhere, but Prince Henry had retained his regard for Catherine. Perhaps her unnecessary suffering had made her into a sort of romantic figure in his eyes, in need of rescue by 'Sir Loyal Heart', the identity he had chosen for jousting. One of Henry VIII's first acts, following his father's death, had been to relieve Catherine's sufferings and take her for his bride. Of course, there were precedents for similar remarriages; they had needed to look no further than her immediate family. Her own sister Isabella had died in childbirth, making way for their younger sibling, Maria, to marry her widower Manuel of Portugal and bear him eight children. On that first wedding day, as a blushing teenager back in Westminster Abbey, she had been given away by the charismatic young ten-year-old. Now he was her husband.

She had first arrived in England in the autumn of 1501 at the age of fifteen, riding into the capital with her hair hidden away under a cap. Prince Arthur had been a slender, dark-haired boy who resembled his father. He was quite different from his robust younger brother, who was popularly considered to have taken after their grandfather, being athletic and blonde like the attractive Edward IV. Catherine had been pleased by her young husband, who was learned and serious, although they found it difficult to communicate at first, using Latin as their main language. The two teenagers had dazzled the assembled crowds in the abbey, dressed in white satin, standing on top of a 6-foot platform for all to see. The ceremony had been followed by a four-course feast in the Bishop's Palace before the wedding night was passed at Baynard's Castle. After weeks of pageantry and festivity, they had set out for Ludlow, on the Welsh borders, where they were to spend the rest of their married life. One day Arthur would be king and Catherine would be queen and fulfil her duty by bearing healthy sons and daughters. But it hadn't worked out that way; they had been married for only four and a half months before the prince had succumbed to illness. Catherine had also been unwell, racked with the terrible symptoms of the sweating sickness, later described by the London physician Dr John Caius; the cold shivers, pains in the limbs, exhaustion, the heat, headache, thirst and delirium. The illness was new in England, first recorded in 1485, and had become known for claiming the lives of young men. While Catherine slowly got better, Arthur had weakened and died. He may have had other underlying health problems too, such as the wasting disease phthisis, as his own doctor suspected, which Victorian historians labelled under the catch-all 'tuberculosis'. If this illness had been considered life-threatening, though, it seems unlikely his parents would have arranged his match or sent him away to Ludlow; his sudden decline came as a surprise and a terrible loss. His parents had been devastated when the news reached them a few days later. It was a good thing that there was an heir in waiting.

Swearing the match had never been consummated, Catherine endured years of penury under her father-in-law, Henry VII, being forced to sell her plate and jewels in order to buy food and clothing as she wondered what would become of her. Then, in the spring of 1509, everything changed. The king died, making way for his second son, Henry VIII, who promptly rescued Catherine from destitution and brought her to Westminster to be crowned at his side, as his wife. Finally she became England's queen. The festivities before the coronation, as recorded by the chronicler Edward Hall, saw the London streets hung with rich draperies and cloth of gold. Behind the barriers erected along the route, the trades and craftsmen of the city stood in line, dressed in their coloured liveries, with the Goldsmiths' stand containing maidens in white dresses. Priests and clerks dressed in their fine copes waved their silver censers as the couple passed by, filling the air around them with incense.[2] The crowd cheered them as they processed towards Westminster. The following morning they were anointed, side by side, and the crowns placed on their heads.

Initially, the marriage proved a success. Henry and Catherine are perhaps most famous for their acrimonious divorce, but that lay twenty years in the future and, in 1509, the young pair were well matched. Henry had proved lusty and strong, keen to share her bed and, within weeks, Catherine had conceived. The pregnancy was announced in November and the enthusiastic couple began to make preparations, ordering a birthing or 'groaning' chair, a copper gilt bowl to receive the blood and placenta and the silver font from Canterbury Cathedral; sheets, cushions and linen arrived by the cartload along with a predictable host of doctors, apothecaries and astrologers. However, these formal preparations concealed a degree of personal unease on the queen's part. It had been a less than idyllic pregnancy, as Catherine's romantic view of the marriage quickly shattered when she discovered that Henry's attention had wandered.

From the time that she suspected her condition that summer, he had not visited her bed. Perhaps he had been acting on the advice of his physicians. Popular belief leaned towards the idea that married couples should not sleep together during a pregnancy, in order not to damage the foetus, so when one of Catherine's ladies-in-waiting, Anne Hastings, disappeared from her court, the queen uncovered the possible affair. It is not clear whether this was, in fact, a physical encounter or just a flirtation: Anne certainly was the recipient of impressive New Year's gifts from the king in 1513. Acting in Catherine's interests, Anne's father and brother had removed her from the king's reach. It was a shock to Catherine and prompted the couple's first argument.

However, the incident blew over and the queen entered her final trimester. The child was due in March and, by mid-January, they had arrived at Greenwich, in order for her to take to her chamber. Then, at seven months, she experienced a little pain in one knee, before unexpectedly miscarrying a baby girl. It was a bitter disappointment for both, but further confusion followed, as her womb remained swollen, leading them to believe she had been carrying twins and would soon be delivered of the survivor. They waited but no child arrived and the couple were forced to admit a mistake had been made. It was probably the result of some undiagnosed infection and caused the inexperienced Catherine a considerable degree of embarrassment, so that she hid herself away from the court and did not re-emerge until the end of May. Disappointed, the couple remained optimistic and the nineteen-year-old king predicted that healthy sons would follow. It seemed that their prayers had been answered when Catherine conceived again soon afterwards. That September on royal progress, Henry gave thanks to St Thomas at Canterbury, the Black Cross at

Waltham Abbey, St Edward the Confessor at Westminster Abbey, St Bridget of Syon and Our Lady at Walsingham. His annual gifts to these shrines amounted to the equivalent of almost £50,000 in today's money: at the time, he may have hoped he was guaranteeing his succession.

The most influential birth manual of the century was produced by a German doctor, Eucharius Rosslin, in 1513. An apothecary in Freiburg, he wrote the *Rose Garden for Pregnant Women and Midwives* based on his own observations of poor midwifery and the unnecessarily high losses of mothers and babies that resulted from their terrible hygiene practices. He advocated patience and consideration; a midwife should sit with a woman and encourage her, placing the emphasis on positive thinking, the 'sweet words' to give the mother 'hope of a good speedie deliverance'.[3] Nutrition was also considered to be important to the labouring woman, who should be refreshed with 'good meat and drink';[4] mixtures of warm wine and beaten eggs were particularly favoured as were spinach, butter and honey. Catherine would have benefited from the presence of a number of physicians and surgeons during her pregnancy. Henry took a keen interest in health matters, often diagnosing himself and writing his own cures, which he shared with members of his court. He would establish the Royal College of Physicians in 1518. It was common for the academic branch of medicine, with its textbooks and theories, to be the preserve of men. When Catherine's time came, though, she would be attended by women, with their generations-old oral tradition and hands-on experience.

They approached the second pregnancy with more caution. That summer, Catherine did not accompany Henry on progress but stayed instead in the safety and peace of the newly refurbished Eltham Palace. In addition to her own experience, she was aware of the dangers of childbirth, having lost her mother-in-law and sister in childbed and knowing that her mother had suffered two miscarriages. Her father's new wife had also delivered a stillborn son as recently as 1509. Practical preparations were inescapable though, and in September yards of purple velvet were ordered to furnish the nursery.[5] By December, she was installed in first-floor apartments at the luxurious palace at Richmond, which had been built by her father-in-law, ready to deliver her child. In the early hours of 1 January 1511 she gave birth to a son, and the kingdom had its prince. Delighted, Henry set off again to give thanks to the Virgin Mary at Walsingham, dismounting a mile away at the Slipper Chapel, where he removed his shoes and walked barefoot to the shrine. Once there, he lit a candle, made an offering of expensive jewels and commanded the royal glazier, one Bernard Flower, to make a stained glass window for the Lady Chapel. It seemed that his prayers had been answered.

When the news was proclaimed, London went into celebration. Days of public rejoicing and partying followed, with bells ringing, wine flowing, cannon at the Tower booming and bonfires burning in the streets. Catherine would be lying-in for at least three weeks as custom dictated and therefore did not attend the elaborate christening on Sunday 5 January, when the processional route to the chapel of the Observant Friars was newly gravelled, strewn with rushes and hung with arras. The child was wrapped warmly and carried in procession under a canopy with great ceremony to be anointed at the font. Expensive gifts were given to Elizabeth Poyntz, the wet nurse, and the French King Louis XII, the child's godfather, rewarded the midwife handsomely.[6] Henry was given a wet nurse but carvers, bakers and cellarmen were already appointed to his household in anticipation of his future needs.[7]

Magnificent jousts, pageants, feasts and tournaments followed on 11 and 12 February at Westminster. A special gallery was built for Catherine and her ladies to watch the proceedings; with the usual lying-in period around three weeks, she was clearly up by then, churched and had recovered enough to travel up from Richmond. No expense was spared; only the Field of Cloth of Gold would exceed it as a celebration during Henry's reign. The royal accounts list the orders for scarlet and crimson velvet for the occasion.[8] Elaborate pageants followed, drawn out in the tilt yard before Catherine and full of spectacle and pomp: here, Henry was famously his wife's Sir Loyal Heart, her initials embroidered everywhere and his response to challengers included the wording; 'the good and gracious fortune of the birth of a young prince that it hath pleaseth God to send … which is the most joy and comfort that might be to … the most renowned realm of England'.[9] The day ended with feasting in the White Hall at Westminster, with riotous performances and celebrations.

Then tragedy stuck and the child died at barely two months old. The reasons are unclear but rates of infant and child mortality at the time were very high. At the end of February, orders were given for his burial; lengths of black cloth for gowns and banners, wax candles and torches for the solemn procession at Westminster. The grief of the new parents was intense, to the extent that well-wishers were advised not to offer condolences, for the risk of triggering their pain. Chronicler Edward Hall described Catherine as having made 'muche lamentation' on hearing the news, like a 'natural woman'.[10] The blessing that God had seemed to extend to their union and the dynasty had been cruelly snatched away. Loss did not drive Henry and Catherine apart; it united them in their desire for a child and they began trying to conceive another soon after. Catherine would go on to bear four more children but only one would survive. That child was a girl, the future Mary I, who would inherit the throne over fifty years later.

Had he lived, the little prince would have become Henry IX of England. Although it is not possible to rewrite history, the implications of his imagined survival help us understand the impact of his premature death. Had Catherine of Aragon borne a surviving son as early as 1511, the well-known story of Henry's six wives almost certainly would not have happened. Without the need to divorce Catherine in order to obtain a male heir, it is likely that Henry would have remained married and taken mistresses. Perhaps he would still have been in thrall to Anne Boleyn, and made her his second wife after the death of Catherine in 1536, but he would not have risked casting doubt on the validity of his first match and consequently the legitimacy of his son. Thus there would have been no reason for him to break with Rome to gain his divorce. While he may have reformed some of the abuses and excesses of medieval Catholicism, the Church of England would not have been established and the progress of the Reformation, so virulent in Europe, would not have got a foothold so quickly under the Tudors. Mary I would not have reigned and her half-siblings Elizabeth and Edward may never have been born. The imagined reign of Henry IX is another historical 'what if' that provides a fascinating alternative path for English history; save for one small twist of fate, perhaps even an infection that may easily be cleared up by antibiotics today, it may have become established historical fact. The life and death of this tragic prince truly did shape the future of his country.

11

Elizabeth, 1533

Anne lay in a 'magnificent and gorgeous' bed, looking up at the tapestries of the life of St Ursula. The Greenwich apartments had been newly carpeted and the ceiling lined for warmth and comfort. To one side, a cupboard housed her silver and gold plate, catching the light from the blazing fire. The royal wardrobe had been emptied of its treasures for her sake: chairs covered and fringed with gold and red velvet, Turkish carpets, blankets and furs. Her nightgowns were made of satin and the cloth of estate, suspended above her throne, was made from cloth of gold. The queen's first-floor lodgings were quiet, overlooking the privy gardens on one side and flanked on the other by the long privy gallery. Greenwich had seen many developments since the advent of the Tudors, turning from a country manor into a red brick palace. Henry VIII had built new stables, octagonal tilt yard towers and a banqueting house measuring 100 feet by 30, with clear windows and a minstrels' gallery. It was a palace fit for the birth of a prince, just as Henry VIII had arrived there, forty-two years earlier. As the end of August 1533 approached, Anne Boleyn withdrew to wait for her baby to be born. All the astrologers had promised her that it would be a boy.

Twelve months before, Anne had not even been Henry's wife, let alone England's queen. Her rise to his side was the result of the passion she had inspired in him and his desire to father a male heir. To make this happen, Henry had divorced Catherine of Aragon, his wife of twenty-four years, and was in the process of breaking with the Pope to establish himself at the head of the English Church. Having attracted him as far back as 1527, Anne had denied him full consummation, with the promise of her fertility and the arrival of a son. Surely it was not too difficult a task to accomplish? She had fulfilled part of her promise by falling pregnant very soon after their first secret wedding in December 1532 and had carried the child to term with no serious complications. Given Catherine's record of stillbirths, miscarriages and infant mortality, it was an encouraging start. The arrival of a prince would secure her position at Henry's side.

As the daughter of Thomas Boleyn, Earl of Wiltshire, himself the child of a wealthy London merchant turned mayor, it had been a meteoric rise. Anne was probably born in 1501, although some sources suggest later. Raised in the refined court of Margaret of Savoy, in the Netherlands, then as maid to the unfortunate Queen Claude of France, she acquired a polish that set her apart from her English counterparts, despite not conforming to contemporary standards of beauty. Her contemporaries described her as having a 'long neck and wide mouth', with 'eyes that are black and beautiful' and having an 'elegant figure'.[1] Anne had first appeared at court in 1522, newly returned from France, dancing in the apposite role of 'Perseverance' at the Château Vert pageant before the Imperial Ambassadors. Dressed in a costume of white satin embroidered with gold thread, she was less interested in Henry than in young Henry Percy, the future Earl of Northumberland, to whom she became secretly engaged. The match was forbidden though and Anne was removed from court, returning in around 1526 to enter Queen Catherine's household. Soon after this, when she caught Henry's eye, he had already been married seventeen years and had possibly fathered two children by her more infamous sister, as well as an acknowledged son by Elizabeth Blount. By 1527, the king was urging Anne to become his next mistress. She refused.

For the next five years, Henry courted Anne in the belief that the divorce from Catherine would soon be pronounced and the pair could soon marry and produce children. A few of his passionate love letters to her survive, detailing his concerns for her during an outbreak of the sweating sickness and her receipt of gifts he sent to her home at Hever Castle, in Kent. He reassured her that 'few or no women have been taken ill … and few elsewhere have died of it' but urged her not to be 'uneasy' over his absence, for those who 'struggle against fate' are further from 'gaining [their] end'. Anne sent him a symbol of her inner turmoil; a 'ship in which the solitary damsel is tossed about' and a diamond, along with demonstrations of her affection. He suffered in the hope of her 'unchangeable affection', promising in astronomical terms that their absence only fanned his desire – 'the more distant is the sun … nevertheless the hotter, so it is with our love' – and longed for them to be together, 'you … in mine arms or I in yours, for I think it so long since I kissed you'.[2] Eventually, after a papal court failed to grant Henry the divorce he desired and Catherine refused to step aside, the king took matters into his own hands.

The wedding was always going to be controversial. Anne and Henry went through a secret ceremony after their return from France in December 1532. It may well have taken place at Dover Castle, or even in Calais, after the Valois king, Francis I, gave their union his blessing. A second ceremony took place early in the following year, before Anne officially appeared at court as queen at Easter 1533. The hostile writer, Nicholas Harpsfield, stated how the marriage was 'secretly made at Whitehall very early before day' with only a handful of witnesses 'to avoid business and tumult'.[3] He goes on to suggest a degree of deception on the king's part, in assuring his chaplain, Rowland, that he had a licence for the match, but this had been issued in order for him to marry a different woman entirely. Harpsfield was correct in his account of the timing; the formal divorce between Henry and Catherine was not pronounced until just before Anne's Coronation, although this mattered little to the king, given that he believed his union with Catherine had been invalidated by her previous marriage to his brother Arthur. Thomas Cranmer, who had been appointed Archbishop of Canterbury under Anne's influence, presided over the divorce court and then recorded the details of Anne's Coronation on 1 June. He denied the rumours that he had officiated at their wedding, which he placed around St Paul's Day, on 25 January, claiming that he had only known about it around two weeks later. He believed that the reason for the secret ceremony 'dothe well appere', although, assuming Elizabeth was full-term, in spite of Anne's miscalculations, she would only have been six weeks pregnant at the time. By the time she was crowned, Anne's condition could not be concealed. Cranmer described how he 'sett the Crowne [*sic*] on her hedde' as she sat upon a scaffold in purple velvet robes, with her hair loose and 'sumwhat bygg with chylde'.[4]

A pamphlet published by Wynkyn de Worde, the first printer to establish himself on Fleet Street, gave a detailed account of the celebrations organised for Anne's Coronation. These began on the preceding Thursday and included barges decked out by the London guilds, hung with banners and cloth of gold, to accompany her from Greenwich to the Tower. Throughout the journey, she was greeted by the traditional rounds of 'innumerable'[5] gunfire, although this went expressly against old teachings regarding the exposure of pregnant women to loud noises and alarms.[6] At least Anne was forewarned and, given her reforming views, she may have dismissed these fears as little more than old wives' tales. She was, apparently, pleased to see the 'wonderful number' of people turned out to see her, never before 'seen in one sight' which 'passeth all men's judgements to esteem the infinite number of them'. Other celebrations included pageants of singing children, Apollo and the Muses, the three Graces, St Anne with her daughter the Virgin Mary and a castle with the heraldic devices of the Tudor rose and Anne's own falcon. The Great Conduit ran with wine all afternoon, all was hung with gold and azure blue, wafers and rose petals were scattered 'and there was great melody, with speeches'. At St Paul's Cathedral, virginal ladies held gold tablets saying 'come my love, thou shalt be crowned', 'trust in God' and 'Queen Anne, when thou shalt bear a new son of the King's blood there shall be a golden world unto thy people'.[7] The verses were written by Nicholas Udall, a protégé of Thomas Cromwell, who described Anne, through her falcon, as shining bright, gentle, 'white as curd', 'of body small, of power regal', courageous, 'sharp of sight', chaste and virginal, most worthy 'to live in bliss always'.[8]

Yet that bliss was to be short-lived. In his love letters, Henry had played the role of 'true', 'loyal' and 'entire' servant to his mistress and would 'cast off all others … out of my thoughts and affections and serve only you'.[9] During their courtship, he allowed Anne a degree of licence which she exploited by refusing him full consummation. Yet once she became his wife, he expected her to conform to contemporary notions of submissive womanhood. He had allowed her to 'win'; but, after their vows were exchanged, the proper power balance had to be restored. The long years of anticipation created a problem in themselves. Anne fell pregnant very quickly and the customs of the day advised against intercourse during that time. The early weeks of marriage, which Henry would have anticipated as a period of physical intimacy, were cut short and the rumours at court suggested he was quickly looking elsewhere for satisfaction, possibly with Anne's cousin Madge Shelton or a mysterious 'Imperial Lady' who was an advocate of Catherine's cause. Imperial Ambassador Chapuys reported, shortly before the birth, that the pair had quarrelled as Anne was 'very jealous of the King and not without legitimate cause' which had led to much 'coldness and grumbling' between them. Although Chapuys loathed Anne, he did admit that these were 'love quarrels' of which 'no great notice should be taken' although it could be seen as an omen.[10] Anne was not a typical submissive female. Her 'power' over the king before 1533 was so assured that she had assumed it would outlast their vows. Yet she failed to recognise that, even when professing himself most in love, Henry's submission had been a form of permission. As he later warned her, according to Chapuys, he could bring her as low as he had once raised her. Once she made the transition to queen, her power began to dissolve. She was no longer the unattainable figure of romance but an obstinate woman who dared to try and rule her husband, such as were ridiculed and 'tamed' in Elizabethan and Jacobean drama.

Shortly before Anne gave birth, Henry had decided, on the advice of his physicians and astrologers, that her child would be a boy. He began to plan a pageant and tournament and sent to Flanders for horses to mark the occasion. Her bed, removed from the royal treasury, which had been given in ransom for the Duc d'Alençon in 1515, had a satin canopy fringed with gold, and was 'one of the most magnificent and gorgeous beds that could be thought of'. Two cradles were moved into the room, one made from carved wood painted gold and another a state cradle upholstered in crimson cloth of gold.[11] The chamber walls were hung with tapestries depicting the life of St Ursula and her 11,000 virgins. The court was abuzz with speculation and prediction, with many expressing pleasure that the future prince would be born under the astrological sign of Virgo, as it would confer stern judgement upon him.[12] On 3 September, a delegation of the king's physicians and astrologers assured Henry that Anne's child would be male; Henry planned that the boy would be named after him, or else called Edward.[13] The plans for her lying-in had been overseen by Anne's chamberlain Lord Cobham and Lord Mountjoy, from his experience of Catherine of Aragon's confinements. Everything was ready; all the queen had to do now was deliver.

The birth approached. Abroad, there were already rumours that Anne had given birth to a 'monster', that Henry was ruled by her and the child would be 'weak' as a result of its parents' sexual indulgence.[14] She entered her confinement at Greenwich on 26 August, suggesting that she expected delivery to take place at the end of September. It would not be the physicians' only incorrect prediction. On the afternoon of Sunday 7 September, Anne gave birth to a baby girl. Mother and baby were healthy but it must have been a blow. Chapuys reported the 'great disappointment and sorrow' of the king and queen and the 'great shame and confusion' of the multitude of advisers who had promised the child would be male. He reported that she was to be named Mary, to further deprive Henry's elder daughter of her title, although this was later changed to Elizabeth, after both the baby's grandmothers. The ambassador was even more damning in his conclusions that 'God has entirely abandoned this king and left him a prey to his own misfortune' and that there was 'general indignation' against the marriage. The tournament was cancelled and the pre-prepared letters announcing the birth were altered by the addition of an extra 's', making 'prince' into 'princess'. Henry was reputed to have said that, with the grace of God, sons would follow. Elizabeth's arrival had huge implications for Henry's existing daughter, Mary, who had been born to Catherine of Aragon in 1516. Now, not only was she considered illegitimate, but she was displaced from the line of succession. This would have been more palatable if she was giving way to a son but the priority given to the little red-haired girl must have been extremely difficult for her. However, soon Elizabeth would be in the same unenviable position as her half-sister.

Anne Boleyn never bore Henry the son he desired. A second pregnancy in 1534 ended in a miscarriage or stillbirth and there was possibly a third in 1535,[15] although the details of this are unclear and would have done little to help Anne's cause, serving as reminders of Catherine's gynaecological history. By the end of that year, though, she had definitely conceived again. This time, they hoped the child would prove to be the son they desired. In January 1536, Catherine of Aragon died, releasing Henry from any fears that he may be forced to reconcile with her and removing the focal point of objections to the Boleyn match. However, it would also leave the way clear if the king were to seek a new wife. It is not certain whether Anne believed this would happen at this point although Henry was already courting Jane Seymour. The Catholic Jane Dormer described how bitter scenes erupted between the two women with 'scratching and bye-blows' and Anne reputedly snatching an image of the king from around her maid's neck.[16] However, Chapuys was not entirely accurate in his description that the king was treating Anne 'as he treated his late queen' and that he had 'latterly made very valuable presents' to Jane, causing Anne to cry and lament 'lest she herself might be brought to the same end' as her predecessor.[17] While Anne was pregnant, she still held the trump card. Then, on the day of Catherine's funeral, 29 January, she miscarried a boy of about fifteen weeks.

Anne's delivery of a daughter is often considered a factor in the failure of her marriage. Certainly, the much-needed son and heir might have bought her more time, even assured her position, but the loss of a son in 1536 was a severe blow. Gynaecological problems were always attributed to the woman and Henry no longer believed Anne would bear him a son. As Henry's romantic vision of Anne rapidly crumbled, she and her faction became vulnerable. Her accusers attacked her as a woman, sexually and morally: adultery, incest and witchcraft were classic weapons used by men to differentiate a female who had transgressed; they formed part of a recognisable social code that signalled a viable target in which even other women, and the king himself, participated. Without Henry's protection, the already unpopular Anne became a scapegoat for social and gender venom, heaped with the abuse usually reserved for perceived upstarts like her previous adversary Thomas Wolsey. She was arrested at Greenwich four months later and executed on 19 May. Her daughter was made illegitimate but survived the dangers of the coming years to succeed to the throne at the age of twenty-five as Elizabeth I. She would reign for almost forty-five years and never marry.

12

Edward, 1537

He called her 'pacific'; a bringer of peace. With her, he hoped he could be truly happy and forget all the trials and problems of the last ten years. She was blonde, comely and docile; hopefully, with God's blessing she would also prove fertile. What Henry VIII and England most needed was a male heir. So far, he had two daughters, Mary and Elizabeth. Decades of marriage had only resulted in a number of miscarried or stillborn sons; in the one case where a baby boy had lived, in 1511, his parents' rejoicing had been cut short by his sad loss, only a few weeks later. The drive for a son had already seen Henry put aside two wives and now he had taken a third. Yet the king himself was no longer the lean, handsome figure who had wrestled bare-chested with King Francis at the Field of Cloth of Gold or spent all the daylight hours in the saddle, pursuing the hart. At 6 feet 2, with a 45-inch chest and a 37-inch waist, he had required a hoist to lift him onto his horse but, after a riding accident at the age of forty-five, he had begun to pile on weight.[1]

Henry VIII had married Jane Seymour on 30 May 1536. Anne Boleyn had died on the scaffold only eleven days before. Jane had been fortunate to be in the right place at the right time, as Henry's marriage was unravelling, and by her very opposite nature to Anne, she had attracted him. They were betrothed the day after Anne's death, which was hardly a romantic beginning, but Jane was twenty-eight and under no illusions about the match. From the start she understood that she was expected to provide Henry with the son he desired. So far, he only had two surviving daughters, princesses Mary and Elizabeth, who, as women, were considered undesirable heirs to the throne. England was still a nation entrenched in patriarchal values. Wives and daughters were ruled by their fathers and husbands, so the thought of a queen ruling alone, without the guiding voice of a man, was unthinkable for some and objectionable for most. A queen would need to choose a husband of similar rank, requiring her to look abroad and opening up the country to foreign, possibly Catholic, influences. Additionally, the status of both Mary and Elizabeth had been called into question as a result of Henry's divorce from Catherine and the reputed adultery by Anne. Henry had proved he could father a son, though. He had an illegitimate boy, Henry Fitzroy, who had been borne by his beautiful mistress Elizabeth Blount and was then seventeen years old. It would have been difficult for Fitzroy to inherit the crown but not impossible, especially after Henry had rejected Rome and established himself as Head of the Church of England. Yet, a legitimate heir was still preferable and, after twenty-seven years, Henry had failed to produce one. Jane had been a year old when her husband's quest for a son had begun. For almost her entire life, he had been trying to father a male heir. It may have felt like her destiny to provide him with one. As her motto, she chose 'bound to serve and obey'.

Henry was impatient. Even in the early days of their marriage, he had kept hoping to hear that Jane had conceived. He would put his hands on her stomach and repeat, 'Edward, Edward,'[2] the name he had already chosen in advance for his son, but it was still early days. Both Catherine and Anne had conceived almost at once, possibly on their actual wedding night, so the delay in Edward's conception, coupled with Henry's advancing age, gave the king cause for concern. By July, he had planned a pilgrimage along the traditional North Downs Way, through the holy sites of North Kent and reaching the shrine of Thomas à Becket at Canterbury and on to Dover Castle. For centuries the location had been associated with the performance of miracles, and within the crypt there was also a shrine to the Virgin Mary, who was known to intercede in cases of fertility. It was said that, less than a century before, Queen Margaret of Anjou had become pregnant after making her devotions there. On 17 July, John Hussee wrote to Lord Lisle that Henry was leaving for Greenwich in the morning and would soon be arriving in Dover.[3] Hussee outlined the royal couple's itinerary and the speed at which they would be travelling: by the 19th they would be at Rochester; the next day would find them in Sittingbourne; on the 21st they would arrive in Canterbury.

With hindsight, the irony of their presence in the city is apparent. Henry's examination into the state of England's monasteries had already begun and was soon to yield damning results. A huge programme of closures would follow, along with the destruction of shrines and tombs, icons and images and a ban would be placed on pilgrimages. Becket's tomb, which had attracted visitors since its creation in 1220, would be destroyed on Henry's orders in 1538. There has been speculation in later centuries regarding the ultimate fate of the martyred archbishop's bones but, in 1538, the Pope was in no doubt of Henry's 'cruelty and impiety' in burning the remains and scattering 'them to the wind'. The shrine was 'despoiled' of its 'numerous vases of gold and precious stones',[4] which entered the royal coffers. When Henry and Jane visited in 1536, this destruction of a long-standing English tradition and its associated cultures of saintly devotion was barely two years away. Was Henry already casting his eyes around at the wealth on display in Canterbury Cathedral as he knelt there to pray beside his new queen? Or was he concerned by the corporeal and venal nature of what he saw? The child that Jane would soon conceive would play a significant part in the continued reformation of the English Church. Henry had begun the process but little Edward, when still only a teenager, would pass far more stringent laws to end the old ways. From Canterbury, they travelled on to Dover Castle. It was there that Henry received the news that Henry Fitzroy had died on 23 July.

Henry was distraught on the loss of his son but, six months later, Jane was able to give him the news he had been hoping for. Early in January 1537, she fell pregnant. Her condition was made public that April, being referred to in Parliamentary proceedings on the third of the month, when provision was being made for Mary and Elizabeth.[5] Three days later, Sir William Eure wrote to Cromwell that the rumours of the pregnancy 'gave the greatest possible satisfaction', with all men 'rejoicing' and, at the end of the month, John Hussee wrote, 'Jesu send her a prince!'[6] In May, Jane wore an open-laced gown to announce the child's quickening at Hampton Court and special masses were said in St Paul's Cathedral for her good health and that of the child. In the early stages of the pregnancy, she developed a passion for quails, which were then out of season. Henry wrote to Calais in search of a supply, ordering the net to widen to Flanders if enough could not be found. When the first of a large consignment arrived at court that May, a dozen were roasted for the royal dinner and a further dozen for supper.[7] Plans for a royal progress that summer were abandoned and Jane remained at Hampton Court instead, to avoid an outbreak of the plague in London. It was still raging early in October when the Duke of Norfolk wrote to Thomas Cromwell that 'the death' was still 'extremely sore' in the capital and the 'young folks', traditionally the worst afflicted, were kept away from the palace gates. Jane had already entered her confinement by then, to await the onset of her labour.

It was around this time that Hans Holbein completed a mural at Whitehall Palace that contained the portraits of Henry, Jane and Henry's parents, Henry VII and Elizabeth of York. Designed to demonstrate the dynasty's lineage, the confidence of Henry's pose suggests his anticipation of the birth of a son, as his astrologers predicted. It is likely that Jane's pregnancy was, in fact, the reason for the work being commissioned. There is no direct reference to her condition in the picture, although this may well have been considered injudicious considering she was in the early stages and there was no guarantee she would carry the child to term. This was the first version of the famous larger-than-life depiction of Henry, facing forward, legs apart, which has been copied so many times as to have become the archetypal image of him. The mural would be lost when Whitehall Palace was destroyed by fire in 1698 but by that time, numerous copies had already been made.

On the morning of 12 October, Jane was finally delivered of a healthy son. It was the eve of St Edward's Day, although it seems that the couple had already chosen this name in advance. Henry was not alone in his delight; celebrations were held all over the country and contemporary letter writers spoke of the 'exceeding goodness' and 'strength of gladness' they felt at the prince's arrival. Hugh Latimer wrote that there was no less rejoicing than if John the Baptist had arrived![8] Initially, Jane appeared to be well. The birth had been arduous, lasting two days and three nights, but later reports that she had undergone a caesarian or that her limbs had been broken to allow for delivery were wildly exaggerated. She was in recovery when Edward was christened three days later in the chapel at Hampton Court, where she sat, wrapped in velvet and furs, to receive visitors in the waiting chamber. The baby's sisters, Mary and the four-year-old Elizabeth, displaced by his arrival, played ceremonial roles as their brother was blessed and anointed. Plans were already being made for the queen's churching when she fell ill a few days later, with one doctor reporting that 'all this nyght she hath bene very syck'.[9] Prayers were said for her at St Paul's but after briefly rallying, her condition rapidly deteriorated.

Six doctors were called in. Among them was William Butts, Henry's chief 'doctor of physic' and one of the founders of his 1518 Royal College of Physicians, and George Owen, who would become chief physician to the newborn child. They witnessed the queen suffer a 'natural laxe', a heavy bleed, on the night of 23/24 October. Post-partum haemorrhaging could be caused by internal injury, perinatal tears or the retention of part of the placenta following delivery. The signs were so disturbing that her confessor was called in and, as anticipated, Jane died that day. Investigating her final days, Thomas Cromwell criticised the decision of those attending her 'who suffered her to ... eat such things as her fantasy in sickness called for', although, by that point, her diet would have had little effect. That day, Henry wrote to Francis I, who had long promised to be godfather to any Prince of Wales, expressing his joy at the boy's birth and the 'bitterness of the death of her who has brought me this happiness'.[10] Henry's third queen was buried at St George's Chapel, Windsor, on 12 November 1537. Her ladies wore white 'kerchers' over their heads and shoulders, as a sign of her death in childbed and the chapel was hung with black cloth. The route was lit by 200 poor men carrying lighted torches early in the autumn morning, when her embalmed body was laid to rest.

Her son, Edward, remained in the royal nursery at Greenwich, before being set up in his own establishment in the north range at Hampton Court, at a cost of £6,500. Having lost so many children, Henry was leaving nothing to chance with this new son. Under the care of Mistress Margaret, Lady Bryan, recently in charge of his sister Elizabeth's household,[11] Edward's world was run under strict guidelines to prevent infection and injury; serving boys and dogs were forbidden as the most clumsy of creatures and a daily programme of washing was followed, with walls, floors and ceilings scrubbed down. No food or dirty utensils were to be left lying around and anyone falling ill was to immediately leave the palace. Visitors needed the king's written permission to approach the cradle and none were allowed to travel to London in summer, in case they acted as carriers of some terrible infection. The prince's clothes were washed, brushed, tested, perfumed and dried before the fire to kill any lurking pestilences. A new kitchen and wash house were constructed especially to serve Edward's establishment and prevent cross-contamination from the rest of the court. His cradle of estate lay in the presence chamber, where he was displayed to visitors who had been allowed access through the heavily guarded watching chamber. He actually slept in the rocking chamber, where a canopy hung over his cradle to protect him from the sun.[12]

Edward was appointed a wet nurse, Mother Jack,[13] whose milk, according to Cromwell, he 'sucketh like a child of his' power. When he was weaned, in 1538, Mother Jack was no longer needed but a dry nurse, Sybil Penn, remained to care for him. Contemporary advice regarding wet nursing advocated the employment of several healthy, abstemious females, whose ideal age would be around twenty-five. The Swiss physician Conrad Gesner wrote in 1541 that wealthy families should employ a range of women in order to guard against illness and the loss of supply. Their milk should be examined before they were employed, to check its colour and consistency; it should be sweet and white and remain in a drop when placed on a fingernail. The German paediatrician Metlinger advocated that, soon after birth, a child should be fed a mixture of human milk and 'mush' until the arrival of its first teeth. After this, the child might receive rice pudding, moistened bread and a little white meat.[14] Whatever Jane's baby was fed and for however long, he grew strong and remained healthy as a child. The year after his birth, Lord Audley described him as being tall, firm and stiff 'and could steadfastly stand'.[15] When Henry died in 1547, his nine-year-old son became Edward VI, followed by his half-sisters Mary and Elizabeth.

13

James, 1566

They had sat down to dinner in the northern turret room of Holyrood Palace, in Edinburgh. It was a March evening. Queen Mary had been tired; she was six months pregnant and listened as her favourite, the short, round-backed David, played the lute and sang. Tonight she was not dining in state, but quietly, with a few close companions; her half-brother, Lord Robert, and half-sister, Mary, Lady Argyll, along with the Italian David Rizzio, her private secretary. She preferred to be in the little room, 12 feet square, adjoining her bedchamber, as it felt more comfortable and intimate. The hour approached eight and the candles were already burning down and the bottles of wine were almost empty. Then, above their own voices, the party heard a clattering noise, coming up the winding staircase which linked the queen's suite with that of the king below. It would not be a surprise if Darnley turned up drunk again, intent on causing trouble, throwing around his wild accusations about her supposed affair with David. Rizzio was the opposite of her husband in many ways; as a Catholic foreigner he was an automatic object of suspicion but he was not handsome and tall, as Darnley was, nor did he possess the youth and strength that had drawn Mary into marriage the previous summer. Still, she would rather be dining quietly with David than put up with another of Darnley's childish rages. The events that followed that evening were recorded by the Scottish Ambassador to England, Sir James Melville.

The door in her bedchamber burst open with a clatter. Footsteps crossed the floor quickly and several figures appeared on the threshold, including the king and his friend, Lord Ruthven. According to Sir Kenelm Digby, Darnley was already in the room, leaning on the queen's chair when they 'overthrew the table, candles, meat and dishes'. Spotting Rizzio, they called on him to leave the room, saying it was no place for him. Guessing at their violent intentions, Rizzio grabbed at the queen's dress and hid behind it, desperate to save his life. Terrified, but remembering her position, Mary declared it was her will, as queen, that he remain there. Her husband replied that it was 'against her honour'. That was when one of them drew a gun. They dragged Rizzio away and Mary could do little but hear his screams as he was murdered and thrown down the staircase, his bleeding body stripped of its fine clothes and jewels, the damask furred gown and satin doublet of his office. Digby has him clasping Mary about the waist, as he was stabbed in her presence. As the queen protested, her husband answered that Rizzio had 'had more company of her, than he, in the space of two months'. Sickened, as he started weeping, Mary said she had had enough of him. However, this was not the time for action on her part. She was due to give birth to his child in three months' time and, as a Catholic in a Protestant nation, she was vulnerable. That night she bit her tongue, but she would get her revenge.[1] According to William Harris, the editor of a 1753 account of the life of her son, James, the story of Rizzio's murder had such an effect on him that 'even through his life he could not bear the sight of a drawn sword'.[2]

Mary had been born in Scotland but she had grown up

in France. After having succeeded to the throne when she was six days old, she had initially been considered as a wife for the English heir, Henry VIII's only legitimate son, Prince Edward. However, the rise of the pro-Catholic faction in Scotland favoured the Auld Alliance and she was betrothed to the Dauphin Francis and sent to the Valois court to be raised with him. The young pair were married in April 1558, when Mary was fifteen and her bridegroom fourteen. A little over a year later, the unexpected death of her father-in-law, Henri II, in a jousting accident, made the young couple king and queen. However, their tenure was short as by the end of 1560 Francis was dead, killed by complications arising from an ear infection. Days before her eighteenth birthday, Mary found herself a widow, known as the 'white queen' for the mourning robes she wore. She returned to Scotland nine months later, to find a complex political and religious situation, with a strong Protestant having gained ascendancy under the lead of her half-brother, the Earl of Moray. Her Catholicism caused many to view her with deep suspicion, including her own cousin, Elizabeth, who had recently inherited the English throne. One of her most vocal opponents was the preacher John Knox, who railed against the rule of 'wicked women' whose rule was 'abominable before God'.[3]

Soon, Mary began to consider remarriage. She was young and reputedly beautiful, with the Scottish Ambassador, Melville, describing her as having auburn hair and chestnut eyes, with the long nose inherited from her father.[4] Her cousin Elizabeth suggested her own favourite, Robert Dudley, Earl of Leicester, whose wife Amy had recently died in mysterious circumstances, but the Queen of Scots was not willing to take on what she dismissed as the English queen's reject. Another candidate she considered was the Spanish

Don Carlos, son of Philip II of Spain. At least he was Catholic but he was showing increasing signs of instability, following a fall down a flight of stairs in 1562. His life had been saved on that occasion by a trepanning operation but the inbreeding of the Hapsburg family was beginning to show. Increasingly wild and unpredictable, he would eventually die in solitary confinement. He did not appeal to Mary as a husband though, and soon she was able to make her own choice. In February 1565, she was reunited with her first cousin, Henry Stuart, Lord Darnley, whom she had met during her widowhood in France, and fell in love, describing him as the 'lustiest and best-proportioned long man that she had ever seen'.[5] He was handsome, accomplished and, at just nineteen, three years her junior. Mary and Darnley were both great-grandchildren of Henry VII and their offspring would have a strong claim to the English throne. The ceremony took place on 29 July 1565, between five and six in the morning, in Mary's private chapel at Holyrood Palace, according to Catholic rites, although Darnley then left Mary to hear Mass alone. Two months later, she fell pregnant.

That autumn, her courtiers began to suspect her condition. By the end of October, it was rumoured that she had conceived, according to Lord Randolph, although he did not know by what 'tokens' this was judged. On 12 November he was more certain, with the 'nurse already chosen', and Mary's choice to travel by litter that December.[6] Doctors of the day may have diagnosed pregnancy by examining her urine, with one text of 1552 describing that of a pregnant woman as a 'clear pale lemon colour leaning towards off-white, having a cloud on its surface'. The practise of mixing wine with urine may have produced reliable results, as alcohol reacts with some elements of urine. Other sources recommended a needle rusting or a nettle turning black when placed in the liquid.[7]

Mary's ill health had caused some distance to open up between her and Darnley, and they increasingly spent time apart. Beliefs of the time would have advised against him sharing her bed, which, given his comments at the time of the Rizzio murder, was a significant bone of contention. That Christmas it was recorded that there was 'some misliking between them'[8] and Randolph reported that Darnley was annoyed at always coming second to his wife. Lord Herries believed that the problem lay with Darnley's arrogance, coupled with his belief that the nobility was behind him, and that the proper ruler of Scotland should be a man, as 'it was a shame a woman should command'.[9] As the queen's husband, the king consort, Darnley was urging to be given the crown matrimonial, meaning he would continue to reign in the event of Mary's death. The approaching birth of her child made this a possibility. By the time of Rizzio's murder the following March, she considered herself to be seven months pregnant, although miscalculations were common in an era that lacked any form of accurate testing and her child would not, in fact, arrive for over three months. In the meantime, she was temporarily reconciled with Darnley, as she waited for her baby to be born.

It was at this time that the profession of midwifery was undergoing its first official regulation. Male medical practitioners had been overseen by Henry VIII's Royal College of Physicians since 1518, but no equivalent establishment existed for women. Those assisting at deliveries were part of a predominantly oral network. Their experience came from observing the births of others and being recommended by family and friends, allowing some women to make a name for themselves in local circles as nurses and midwives. The line between medicine and witchcraft could often be blurred, though, giving rise to accusations that midwives retained items such as placenta, birth cauls and umbilical cords for superstitious practices or to sell on. Popular custom held that a piece of dried cord, worn about the neck, could ward off evil and that cauls were particularly effective in preventing drowning, so were commonly sold as talismans to sailors. Careless and rapacious midwives had been criticised by German apothecary Eucharius Rosslin in his 1513 *Rose Garden for Pregnant Women and Midwives*, which had been translated into English in 1540 as *The Birth of Mankind*. The years of Mary's pregnancy and her child's infancy witnessed the first midwife oath, sworn in 1567, by an Eleanor Pead of Canterbury. Its details reflect some of the fears of mothers and the suspicion of Catholic ritual and use of relics. As a first-time mother, Mary would have shared some of them.

Before the midwives of 1567 swore any oath, they were obliged to provide recommendations of their past work and prove they were members of the Church of England. Then, for a fee, they made a promise before the Archbishop of Canterbury, who, in 1567, was Matthew Parker. They were not to desert a poor woman in labour in order to attend on a rich one, who might reward them more handsomely. When delivering a child, they were bound to help preserve life and not 'dismember' it any way in order to make for an easier birth or to save the mother. When necessary, they would administer 'the sacrament of baptism' using 'apt and accustomed words' and see that those who did not survive were given a proper burial. They were not to 'use any kind of sorcery or incantation' and were to report those who did.[10] Mary's midwife was Margaret Asteane, who had been provided with a gown of black velvet that May. The queen took to her chamber at Edinburgh Castle on 3 June, where a bed hung in blue taffeta and velvet had been prepared, along with ten ells of Holland cloth for the cradle. On 15 June, a false report of her delivery spread through the city but her son did not arrive until four days later, on the morning of 19 June, in a tiny room off Mary's main bedchamber. According to Antonia Fraser, one of the waiting women, Margaret, Countess of Atholl, attempted to alleviate her mistress's birth pains by use of witchcraft. By unspecified means, she tried to divert the rigours of labour to Lady Reres, who lay in bed to suffer for the queen.[11] Whether or not this worked, Mary's son arrived between ten and eleven in the morning, with a thin caul stretched over his face. He was given to Lady Reres to suckle while his mother recovered.

Edinburgh rejoiced at the news, with rounds of gunshot and bonfires. When the messenger reached Elizabeth in England, she uttered the famous response, 'Alack, the Queen of Scots is lighter of a bonny son and I am but of barren stock.'[12] The boy, named James, inherited a double claim to the English throne and was now the most likely heir to Elizabeth. In 1566 she was thirty-three, still young enough to marry and bear a child, yet her outbreak of smallpox in 1562 had been a timely reminder of her mortality. Mary was delighted with her son, taking the unusual step for a queen of having him sleep in her room and watching over him at night.[13] That summer, James was established in his own household at Stirling Castle, the traditional location for royal nurseries in Scotland. Mary herself had been crowned there in 1543, while the new quadrangular palace, founded by her parents, was in the process of completion. The new nursery was hung with tapestries and equipped with silver and gold buckets; the cradle had a mattress of fustian, a feather bolster and coverlets of blue plaid. Lady Reres was to sleep in the room, with her own bed of blue plaid and a canopy to go over it.[14] At Christmas, Mary held three days of entertainments for the little boy, in the Great Hall at Stirling, where guests sat around a round table, a child dressed as an angel was lowered in a huge globe and food was dragged in by satyrs and nymphs on a mobile table. The night was concluded with the first fireworks display Scotland had ever seen.

In February 1567, Mary attended the wedding at Holyrood Palace of one of her close servants. At around two o'clock in the morning, two explosions were heard within Kirk o' Field, caused by barrels of gunpowder placed under Darnley's chambers. He, however, was found beside his valet on the lawn outside, his body untouched by the blast. An illustration, drawn up for Elizabeth's minister William Cecil, showed the two men, larger than life, stripped naked in the orchard. It was clear that he had been murdered and an enquiry confirmed that death had been caused by strangulation. Suspicions had already been raised by the closeness of Mary and her new favourite, the Earl of Bothwell. After the shoes of one of the earl's supporters were found at the murder scene, the finger of blame was pointed firmly at the queen.

After this, Mary's life rapidly imploded. In April, on the way back from visiting her son in Stirling, she was abducted by Bothwell and, the following month, became his wife, following his hurried divorce twelve days earlier. It remains unclear whether Mary was a willing participant in this or if she was forced. Four weeks later, Parliament raised an army against them and captured Mary, taking her to Edinburgh, where she was accused of adultery and murder. In prison that July she miscarried twins and, the following day, was forced to abdicate in favour of James, then just over a year old. He became James VI, under the regency of his half-uncle, the Earl of Moray, and never saw his mother again. Mary fled to England, where she hoped her cousin Elizabeth would help restore her to the Scottish throne. Instead, she remained in captivity until evidence of her involvement in a plot against the English queen finally ended years of Elizabeth's procrastination and prompted her to sign a death warrant. Mary, Queen of Scots, was executed at Fotheringhay Castle on 8 February 1587.

14

Henry, 1594

Many miles away in England, the throne rested on a fragile, ageing pair of shoulders. Queen Elizabeth, once red-haired and radiant, was now bald under her jewel-encrusted wigs and, it was rumoured, her love of sugar had rotted her own teeth away so that she now wore a wooden set. She had never married and, in the summer of 1593, was approaching her sixtieth birthday. The country needed an heir and the most likely candidate was James VI of Scotland, the great-grandson of Margaret Tudor, sister to Henry VIII. For centuries, England and Scotland had been at war, with the battles of Flodden Field and Marston Moor forming a powerful part of both countries' legends. All three of Elizabeth's cousins, Jane, Katherine and Mary Grey, were dead, and there were no rival claimants with as strong a pedigree as James. He had reigned undisputed since the dramatic events surrounding the abdication of his mother, Mary, Queen of Scots, when he was nine months old. After almost two decades in captivity, she had been executed on Elizabeth's orders, after having been involved in a treasonable and murderous plot against her cousin. As a Protestant, James was a more acceptable potential heir to the joint thrones of both countries. Now, the young king had outdone the English queen on two counts: he had married and fathered a child. His wife, Anne of Denmark, was expecting a child in the spring, a child who might one day be the king or queen of a united England and Scotland.

James and Anne had been married by proxy on 20 August 1589. His representative, George Keith, sat beside the bride on the marital bed and spoke the vows for his king. She was fourteen, eager for the match, and passed her engagement in sewing shirts for her fiancé, believing herself to be in love. James was twenty-three and, apparently, equally keen for the match, having 'left nothing undone to make all in readiness to receive the queen and her company honourably'.[1] Sir James Melville recorded the circumstances of their meeting in his memoirs, as a difficult sea crossing in bad weather sent Anne's fleet back to Norway, leaving the king 'impatient and sorrowful', unable to sleep or rest. He ordered national fasting and prayers before setting out in person to fetch her. Three other ships were lost in such 'extream stormy' conditions that 'they were all in great hazard' but James landed safely, while Anne was still waiting for the 'turning of the wind'. They were married in the old bishop's palace in Oslo that November and thought it wisest not to brave the sea again until the following spring. The Danish Admiralty, accompanying them home, were rewarded with gold chains and medals bearing James's image. Queen Elizabeth had given her approval to the marriage, offering all 'the best blessings' as she had felt an 'inward zeal' towards Anne's parents since her childhood. Upon their return to Scotland the following year, she wrote again to wish their contentment to be 'long and prosperous'.[2] Anne's Coronation was arranged at once and took place on 17 May 1590, soon after their arrival.

Three years passed before Anne conceived, but she was still very young. This did not prevent James's enemies whispering about his perceived preference for male company, nor her fertility levels. When she realised she had fallen pregnant, in

1. Site of the Battle of Hastings, East Sussex. In 1066, William the Conqueror landed on the south coast of England and defeated the forces of King Harold. The following decades saw tension between the invading Normans and the Anglo-Saxons, even after Harold's granddaughter Edith married the Conqueror's youngest son, Henry I. She changed her name to the Norman Matilda and the daughter she bore in 1102 symbolised the union of the old and new England. (John Mappley)

2. The entrance to Abingdon Abbey, Oxfordshire. In 1102, Queen Matilda gave birth at the royal manor of Sutton Courtenay, 2 miles from Abingdon Abbey, where her doctor, Faricius, was abbot. Faricius made enough money from working as a doctor to make significant improvements to the abbey, although it prevented him from becoming Archbishop of Canterbury. (Bill Boaden)

Above left: 3. Henry I, King of England 1100–1135. The first royal baby to be born after the Conquest, William I's younger son was criticised for marrying an English woman, and he and Queen Matilda were derisively called by the Anglo-Saxon names of Godric and Godiva. (Amy Licence)

Left: 4. Henry II, a modern sculpture from the front of Canterbury Cathedral. Henry Plantagenet, Duke of Normandy, was the son of Empress Matilda and husband of Eleanor of Aquitaine. Eleanor gave birth to their first child, William, at Poitiers in 1153, while Henry was fighting to secure his English inheritance. (Amy Licence)

Above right: 5. Medieval herb garden at Priory Park, Southend-on-Sea, Essex. Many of the early herbal manuscripts were produced and held within monastic establishments. These were repositories of medicinal knowledge, with monks and nuns cultivating extensive gardens to grow the plants they used to tend their patients. (Amy Licence)

6. Wallingford Castle. William of Poitiers, son of Henry II and Eleanor of Aquitaine, would have become William III but he died at the age of two when staying at Wallingford, on the Thames. (Chris Woodrow)

7. Caernarfon Castle. Edward II was born amid the construction of the castle in 1284, which formed part of his father's defences after defeating the Welsh. His mother, Queen Eleanor, may have laboured within the Eagle Tower, but as this was still being built, she is more likely to have laboured within a temporary, timber-lined tent. At the age of forty-two, she would not bear another child. (Kay Mumme)

8. The Black Prince's Gauntlets, Canterbury Cathedral. Edward of Woodstock was born in 1330, the eldest son of Edward III and Philippa of Hainault. A seasoned military campaigner of the Hundred Years' War, he also excelled at jousting and might have been a king in the same mould as Henry V. These gauntlets are replicas of the real items, held in a glass cabinet in the cathedral. (Amy Licence)

9. Tomb of the Black Prince, Canterbury Cathedral. Edward of Woodstock, later known as the Black Prince, would have become King Edward IV but he predeceased his father by one year. This magnificent tomb, created by master mason Henry Yevele, followed the prince's own specifications. His son went on to become Richard II. (Amy Licence)

Above left: 10. Monmouth Castle. Here, in 1386, in the tower over the gatehouse, heiress Mary de Bohun gave birth at the age of eighteen to a son, who was named Henry after his father. (Philip Blayney)

Above right: 11. Prince Hal, Stratford-upon-Avon. When he was born at Monmouth Castle in 1386, Henry's chances of becoming king were slim. However, in 1399 his father, Henry of Bolingbroke, would seize the throne from his cousin, Richard II, and reign as the Lancastrian Henry IV; after his death, his son went on to rule as Henry V. (Simon Rowe)

Below: 12. Tomb of Henry IV, Canterbury Cathedral. Henry IV was laid to rest alongside his second wife and queen, Joan. His first wife, Mary de Bohun, who had borne his son, Henry, later died in childbirth and never saw her husband and eldest boy become king. (Amy Licence)

Above left: 13. Candle burning at the site of Thomas à Becket's shrine. Here stood the most famous shrine in medieval England, bearing the relics of the martyred Saint Thomas, murdered in Canterbury Cathedral in 1170. A constant stream of pilgrims visited the glittering tomb and miracles were reported, relating to the cures of all illnesses including infertility. It was here in the 1450s that Queen Margaret of Anjou prayed, hoping the saint would intercede on her behalf and that she would conceive. The shrine was demolished in 1538. (Amy Licence)

Above right: 14. Margaret of Anjou and Prince Edward, statue in the Jardin de Luxembourg, Paris. After eight years of marriage to the ascetic Henry VI, Margaret finally bore a son, Edward of Westminster. His father, though, had descended into madness and was unable to recognise the boy, fuelling rumours that he had been fathered by one of Margaret's favourites. (Deborah Esrick)

15. Pestle and mortar. An expectant mother might ask an apothecary (or chemist) to mix her up a potion to ease her aches and pains, which might include unusual ingredients such as lion's grease or powdered unicorn horn. As Chaucer suggests, the relationship of demand and supply between physician and apothecary was mutually beneficial, keeping each in business. (Amy Licence)

16. Edward V, from a window in Canterbury Cathedral. Elizabeth Wydeville bore her son in sanctuary in 1470, without knowing whether her husband, Edward IV, would ever return to England. The arrival of a boy after three girls had great significance for the line of succession. Edward (right) appears before the three feathers motif of the Prince of Wales, while his brother Richard (left) has the falcon and fetterlock symbol of the House of York. The boys disappeared in the Tower of London in 1483. (Amy Licence)

17. Winchester deanery. Henry VII chose the city of Winchester for the delivery of his first-born child by Elizabeth of York in September 1586. It proved to be a boy, whom they named Arthur, as an embodiment of the old legends for the new Tudor regime. (Michael Leutas)

18. Edward VI. Finally, in 1537, Jane Seymour gave birth to the male heir that Henry VIII had desired for almost two decades. It was a long and difficult delivery but Jane appeared to be recovering well. After a week, though, her health deteriorated and she died a few days later. Her son reigned for seven years after his father. (Amy Licence)

19. Edinburgh Castle, Scotland. It was here, in June 1566, that Mary, Queen of Scots, gave birth to her only child, a son, labouring in a bed of blue taffeta and velvet. Soon, Mary was forced to abdicate in his favour; the boy would go on to unite Britain as James VI of Scotland and I of England. (Michelle G. Turner)

20. St Augustine's Abbey, Canterbury. James's second son, Charles, became Prince of Wales after the death of his elder brother Henry in 1612. Thirteen years later, he succeeded as Charles I and married the French Princess Henrietta Maria at St Augustine's Abbey in June 1625. (Carrie Ahrens)

21. Merton College, Oxford. During the English Civil War, Queen Henrietta Maria lodged here when London fell to the Parliamentarians. It was here that she conceived her final child Minette and, heavily pregnant, had to flee as the city came under siege. (John Hackston)

Top left: 22. George III. Born at seven months, George was the eldest grandson of George II but was not expected to survive. He went on to reign for sixty years and fathered fifteen legitimate children. (Paul Carrington)

Top right: 23. The waters, Bath Spa. During the seventeenth century, taking the water cure at Bath was considered beneficial for female ailments, including conception. Henrietta Maria visited here and Mary of Modena fell pregnant after bathing in the city's Cross Bath. (Paula Funnell)

Middle left: 24. Princess Charlotte death token. In 1817, Princess Charlotte went into labour with her second child at the age of twenty-one but, weakened by a combination of her diet and blood-letting, she failed to progress. Both she and her son were lost. (Ann Longmore-Etheridge Collection)

Bottom left: 25. Princess Charlotte memorial tea cup. (John C. Martine)

THE YOUNGLING OF THE FLOCK.

Top left: 26. Victoria and Albert. Queen Victoria was a reluctant mother, finding that pregnancy interfered with her relationship with her husband. It appears that neither she nor Albert were aware of, or chose to practice, any form of birth control, so that she ended up bearing nine children. (Amy Licence)

Top right: 27. 'The Youngling of the Flock'. An engraving of a painting, featured in an 1851 book of poetry, typical of the increasingly sentimental attitude towards Victorian children. In reality though, poor nutrition and hygiene cost the lives of many, even if they managed to survive the birth process. (Andy Brii on flickr)

Middle right: 28. Nineteenth-century baby rattle. Well-to-do Victorian babies may have cut their teeth on this silver rattle with its bright orange piece of coral to be held or chewed. (East Lothian Museums)

Bottom right: 29. Clarke's miraculous salve. A nineteenth-century cure for many ailments including 'bad breasts' occasioned by the pains of breastfeeding. Queen Victoria loathed breastfeeding to the extent that her daughters hid from her the fact that they were suckling their babies; when she discovered, she called them 'cows'. (Amy Licence)

Above: 30. York Cottage, Sandringham Estate, Norfolk. Here, Princess Mary of Teck gave birth to her second son, Albert, the future George VI. Unfortunately, he arrived on the anniversary of the death of his great-grandfather and namesake, Prince Albert. (Martyn Pearson)

Right: 32. Buckingham Palace. The scene of many royal wedding celebrations with the bride and groom appearing on the balcony for the famous kiss, pictured here shortly before the First World War, as princes Edward and Albert would have known it. (Leonard Bentley)

Opposite page, bottom: 31. George VI and his wife Elizabeth, featured in a stained-glass window in Canterbury Cathedral, flanked by their two daughters, Elizabeth and Margaret. The family lived a fairly uneventful domestic life until the abdication of Edward VIII altered the line of succession. (Amy Licence)

Bottom left: 33. Elizabeth Bowes-Lyon with the future Elizabeth II. (Elizabeth Norton)

Bottom right: 34. George VI and his wife Elizabeth, a recent statue in the Mall, London. Elizabeth, better known to many now as the Queen Mother, wears the robes of the Order of the Garter. She had reservations about marrying into the royal family, unsuspecting that she would one day be queen of a nation engaged in a Second World War. (Marc Pether-Longman)

35. Princess Diana on her wedding day. She would conceive her first son, Prince William, while still on her honeymoon. (Vin Miles)

36. Mug celebrating the Royal Wedding, 1981. Prince Charles and Lady Diana Spencer are depicted on this mug, typical of those produced to satisfy consumer demand for the fairytale royal wedding. (Shani Thorpe)

37. Charles and Diana's wedding cake took three and a half days to make in the Royal Naval College kitchens at Chatham. A spare was also produced, just in case. (Alwyn Ladell)

38. 1981 Royal Wedding souvenir badge. It is estimated that 750 million people watched the event live on television. (Stuart Williams)

39. Flags hung up in Regent Street in 2012 to celebrate the Diamond Jubilee of Queen Elizabeth II. (Simon Leach)

40. Queen Elizabeth, Prince Philip and their four children, Charles, Anne, Edward and Andrew, hung outside the Sea Containers House on the Thames, in celebration of the 2012 Diamond Jubilee. (Simon Leach)

early summer 1593, she was eighteen years old. The news came as a relief to all, in dynastic and personal terms. James's sexuality has been the subject of debate for centuries, fuelled by varied interpretations of his behaviour, such as the letters and caresses he exchanged with favourites, 'as if he had mistaken their sex and thought them ladies'. Commentators such as the Countess of Nottingham, writing to the Danish Ambassador, remarked upon his 'coarseness' and 'baseness', while Coke described him as 'addicted to hunting and drinking'.[3] During 1593–5, he was reputed to have been romantically involved with Anne Murray, Lady Glamis, which coincided with the pregnancy. Whatever James's sexual preferences were, they appear to have had little impact on his ability to father children and, in the initial years of the marriage, he gave every appearance of being devoted to the wife he had plucked from the tempestuous seas. The nature of their relationship is still elusive, with Anne frequently excluded from accounts that deal with James and his favourites; she is absent entirely from the 1651 *The Narrative History of King James, for the First Fourteen Years* and remains in the margins of the Ralph Winwood papers, published in 1725; modern depictions of the couple still reduce her to the vapid and pleasure-loving stereotype.[4] As a Queen of Scotland and England, a Catholic and a mother, she had an importance that remains to be fully explored.

As her child grew, Anne would have been aware of her husband's views about the practices of midwives and the use of pain relief. A verse in Genesis, where God said to Eve that she would 'bring forth children in sorrow', had historically been interpreted as a ban on attempts to alleviate that suffering, although there was an equally long tradition of the use of herbs, baths, fumigation and oils.

This was reinforced by Percivall Willughby's seventeenth-century *Observations in Midwifery*, which quoted the Bible and stated that midwives should 'endeavour to mitigate their women's sorrows and no way augment them'. He advocated an active labour, allowing the mother to 'walk gently' and keep warm, as well as 'anointing the places concerned with travail' with 'fresh butter, goose grease, hen's or capon's fat'.[5] Distilled roses and lilies were commonly used by mothers, as were thyme, cyclamen and musk. Women were given powders to make them sneeze and expel the foetus more easily, while enemas and the channelling of vapours into the womb were considered to aid dilation. Others clasped talismans, such as eagle stones, which contained a stone within a stone, or the old Catholic tokens such as girdles, relics and Agnus Dei, although these practices had been curtailed since the reformed church had introduced the midwife's oath. Despite her religion, these would have been out of the question for Anne, along with other, more controversial methods of lessening her pains. James was particularly suspicious of witchcraft. In 1589, when he had sent for Melville's sister-in-law, being 'discreet and grave', in order to wait upon Anne, she was drowned when the boat carrying her had been wrecked by storms, reputedly 'procured' by two witches, who confessed to the king. The time he had spent in Denmark with Anne introduced him to a country where witch trials were already advanced. On returning to Scotland, he attended the North Berwick witchcraft trials and, in 1591, when midwife Ursula Kemp administered a potion to Eufame Macalyane of Edinburgh containing opium and body parts from a local graveyard, James approved the death sentence for both.[6]

Anne went into labour at Stirling Castle, where she was delivered of a son on 19 February 1594. There is little evidence to suggest how the birth went, beyond the fact that mother and child were healthy and recovered from the process without significant problems. In historic terms, it was a significant time to bear a child, with an improvement in the prognosis for mother and baby. Although women appear to have been undergoing caesarian sections since Roman times, this practice had ceased during the Middle Ages, except when babies were being saved in cases of maternal mortality. The first recorded case of a successful intervention had recently taken place in the 1580s in Switzerland, when a pig-gelder named Jakob Nufer operated on his wife, who reputedly survived to bear five more children. While the sources of this are not conclusive, a child of the same name is recorded as having been born in Germany in 1587 to a Jakob and Anna.[7] Also, in the late sixteenth century, physician Peter Chamberlen developed a rudimentary pair of forceps, to aid live delivery, although these were kept closely guarded and locked away, not being made public until a century later. It was 1670 when the secret was revealed and forceps were developed for use during difficult births. In spite of these developments, the act of birth would remain dangerous, for mother and child. As Joseph Hall, Bishop of Exeter in the seventeenth century, stated, 'death borders upon our birth and our cradle stands in the grave'.

Whatever the details of Queen Anne's delivery, the royal couple were pleased that she and the child, named Henry Frederick, had come through the ordeal unscathed. James ordered the building of a new Chapel Royal for his christening, which was completed in seven months. Henry was duly baptised there, on 30 August, with celebrations afterwards in the Great Hall, the largest banqueting hall in Scotland, dating from 1503. James would not have remembered the Christmas celebrations his mother had organised there to celebrate his first Christmas in 1566, but he put on an equal display for his own son's baptismal feast, with dishes arriving on a model ship of state, 5 metres by 12, firing brass cannon and sailing on an artificial sea.

However, an unpleasant shock was in store for Queen Anne. It was customary for royal babies to be removed from their parents and established within their own household but the king wished to prevent his wife from influencing their son at all, in case she should impart to him any aspect of her Catholicism. She was to have no say in his upbringing at all. The baby was placed with Helen Little, James's own nurse, in the oak cradle where he had lain as a baby, before being placed under the care of the Earl of Mar at Stirling Castle. James wrote to Mar 'upon the trust I have in your honesty', insisting that in the event of his own death Mar should not relinquish Henry to 'neither the queen nor the estates' but 'deliver him till he be eighteen years of age and that he command you himself'.[8] Anne fought to gain more access to her boy, demanding the issue be debated in the Council, but James refused on every point, causing many bitter public scenes. In July 1595, Anne was already pregnant again but the strain of the arguments caused her to suffer a miscarriage. This brought an end to their fighting but left a permanent mark upon the marriage, which John Coleville described as 'lurking hatred disguised with cunning dissimulation'. James, though, took a close interest in the education of his son and his training as a future king. In 1599, he wrote *Basilikon Doron* or 'royal gift', a long letter addressed to Henry, outlining how to be a good, godly monarch. In it, he advised the five-year-old prince to choose a wife of the same religion, avoid Papists and leave his kingdom entirely to his eldest son.

A book of ordinances was written for Henry's household

in May 1610, when he was sixteen. For breakfast, he was given a daily allowance of fine white bread, beef, mutton, chickens, beer and wine. It appears that the prince was not bound by the usual rules of consumption on fish days, with menus including veal, lamb, mutton and a range of poultry and small birds, alongside the usual carp, pike and whiting. Perhaps this was in deference to his youth, as well as his status, as the diet for his household officials on such occasions contained no meat dishes at all, with his chamberlain, comptroller and treasurer eating cod, plaice, sole, gurnard and other smaller delicacies. Henry had twenty-one gentlemen of the Privy Chamber 'in extraordinary' and seventeen more 'in ordinary'. He had a music teacher, a dance teacher, a keeper of his library and a physician, Doctor Hammond, who received the huge sum of £140 a year. There was also an apothecary, Ralph Claitone, paid just over £30, and a surgeon, Lewis Rogers, who earned £48 annually.[9] Sir Charles Cornwallis described the young prince as about 5 foot 8, with a 'strong, straight, well-made body' and wide shoulders, a majestic countenance, auburn hair, long-faced with a broad forehead and grave eyes; his smile was gracious but his frown was terrible. He was loving, affable and honest, his 'favour like fun', shining on all alike, unable to flatter, fawn or 'use those unkindly who deserved his love'. He was considered the 'darling of the English nation', his 'court filled' and most 'highly beloved'.

Yet Henry was never to become the cultured king he promised. He had fallen ill of an unspecified disease in October 1612 and died on 6 November at St James's Palace. Although the physicians of the day unanimously denied it, the rumour persisted that his end had been exacerbated by poison.[10] Simonds d'Ewes recorded that the 'unbounded grief of all classes' for Henry's loss, even including women and children, has perhaps 'never been exceeded'. Described as a youth with a strong constitution, d'Ewes speculated that he should have recovered from the 'sports and recreations' in which he was supporting the marriage of his sister, Elizabeth, to the Elector Palatine, except that during a tennis match, he consumed some grapes 'supposed to have been poisoned'. He concluded that the 'fairest hopes of the nation were destroyed',[11] much as did Wilson's 1653 *Life of James I*, in which Henry had 'a spirit too full of life and splendour to be long shrouded in a cloud of flesh'. His light 'cast so radiant a lustre' that its loss darkened others and lost 'the benefits of its own glory'.[12] His death meant the crown passed to his younger brother Charles, then aged twelve. Slight and small, he had developed a stutter and the severe rickets he had suffered from as a small child had rendered him incapable of learning to walk without reinforced boots. He looked to prove a very unlikely king indeed.

15

Henrietta, 1644

Henrietta Maria had a magnificent trousseau for her new life
as Queen of England. As the daughter of Henry IV of France
and sister of the reigning Louis XIII, no expense had been
spared. There was a black dress embroidered with silver
and gold, one of cloth of silver trimmed with gold flowers
and another of grey satin with a long train and hanging
sleeves. Then there was the violet velvet mantle, lined with
ermine and covered with gold fleurs-de-lis, the four-dozen
lace-trimmed chemises, silk stockings, gold slippers with
rosettes, perfumed leather gloves and fur-lined boots. Her
own bed came with her too, with embroidered crimson
curtains, layers of quilts and toppings of white plumes.
Among her train were her fool, Mathurine, musicians,
cooks, a surgeon, an apothecary, a perfumer, a tailor, an
embroiderer, a jeweller and a clock-maker. She rode out
of Paris in May 1625, in a red velvet litter drawn by two
mules decked out in red with white feathers, heading for the
Channel.[1] A sailor reported having seen her viewing the sea
at Boulogne on 8 June, 'in good health and very merry'.[2]

Her journey and reception in England did not go quite
as planned, though. On 11 June, after the French ships
had been dispersed by a storm, the merchants of Deal were
commanded to sail to Boulogne to accompany their queen
to England in safety. The next day, the princess had put to

sea as her arrival was expected 'this night at Dover'.[3] The fleet arrived at eight o'clock in the evening amid the rain. Charles was waiting in Canterbury, about 20 miles away, so his queen spent the night in the formidable bastion of Dover Castle. The French party were less than impressed. Insufficient rooms had been provided, meaning that her 'little army' of 4,000 attendants[4] had to find lodgings in the town, and those that were set aside for her use were dark and gloomy. The famous architect Inigo Jones had been working to improve them but the standard still fell short of the French princess's expectations. There was little choice for the moment, though, and she retired to bed.

Henrietta Maria was fifteen years old. Standing at under 5 feet in height, she was described by the English Ambassador as 'the loveliest creature in France and the sweetest thing in nature'.[5] The pair had been betrothed while Charles was still the heir to the throne but, in March 1625, his father, James, had died. Henrietta had been styling herself 'bride of the Prince of England' but now she was going to be married to a king. Charles arrived at Dover the following morning and an emotional scene ensued, in which Henrietta Maria wept and he reassured her that she had not 'fallen into the hands of strangers' but that this was God's will. The ceremony had taken place, in proxy, that May but now they proceeded to Canterbury, where they were married again, in the Great Hall at St Augustine's Abbey on 13 June. This was followed by a banquet at the nearby house of Lord Wootton before they spent their first night together in the abbey. The courtier, Endymion Porter, reported in a letter to his wife that 'last night the king and queen did lie together at Canterbury'.[6] The following morning, their intimate attendants noticed that Charles was 'very jocund' while his new wife seemed 'not well at ease', even 'moribund'.[7]

This proved to be prophetic, as the first years of the marriage were not easy. However, following the assassination of Charles's favourite, George Villiers, Duke of Buckingham, the couple grew closer. Henrietta Maria bore a stillborn son in March 1629, before delivering a second boy, Charles, in May 1630. Other children soon followed, so that by 1640, they had six surviving children out of eight pregnancies; three boys and three girls. The royal couple had grown close and, by many accounts, had a happy, loving family life; during the 1630s they increasingly withdrew from public life and criticisms were made of Henrietta for her Catholicism. That was when everything began to change.

Tensions had been brewing between the king and Parliament over religion, taxes and the way that royal power was exercised. Henrietta was thirty-two in 1642, when Civil War broke out. She was out of the country raising money for their cause when the first battle was fought that October at Edgehill, where royalist troops clashed with the parliamentarian rebels angered by Charles's attempts to rule without them and then to arrest some of their members. Early in 1643 Henrietta returned to England, but if she had entertained any ideas about returning to her old life, she soon realised this was impossible upon learning that her chapel at Somerset House had been destroyed and boarded up. Charles had established an alternative capital at Oxford, so the pair were reunited there in July after a separation of sixteen months. The city welcomed her and she was offered lodgings in Merton College, where Charles visited her each afternoon. It was from Oxford that Charles and his armies set out to confront the forces of the parliamentarian Robert Devereux, Earl of Essex, at Newbury in September. It proved to be another indecisive encounter but Henrietta was relieved when her husband returned safe and sound. The following month, she fell pregnant with her last child.

Henrietta's last pregnancy was complicated by her own ill health. Suffering from frequent headaches and toothache, her condition worsened as the months passed. By the spring, Essex was threatening to besiege Oxford and it was no longer safe for her to remain there to deliver her child. With skirmishes breaking out all over the country and the Scots on the verge of invasion, any travel would have been difficult, let alone for a woman in the later stages of pregnancy. Charles tried to persuade her to remain in the city but she did not feel safe there and, suffering from a feverish cold, which created pains in her joints, she fled and headed for the comparative safety of the west. It must have been a worrying time for the queen. Under such circumstance, it would have been difficult for her to heed the advice of manuals like *The Expert Midwife* of 1637, which advised, 'Let them take heed of cold and sharp winds, great heat, anger, perturbations of mind, fears and terrors.'[8] Contemporary views stated that mothers who suffered from shock and trauma during their pregnancies were likely to produce 'monster births' such as those recorded in England in 1609, 1613 and 1640. The story of a French woman who had been born with a pig's face was prevalent during 1638–9, with five versions of her tale being published in London in one week of December 1639 alone. It was also recounted in a broadsheet ballad and a chapbook, both published in 1640. As a devout Catholic, Henrietta drew upon her faith and, in the event, her child was considered to be 'a pretty baby', which the superstitious would have considered as vindication of her flight.

The queen arrived at Bath on 21 April to take the waters but found herself unable to rest. She attempted to find herself a safe haven in Bridgewater before settling into the house of the Earl of Bedford, in Exeter. From there she wrote to summon her Swiss physician, Sir Theodore Turquet de Mayerne, the author of a manuscript of recipes that was later published as *Archimagirus Anglo-Gallicus*. Mayerne was a trusted royal employee, having been the physician of Anne of Denmark from 1610 and, according to Colonel George Monck, 'one of the first physicians in the kingdom'.[9] Charles also wrote to Mayerne, asking him, 'For love of me, go to my wife.'[10] Mayerne was in London at the time but Parliament gave permission for him and another doctor, Sir Matthew Lister, to travel to Exeter to attend the queen. They undertook the seven-day ride in her royal coach.

While Henrietta Maria awaited their arrival, her attendants would have used various methods in trying to alleviate her sufferings. The early seventeenth-century herbals and household manuals, such as Gervase Markham's *The English Housewife* of 1615 and Culpeper's *The English Physician* of 1652 and the *Directory for Midwives* and *Complete Herbal* of 1653, reflect the knowledge of the era and the treatment the queen would have received. Her attendants in Exeter would have known 'the time of the year, month and moon' to sow and collect herbs, in their 'best flourishing … height of goodness' according to Markham, as well as 'some approved medicines and old doctrines … for the curing of ordinary sicknesses'.[11] Culpeper's herbal was even more accessible, listing the relevant herbs used for specific childbirth conditions. Motherwort was recommended for pregnancy as 'you can desire no good to your womb but this herb will effect it'; it could help restart the courses, cleanse and help cool the womb and ease labour. Other good herbs for an 'easy and speedy delivery' included bay leaves, betony, fennel, feverfew, horse-tongue, jessamine, mint and turnsole. However, it also recommended expensive powdered ingredients like ivory, pearl and coral. As she awaited her doctors, Henrietta must have prepared herself for the worst possible outcomes too, taking Mass and acquiring horse parsley, basil, bay leaves, chervil, toad-flax, pennyroyal and savine, in case complications arose and she or her child were lost.[12]

Mayerne and Lister arrived in Exeter in time to attend the birth. News was already reaching the queen that Essex had pursued her and was planning to march on the city, although by that point she had little option but to remain put and deliver her child there. Henrietta was tiny, standing at less than 5 feet tall. Cases where a woman's pelvis would not allow for the delivery of a large child frequently resulted in maternal and infant deaths. A manual for midwives, completed in the early decades of the next century, recommended that 'if the woman be too small' she should be kept upright, for 'the more free respiration', and/or walk about the room, according to her strength. If necessary, she should be supported under the arms. While she waited, she should be 'comforted and refreshed' with fresh, soft eggs, good broths, jellies, toast and a little wine and water. Only when her waters broke should she take to her bed.[13] After a difficult labour, a large, healthy baby girl arrived on 16 June 1644, at Bedford House. She was named Henrietta but would later be called Anne and Minette. Her mother wrote to Charles I that she had felt as if she was 'so tightly squeezed in the region of my heart that I was suffocating'. She could hardly move and was unable to stand; her legs and knees were 'colder than ice' and she had lost the sensation in one arm and sight in one eye.[14] It was Mayerne's professional opinion that the queen would not live long and modern medical opinion has suggested that her aches, tightness and coldness imply a diagnosis of tuberculosis, in a 'sub-acute phase'. Interestingly, her French doctors would prescribe her asses' milk to drink, which was the contemporary cure for the disease.[15] Other cures for post-partum complications could be less useful, like Culpeper's advice that keeping a bur leaf on the woman's head for a year would draw a prolapsed womb back into its rightful place.[16]

Yet Henrietta Maria was determined and she had not given up. Entrusting her baby to Anne Villiers, Lady Dalkeith, she left her sickbed on 1 July, after only two weeks' recovery, and disguised herself in 'ordinary clothes'. Very weak, 'the most worn and weak, pitiful creature in the world', she managed to escape from the city but collapsed after 3 miles and was forced to hide in a hut while the parliamentarian soldiers passed by, discussing her escape.[17] Eventually, friends helped her to ships waiting in Falmouth Bay but enemy vessels fired on them as they tried to sail to safety. With cannonballs crashing around them, the queen gave the order that, if they were about to be taken prisoner, the captain should set light to the gunpowder store in the hold and blow them all up. Managing to flee, they then encountered a terrible storm before landing on the French coast and being attacked as pirates before the English queen could declare her identity. She headed for the spa at Bourbon l'Archambaut but the journey took a month and, once she arrived, Henrietta Maria collapsed with a fever and an abscess in her breast. She wrote to Charles that she had 'done all [she could] for her life'.

Events in England were progressing in her absence. On 2 July, the day after the queen had fled Exeter, royalist forces were defeated by a combined Scottish and Parliamentary force at Marston Moor, meaning that the king lost control of the north of England. Left behind in Exeter with Lady

Dalkeith, a wet nurse and a small household, baby Henrietta was of little interest to the parliamentarian forces. She had been strong and healthy at birth but soon feel prey to the 'convulsions', or fits, which so often proved fatal to babies of this era. Midwife Jane Sharp wrote in 1671 that fitting could be caused by fevers and feeding, with some babies convulsing from 'sucking too much milk'. She recommended that infants should not be bled or given strong medicines but, instead, should be given a 'glister' of mallow, rose oil, violets and camomile, administered warm in a little milk and water. The wet nurse should also be given treatments but only very weak ones, as strong substances could 'endanger the child that sucketh the breast'. Convulsions could also be the result of griping in the belly, occasioned by bad milk, wind or worms. The baby's stomach could be soothed by laying across it a piece of wool, dipped in a warm mixture of olive oil, lavender, fennel and cumin. Rhubarb, aniseed and almond were also recommended as oils or syrups for the relief of wind.[18] Henrietta recovered sufficiently to be baptised in Exeter Cathedral on 21 July.

For a brief time, Henrietta and Lady Dalkeith lived in Oatlands Palace, near Weybridge in Surrey, but the escalating civil conflict made it a dangerous place to be. In 1645, Charles's army had been completely defeated by Oliver Cromwell's New Model Army at the Battle of Naseby. The king retreated to Oxford for the winter, but the following spring the city came under siege again, forcing him to escape and flee to London in disguise. In 1646, Lady Dalkeith smuggled the two-year-old Henrietta out of London and to France, where she was reunited with her mother. Charles I surrendered to the Scots, who agreed to invade England on his behalf, but their defeat and the king's capture led to his trial in 1648. Charles's refusal to recognise the court or enter a plea did not prevent Parliament from finding him guilty. He was executed on 30 January 1649. Henrietta, also known as Anne in France, was brought up as a Roman Catholic by her mother, living first at the Louvre, then in the Palais Royal, with Louis XIV. After the death of Oliver Cromwell, the English monarchy was restored in 1660 under Henrietta's eldest brother, Charles II. The queen and her daughter returned briefly that year, before Henrietta returned to France, to be married to Louis's younger brother Philippe, Duke of Orleans. She bore two daughters and died in 1670 after suffering from a pain in her side and drinking chicory water, which she believed had been poisoned. She outlived her mother by nine months.

16

James, 1688

She might be a queen but that was no guarantee of privacy. Her child had been conceived in the secrecy of the marital bed but, when it came to giving birth, the bedroom was full of expectant faces. Worse still, while she sweated and laboured before all these witnesses, the palace was still alive with rumours. The Protestants whispered that the baby had not been fathered by her husband, King James II, but was in fact illegitimate and that, should any complications arise, a substitute child would be smuggled in, hidden in a bedpan. The Catholics, keen for a male heir to act as a figurehead for their faith, eagerly awaited his arrival. There was also Princess Anne, James's daughter from his first marriage, who should be able to testify that the delivery was straightforward. As Queen Mary's contractions intensified, the faces in the room grew blurred but she could still hear them chattering above her cries. For a Queen of England, the situation was more than undignified; it was insulting.

The Italian princess, Mary Beatrice of Modena, had been married to James at the age of fifteen. She had little known what a volatile political environment she was about to enter and the long-lasting effects it would have on her life and those of her children. During his brother's reign, James and his first wife, Anne Hyde, had converted to Catholicism, although this was controversial and had been kept secret. Theirs had been a love match, forbidden by her father, although the couple went on to wed while she was pregnant. James's second match was a matter of diplomacy. The ceremony had been conducted by proxy in September 1673 but Mary had not arrived in England nor seen her future spouse until November. At forty, he was old enough to be her father; in fact, Mary was only four years older than his eldest child, a daughter, who bore the same name. Perhaps she had already heard the tales about his exploits with women or his infamous inability to conceal his 'ogling' glances at them. He certainly looked splendid, dressed in a fashionable gros point de Venise lace cravat and cuffs, with a grey coat embroidered in gold and silver thread.

Mary also found very quickly that her marriage was an unpopular one. The year of her marriage, 1673, had witnessed the passing of the Test Act in England, whereby holders of office were bound to swear an oath denouncing certain Catholic practices. James had publicly refused to do so and relinquished his position of Lord High Admiral, which was tantamount to declaring his conversion. When the new queen arrived, she was widely viewed as acting on the Pope's orders to restore Catholicism and was treated with deep suspicion. Many Protestants looked instead to James's eldest daughter, Mary, who had been married to William of Orange. She and her younger sister Anne had been raised in the Protestant faith, against a backdrop of increasing religious conflict and intolerance. Between 1678 and 1681, national anti-Catholic feeling had been fanned by a fictitious Popish plot, orchestrated by Titus Oates, in which Jesuit priests were planning to assassinate James's elder brother, Charles II. James had already seen his fair share of conflict and knew how fragile a reign could be. He had spent two years in Parliamentary custody as Prince of York, during the

English Civil War, before escaping to join his elder brother at the Hague. Months later their father had been beheaded.

The royal couple had a history of infant mortality. James's first wife had borne him eight children but only two girls had reached adulthood. Mary of Modena had already had ten previous pregnancies and failed to produce a surviving heir. Five children had been born live and five stillborn, while one daughter, Isabel, had survived the dangerous first years only to die at the age of four. In 1671, Jane Sharp, author of *The Midwife's Book*, advocated certain steps to help prevent miscarriage. Depending upon her individual balance of humours, an expectant mother should drink wine boiled with thyme, eat ten juniper berries every morning, sweat in a stove, drink a dram of wine mixed with galingale and cinnamon. She diagnosed that the most common cause of barrenness and foetal loss were due to the 'dryness' of young women's wombs. This should be corrected by 'cooling drinks' and pastes made from barley, ground almonds, white poppy seeds, cucumber, melon and citrus fruits. The oil of nightshade and ground mandrake seeds could also help, if a woman was possessed of a particularly hot, dry womb.[1] Mothers could also employ the power of prayer and take the various cures available at spa resorts, such as Bath, Tunbridge Wells, Harrogate and Epsom.

In 1687, Mary visited Bath in the hopes that 'taking the waters' would aid her fertility. By this time, she had no surviving children left. The warm mineral spring had been drunk by those seeking a cure since Roman times and, while she was there, Mary bathed in the famous 'Cross Bath'. James joined her in the city on 6 September, and by the autumn she suspected she had conceived again. Her personal hopes for the fate of this new infant ran parallel with national concerns about its potential upbringing. The news was received with great joy by the king and his friends, given her previous gynaecological record and the four years that had elapsed since her last conception. That November, Italian diplomat Francesco Terriesi wrote to the Grand Duke of Tuscany, hoping for an heir to 'put an end to these disorders'. Mary's pregnancy had not yet been confirmed but he believed it 'would be the best antidote against the fire the Prince of Orange has kindled'.[2] A male heir to the throne would become an important new focal point for English Catholics, allowing them to anticipate the future promotion of their beliefs.

In January, after her condition had been made public, Terriesi described how the news had caused 'great surprise' among those who had 'little calculated upon such an accident'. Ominously, Terriesi also reported that the followers of William of Orange refused to believe it or 'impudently declare[d] it to be a fiction'. Although she was making 'good progress' the Italian reported how Mary had been dismayed by certain satires published against her, as she had 'never given cause to anyone save to worship her'.[3] The diary of the Earl of Clarendon, James's former father-in-law, recorded the surprise of those close to the queen regarding the public reaction to her pregnancy. It was 'everywhere ridiculed, as if scarce anybody believes it to be true'. One of these satires, an engraving by Granger, portrayed the queen seated by her child in the cradle, being embraced by a swarthy-looking father, Edward Petre, her husband's Jesuit confessor. Petre was deeply unpopular and the Pope had refused all James's attempts to promote him to cardinal. In recompense, the Jesuit was appointed to the Privy Council and, at the time of Mary's pregnancy, the public dislike of him had reached new heights.

That February, a sensational London murder, of a butcher by his wife, gained the popular imagination. As reported by

Terriesi, the woman was a midwife and rumours immediately sprang up that he had uncovered the plot by which she was to smuggle a live child into the queen's bedroom and pass it off as Mary's newborn child.[4] In a letter to William of Orange, Lord Danby observed that 'many of our ladies say ... the queen's great belly seems to grow faster than they have observed their own to do' and that Princess Anne, her step-daughter, should be on hand to see that the midwife did her duty.[5] Other contemporaries, however, believed that the pregnancy was genuine. The letter of one Hoffman, writing to the Emperor, is preserved in the Vienna archives and included hope that the queen would carry this child to term. 'Contrary to her usual habit' of being ill while expecting, he wrote, Mary was 'keeping so well ... that there is every hope of her fortunate deliverance'. It appears that she had already made plans for lying-in at Windsor and was anticipating the baby's arrival in mid-July. Her 'prosperous health' was confirmed by Nuncio d'Adda, who also reported her continuing distress at the satires, printed in Holland, claiming that she was actually wearing a cushion under her dress.[6] However, worse news was to come that May, when she learned of the illness of her brother, the Duke of Modena and, for a while, her doctors feared she would miscarry. Soon though, Mary was able to write to her step-daughter, Mary, Princess of Orange, to reassure her that, although she had been frightened, she had recovered and was expecting to enter confinement in about six weeks. She was dissuaded from her plans for lying-in at Windsor, as the persistent rumours made a more public occasion necessary. A suite of rooms was prepared instead at St James's Palace, away from the glare of the sun but right in the public gaze. Here, it would be impossible for Mary to practise any deception, even if she had wanted to.

Prince James was born on Sunday 10 June 1688. The estimated date of his arrival had been miscalculated but, as Terriesi pointed out, it was nine months since the royal couple's sojourn at Bath. Mary had not felt at all unwell, sitting up late the previous night playing cards and retiring to bed as usual. She slept in a bed hung with richly patterned blue-and-violet Genoa velvet, displayed in the 2013 Secrets of the Royal Bedchamber exhibition at Hampton Court.[7] Her labour started at eight the following day and lasted only two hours; the baby was healthy, 'admirably formed and promises to live', according to Abbe Rizzini, while Clarendon wrote that he was a 'fine child to look upon'.[8] Terriesi described how her chamber was 'public at the time of the birth to all ladies who chose to enter and the ante-chamber to all men', and that as many as 200 well-wishers and 'malcontents' were present. The Lords of the Council wrote to inform the colonies that the queen was 'delivered of a prince about ten o'clock this morning'. The governors were to 'proclaim the fact, and appoint a day for public thanksgiving and for public rejoicings suitable to the occasion'.[9] James presented the midwife with a purse containing 500 guineas and, in spite of falling ill, the baby survived its first night after having been given 'remedies'. A number of wet nurses were lined up ready and the boy's household was established, containing 'two day nurses, four rockers, a laundress, seamstress and two pages'.[10] Two days later, in the queen's bedchamber, the child was baptised James Francis Edward Stuart, with Pope Innocent XI as his godfather. Terriesi concluded that, finally, 'all the mischievous deceits invented by the malicious representing a false pregnancy must now be dispelled'.

A celebratory ballad was printed at the Golden Ball, Pye Corner, in Smithfield, by a P. Brooksby. The pro-Catholic writer urged all loyal and content subjects to rejoice and welcome the boy, who had been sent by Heaven to their 'languishing nation'. Many had 'long prayed' for his arrival, news of which was brought on 'loud wings of fame ... the glory of Britain aloud to proclaim'. The ballad paints a misleading picture of overwhelming joy in London, with 'all tongues' expressing their 'true thankfulness' and cannon booming out, while 'lords, dukes, earls and commons all, in e'ry degree did their loyalty show'. Not 'one in ten thousand failed' in loyalty. The young prince was designed for great action: 'to valour, to justice, to goodness inclined'.[11] Whoever the anonymous writer was, the work was a gallant effort to stir a sense of national pride but it did not reflect the true mood of the city. Also printed, in the same year, was the thinly veiled pro-Protestant *A New Song of an Orange*, which would 'cure al the ayls in England and Wales'. When it came to 'religion, property, justice and laws', there was nothing 'better to stop a man's mouth than an Orange'![12] Another states that 'the Jesuits swear the midwife told tales and ruined his Highness the Prince of Wales', and that the whole business was a 'forged device' that had created, or substituted, a prince 'in a trice'. Mary had apparently conceived by using holy water and a smock from Rome and the child was born with a stamp or 'tile' on its side, to show its royal provenance.[13]

The person to whom the idea of a fake pregnancy mattered most had not even been in the country at the time of the birth, let alone the queen's bedroom. Despite the presence of the witnesses, intended to place the delivery above suspicion, the supporters of William of Orange continued spreading more reports of deception. Stories circulated that the queen had miscarried, or borne a daughter, and that the bedpan had been the means of smuggling a 'base-born' boy into the room under the noses of all assembled. Others questioned the boy's paternity. One spy reported to William that 'the business of the new prince is so much suspected in Scotland' that it was greeted with 'great solemnity' and that the hat-waving official who delivered the news found a suspicious and silent audience.[14] James and Mary were angered and upset by these reactions but they had no idea just how far the tide of Protestant opinion had turned against them. On 30 June, seven members of Parliament sent an invitation to William to invade England and claim his father-in-law's throne.

Unaware of this, Mary wrote to her step-daughter, William's wife, describing how she had been delivered early and that the child was strong. The answers she received were cold and distant, echoing the worst of the suspicions the queen had already encountered: 'All the king's children,' the princess wrote, 'shall ever find as much affection and kindness from me as can be expected for children from the same father.'[15] This was soon followed by a list of eighteen personal questions as William was, in fact, conducting his own enquiry into the birth, with his sister-in-law, Anne, as chief witness. Her answers to the questions regarding the pregnancy and labour were sufficient to convince William that there was cause for suspicion. Hostile witnesses who had been present in the birth chamber changed their story to refute the child's legitimate arrival. When the English Ambassador at The Hague held a reception to celebrate the prince's birth, no one attended.[16] Saddened, Mary was recovering from the birth and appeared for the first time to dine in public and attend chapel in mid-July.

A further problem arose regarding the baby's feeds. Apparently, Mary had intended to feed him with water gruel and boiled bread but he was unwell and her doctors prescribed a paste made of oat and barley meal. Imperial Ambassador Hoffman reported that the boy was being given 'all the remedies to be found in apothecaries' jar and drawers except milk', including Canary wine and Goddard's drops. The one thing he was not given was milk, with the doctors declaring he would not last half an hour if he was breastfed. It was common at the time for nursing mothers to withhold the breast for a month, as it was thought that feeding should not take place until post-partum bleeding was over. Babies were fed with animal milk, or honey and sugar water, but without the protective immunities offered by colostrum, the first milk, or the process of sterilisation, this resulted in many infant deaths. Newborns were suckled on linen pouches, horns, clay jugs and pickled cow nipples, which were full of germs.[17] Perhaps this could account for some of the infant losses the royal couple had already suffered but, in 1688, their son was more fortunate or more strong. Eventually, James overruled the doctors and a wet-nurse, a tile-maker's wife, was brought to the Richmond Palace nursery in such haste that she had on a petticoat, waistcoat, old shoes and no stockings![18] By mid-August, the baby was 'restored thanks to a natural diet'.

The religious conflict only intensified, with the new Prince of Wales at its centre. On 22 October, James called an unprecedented meeting of Parliament, noblemen, judges, clergymen and London's Lord Mayor, intent on dispelling the whispers that had arisen. Finally, he had become aware of the extent of the threat to his kingdom, in the shape of his son-in-law. In the belief that William was about to invade England, he stated that the son 'which with God hath blessed' him was rumoured to be a 'supposed child', whose arrival was sworn to, under oath, by forty witnesses.

On 5 November, William of Orange landed at Brixham with 15,000 men. James, Mary and their tiny son fled to France. The baby James, known to history as the 'Old Pretender', was brought up in Paris and on the death of his father, in 1701, was proclaimed by Catholics as James III of England and James VIII of Scotland.

17

George, 1738

As soon as her labour pains started, she knew something was wrong. Augusta, Princess of Wales, was not due to give birth yet; in fact, her second child should not be arriving for another two months, according to her physicians. The early June sunshine slanted in through the window, but her estimated due date fell in the height of summer, in August. There was no denying, though, that her contractions were real and increasing in intensity. Still only eighteen years old, she had hoped this second child would arrive smoothly, in comparison with her first. When she had gone into labour with her daughter, last summer at Hampton Court, her husband had hurried her away to St James's Palace, perhaps to ensure his parents, George II and Queen Caroline, were not present at the birth. Now it seemed that she would be going through the ordeal again in unexpected circumstances, although, at least, her baby would be born at the marital home, Norfolk House. The young Princess Augusta must have worried whether a child born so early could be expected to survive. Perhaps she began to prepare herself for the worst.

Much had changed in England in the fifty-year interval following the 'glorious revolution' for which the birth of Mary of Modena's baby, James Stuart, had been the catalyst. The invasion of William of Orange had been successful politically,

although, on a personal level, he and his wife Mary had failed
to produce a surviving child. The throne had then passed to
Mary's younger sister, Anne, who had also suffered heartbreak
as a mother, outliving all seventeen children she bore. As a
result, Parliament looked abroad for its next king, to Germany
and the house of Hanover. The crown went to the great
grandson of Charles I, through the marriage of his daughter
Elizabeth to Frederick of Bohemia. On the death of Anne
in 1714, George I arrived in England with his wife and two
children. The elder, the future George II, was already married
with a son, Prince Frederick, who had been born in Germany.

When it came to choosing a wife for Frederick, his parents
looked to their home country. Augusta of Saxe-Gotha,
a German princess, had arrived in England at the age of
sixteen, speaking barely any English. She had been married
to the twenty-nine-year-old Frederick on 27 April 1736
in the Chapel Royal at St James's Palace. The union
seemed to be a happy one and, seven months later, she had
conceived. However, Frederick had a poor relationship
with his parents, which would complicate matters in the
coming months. An air of secrecy had been deliberately
created around the pregnancy and the king and queen had
not learned of her condition until three weeks before the
princess's confinement. Even the midwife, Mrs Cannon, and
the attendant doctor, Dr Hollings, had not been permitted
to make the information public. During her final trimester,
the prince repeatedly moved Augusta between Hampton
Court and St James's Palace, causing his father, George II,
to chide him that removing her 'under the pains and certain
indications of immediate labour' was 'to the imminent
danger and hazard both of the princess and her child'. The
king interpreted his son's actions and secrecy as a 'deliberate
indignity' and slight to himself and his wife, Queen Caroline.

Following the birth of his daughter, Frederick wrote to his parents, offering the explanation that no midwife had been at hand at Hampton Court and that he had acted on medical advice when removing his wife to London.[1]

The king's concern is understandable. This had been Augusta's first pregnancy and, coupled with her youth, it was important that she and the baby received the best possible medical care. Her survival and health, as well as that of a potential future monarch, were at stake. Relations between Frederick and his parents had been difficult for a long time, with George and Caroline reputedly believing their son to be 'the greatest villain ever born', while Prime Minister Robert Walpole condemned him as a 'poor, weak, irresolute, false, lying, dishonest, contemptible wretch that nobody loves, that nobody believes, that nobody will trust'.[2] Secrecy surrounding the birth could raise insurmountable problems for the succession. Mary of Modena's crowded birth chamber of 1688 was still within living memory, with all the lessons it could teach about the need for openness and publicity when it came to royal deliveries. The circumstances surrounding Augusta's first pregnancy must have incited unwanted public speculation. Frederick's actions in the summer of 1737 caused his parents concern as Augusta began to labour for her second child.

A girl, named after her mother, arrived on 31 July 1737 and the princess recovered well. Her mother-in-law, the queen, was relieved that the child was female, as it would not succeed to the throne and, therefore, the secrecy of its delivery would be less problematic. When it came to the arrival of a prince, all must be above board. Augusta was soon out of bed and her little daughter was handed over to a wet nurse. She must have conceived again about four months later, in November of that year, as the arrival of her second child was predicted for August 1738. However, once again, all did not go quite as planned. Her labour began at the start of June, only ten months after her previous confinement. It is possible that the dates were slightly miscalculated but the implications of this are an earlier conception, during her post-partum recovery. This is not impossible but it seems more likely that, as her doctors suspected, her second child would be premature. That June, rapid preparations were made to ensure her chambers were adequately provided, according to her need and the season. John Maubray's 1724 midwifery text, *The Female Physician*, advised that in summer confinements, when the heat 'scorches so much as to dissipate the woman's strength', she ought to labour in a ground-floor chamber, strewn with wine and willow leaves, rose water and a little vinegar 'as is customary in hot countries'.[3] Her rooms at Norfolk House were made ready.

It appeared that Augusta's child was arriving after a pregnancy of seven months. *The Female Physician* identified a few possible causes for babies arriving prematurely, some of which seem rather unlikely today and conflict with modern gynaecological understanding. Comparing 'human seed' to grain, the author states that different seed can ripen at different times, allowing for pregnancies of seven, eight and even eleven months because 'women bring forth the children of different fathers at different times'. Arrival time could also depend upon the 'formation and perfection of the foetus', as some matured more quickly than others and could also be affected by the temperature of the womb. This was considered to vary between women, determined by constitution, habits and lifestyle, causing some to 'fructify and ripen sooner than others'. The phases of the moon were also thought to exert an influence, with the author citing Pliny's comment that 'none are born in the seventh month but they who have been conceived in the very change of the moon'.[4] According to NASA data recording the lunar cycle, a full moon did in fact fall on 7 November 1373, almost exactly seven months before George's birth.[5]

Eighteenth-century beliefs regarding premature babies differ considerably from those of the twenty-first century. Those who arrived after a seven-month pregnancy were considered to be 'weak and infirm' but, according to astrology, it was an auspicious time to be born. The moon was thought to preside over the seventh month, giving the foetus a 'certain fatness, thereby relaxing and easily distending' the womb. If birth occurred at the end of that month, the child may 'continue both healthy and lively'. The seventh was also considered a significant month for birth because of the many numerological occurrences; Maubray cited seven spheres of heaven and seven days of the week, as well as a range of biblical examples, and concluded that the number 'may properly portend here, perfection in maturity and completion in vitality'.[6]

In spite of this medical confidence, it must have been an anxious time for all involved, considering that the princess may be about to deliver a future King of England in potentially difficult circumstances. All depended upon the baby's gender. If it survived but suffered some birth defect or frailty as a result of its premature arrival, the implications for the royal family would have been considerable. The health of the monarch was metonymic with the welfare of the nation and the empire; a healthy king signalled a healthy country. An essay that appeared in the *Gentleman's Magazine* of August 1732 highlighted the importance of a prince as a figurehead, to restore the nation's 'lapsed powers to their primitive health and strength' and make his subjects 'imitate his divine perfections and transform us into his likeness'. As part of his education, a prince was advised to read the lessons of history to 'learn the causes of the rise and fall of monarchies'.[7] Previous kings and heirs had been deposed, even executed, because of their perceived unsuitability as rulers. The ill-fated Charles I had been a frail child, with poor health, unable to walk unaided and developing a stammer. Any future Hanoverian king must arrive in circumstances that were above reproach and be in perfect health in order to stand a chance at inheriting and retaining the throne. The possibility that a premature male child, with some physical or mental defect that would render him incapable of rule or complicate the succession, would have presented a serious concern. 'Freaks of nature' and 'monster births' were still as feared as they always had been and public interest had been excited by the sensational Mary Toft case of 1726. The Surrey woman was exposed as a fraud after having claimed to have been delivered, by John Howard, an 'eminent surgeon and man-midwife', of a number of rabbits, having become fixated by the animals during her pregnancy. Her story was depicted in cartoons and told in pamphlets, such as the 1727 one titled *Much Ado About Nothing: Or a Plain Refutation of all that has been said about the Rabbit Woman of Godalming*. It was in this context that Queen Charlotte had expressed relief that Augusta's 'poor, ugly little' first child had proved to be a 'she-mouse' rather than a prince.

As her labour advanced, Augusta would also have been aware of the circumstances surrounding the recent death of her mother-in-law, the queen. Caroline of Ansbach had died on 20 November 1737, after being taken ill a few weeks before. It would have served as a reminder to the princess of the long-term risks associated with childbirth, which could ultimately be fatal. While delivering her final child back in 1724, Caroline had suffered from an umbilical hernia that had troubled her since. Six months after the birth of her granddaughter, her womb had finally ruptured and an emergency operation had failed to save her life. Augusta was only eighteen, young and healthy; she had the best possible chance of survival yet she was aware of how dramatically the process might go wrong and leave mother and child with permanent injuries, if they were fortunate enough to survive.

The combination of a female midwife, Mrs Cannon, and the male Dr Hollings is an interesting one for the time, given the rise of the male midwife or accoucher. It was a fashionable but controversial role. As early as 1706, midwife Elizabeth Nihill was writing that men 'lack the shrewd prognostic or acute sense' of the 'experienced woman who much sooner perceive the danger before it is too late and are neither with-held with a false shame'. According to Nihill, the 'great object of the man-midwife' was to 'impose so false a notion upon his patient, as that his partial knowledge is sufficient to everything'.[8] Equally, in choosing Mrs Cannon, the Prince and Princess of Wales were following advice of one of the most prolific professionals of the period, Sarah Stone. Delivering babies in Somerset, Stone's position as the daughter and mother of midwives is a reminder of the oral nature of female knowledge, passed between generations in the same geographical region. Her knowledge overlapped with the usual male preserve of surgery, as she attended female autopsies and studied anatomy, causing her to be summoned instead of them to all the difficult local cases. Outspoken against male midwives, she published her *Complete Practice of Midwifery* in the same year as Augusta's pregnancy.

The *Gentleman's Magazine* for 1733 lists the promotion of a Joseph Atkinson, who was described as a 'man-midwife', but also includes a letter that presents the profession as a triviality, on a par with a 'confectioner or a boot-catcher in some ale house'.[9] A list of books published that September included an entry that highlighted the dangers of male intervention in what had been predominantly female territory; *The Man-Midwife Unmasked or Dr D*— did little to improve the reputation of male practitioners by portraying the allegations of rape levelled at an accoucher. In 1738, a verse version of the story appeared, titled *The Lady's Decoy: Or, the Man-Midwife's Defence: Occasion'd by the Revival of a Bill of Indictment Against the Famous Doctor D*—.[10] This portrays a fictitious doctor being charged with rape after taking advantage of the women in attendance on a birth, although he was not punished as the jury had doubts over the innocence of his accuser. Some were still suspicious of the accouchers' motives and education; one cartoon of the early eighteenth century depicted a hybrid figure, half male, half female, while pamphlets and popular texts repeated the stereotypes of the 'murdering midwife' and 'lewd male-midwives'. Equally, men attacked the stereotype of the gossiping females crowded around the labouring mother. Bernard Faust, a man-midwife, in 1784 wrote, 'How marvellous it is when mothers leave the windows of their bedroom open. Then the stand-offish old women, who otherwise crowd around the mother in a room they have heated to boiling point, will now stay home.'[11] The most important male midwife of the era was the Scottish surgeon William Smellie, who wrote a manual on the art of delivery and developed the forceps that had been invented by the Chamberlen family. He trained other men in gynaecology and midwifery in his London school using an 'obstetrical manikin' designed for the purpose. It is probable, though, that a female midwife was employed for Augusta's second delivery, alongside a male doctor, maybe even the previous pairing of Mrs Cannon and Dr Hollings.

The future George III was born to Frederick, Prince of Wales, and Princess Augusta between seven and eight on the morning of 4 June 1738, at Norfolk House, St James's Square, London. The fears regarding his health and development proved unsubstantiated. After his arrival, he would have been lain on his side as his umbilical cord was cut, in order to prevent him being choked by the humours rushing to his mouth or nose. He would then have been washed in warm wine, milk or ale, with particular care that his 'head, armpits and groin' were cleansed with sponges, before being examined and swaddled. Sometimes butter or the oil of almonds were used when a newborn was especially covered with 'viscous matter'. His ears and nostrils would have been 'unstopped' with 'small tents of fine rags, wet therein', his eyes wiped with a 'soft dry cloth' and 'the mouth, tongue and jaws may be cleansed by the finger'.[12] It was thought that he would not survive so he was baptised the same day, by Thomas Secker, rector of St James's. But the baby did not die, instead he grew stronger.

A year later, George had developed into a strong little boy. To celebrate his first birthday, a small army of sixty boys, all under twelve years old, chosen from the families of prominent citizens, 'formed themselves into a Lilliputian company of foot soldiers' and were brought to Norfolk House 'in the true military costume in hackney coaches'. They marched inside 'with drums beating and colours flying and a full band playing' and kissed the hand of the little prince, who had been dressed in a military style, with hat and feather. He was then invited to become their colonel. George's father, Frederick, never became king as he died in 1751, when his eldest son was twelve. His father, George II, survived for another nine years, before his death allowed his grandson to succeed to the throne as George III. While he grew into a physically healthy adult, the 'madness' for which this George became famous may have been attributable to the hereditary illness porphyria, although it has recently been suggested that he was, in fact, being slowly poisoned by the arsenic found in beauty treatments or certain shades of green paint. It has also been claimed that the purple colour found in his urine, which had been taken as an indicator of porphyria, may have been present as a result of the gentian he was prescribed. Other indicators suggest he may have suffered from bipolar disorder. At the end of his long reign, following a series of debilitating episodes, his health had broken down sufficiently for his son to assume power as regent.

18

Amelia, 1783

He was going to lose America. Since the landing of the pilgrim ship, the *Mayflower*, at Cape Cod in November 1620, it had long been a valued addition to England's expanding colonial empire but now the territories were slipping out of his fingers. George III had been on the throne for thirteen years when the American people rejected the imposition of more levies, saying that it was illegal to tax them without giving them representation in the English Parliament. The conflict had erupted over that very English commodity, tea. Following the Tea Act of 1773, the revolutionary 'Sons of Liberty' had boarded ships owned by the East India Company in Boston harbour and thrown its cargo of crates into the water. Full-scale conflict had broken out two years later, with George accused of 'destroying' his American subjects' lives. In a symbolic attack, a gilded statue of him on horseback, which stood on the Bowling Green on the tip of Manhattan Island, was pulled down and its head was sawn off. The metal was melted down to make 42,000 bullets to fight against English tyranny.[1] By 1783, it was clear that American Independence had been won, following the surrender of General Cornwallis after a three-week siege at Yorktown. Despite the news from across the Atlantic and the advice of his Prime Minister, George refused to give up the fight for America and, after his own

Parliament voted against him, considered abdicating the throne.[2]

While 342 chests of tea were being dumped in the harbour at Boston, the drink was becoming increasingly controversial among George's female subjects. In 1757, Jonas Hanaway published a series of letters claiming that tea consumption lay at the heart of a number of health complaints experienced by women, including 'weak digestion, low spirits, lassitudes, melancholy and nervous complaints'. Just like gin, or Mother's Ruin, poor mothers purchasing tea were taking food out of the mouths of their children, leading them to starve to death. Hanaway considered tea-drinking particularly repellent among breastfeeding mothers, who were passing on this 'liquid fire' to their infants. The anonymous pamphlet *The Good and Bad Effects of Tea Consider'd* attacked the ritual of afternoon tea, when 'artful hussies' neglected their children, while one French doctor believed drinking tea would heat the womb and have a negative effect upon a woman's ability to conceive.[3] This was contradicted in many of the midwifery manuals of the day, such as F. Churchill's 1867 *Manual for Midwives and Monthly Nurses*, which advocated washing sore nipples in strong green tea, feeding weak tea to women in the second stage of labour and giving it to convalescent mothers.[4] Firms such as Phipps and Robinson of London manufactured luxurious silver tea caddies and scoops for the aristocracy but tea was rapidly becoming the nation's drink of choice. When the East India Company stopped importing Chinese porcelain in 1791, it necessitated the manufacture of a new, hard-wearing English bone china that could be mass produced and which subsequently found its way into every home.[5] The role of tea as a symbol of England's loss of America and its reputed effects upon female reproduction were of particular relevance to George III and his family, as late in 1782, around the time they received news of the Yorktown surrender, Queen Charlotte had conceived her fifteenth child.

George had succeeded to the English throne at the age of twenty-two, following the death of his grandfather, George II. He had been happily married to Charlotte of Mecklenberg-Strelitz for twenty-one years, despite only having met her on their wedding day. The relationship had survived George's infamous episodes of madness but the years 1782–3 were to prove especially difficult for the devoted couple. In August 1782, they had been devastated by loss of the twenty-month-old Prince Alfred, after an inoculation against smallpox made him ill. The queen had conceived in the months following but when she was in her second trimester, in May 1783, they also lost the four-year-old Octavius in the same manner, following a smallpox vaccination. The vaccine had been developed in reaction to the widespread epidemic of 1721 but while many survived, deaths from it had already been recorded and it would not be perfected until the work of Edward Jenner in 1796. The additional death of Octavius, to whom his father had been very close, coupled with the loss of America, represented a huge blow to George. Having borne fourteen children over a period of eighteen years, Charlotte had enjoyed an exceptionally high rate of infant survival, with all her elder offspring surviving into adulthood, so the loss of these two sons as a result of the decision to inoculate them must have been difficult to accept. The one glimmer of hope, though, was the child that the queen carried in her womb. This latest pregnancy began to represent a possible happier future in their minds, although at the age of thirty-nine, she was comparatively old in eighteenth-century childbearing terms.

The prognosis for Charlotte was fairly encouraging though. Statistics collected in 1781 by man-midwife Dr Robert Bland at Westminster General Infirmary showed a good rate of survival among most mothers. Bland explained that only 1 in 30 women had 'unnatural labours' with feet, bottom or arm presenting first, and as few as 1 in 210 had a uterine haemorrhage before or during labour. Even then, those mothers had a 2 in 3 chance of survival, although rates of death from puerperal fever were high. Laborious or difficult labours were experienced by in 1 in 18, and 1 in 41 of those were in danger but maternal mortality only occurred in 1 out of 270 cases. Most mothers admitted to Westminster hospital were aged between twenty-six and thirty, with just over 10 per cent falling into the same bracket as the queen, being aged between thirty-six and forty. Six women arriving to give birth were as old as forty-six.[6]

Of course, maternal survival rates were also affected by a woman's record of conception. For her previous fourteen pregnancies, Charlotte had experienced no difficulties in falling pregnant. The average interval between the birth of one child and the conception of the next was seven months, although in six cases, it had taken place in four months or less. The largest break between the births of any of her babies was that between Alfred and the final pregnancy, of two years, two months. This may indicate that Charlotte, having first conceived at the age of seventeen, experienced dwindling fertility in her later thirties, followed by a relatively early menopause. The Westminster statistics show a much poorer rate of survival for the families of lower-class women, with Bland concluding that out of those babies that survived birth, 5 in 12 went on to die before their second birthday, as a result of the 'poverty of their parents'.[7]

Alfred and Octavius had not been lost as a result of

poverty; their inoculations had been carried out at the request of their parents, making this a perpetual source of regret. The death of Prince Alfred coincided with Charlotte entering her final trimester. This was considered a period of significant danger and the queen would have had to temper her grief and not allow it too great an expression in order to preserve the new life she was carrying. A quiet life was advised. Dr John Maubray described this period as the 'finishing maturation months of the infant'. As the child increased in 'bulk, vigour and activity' it would cause the mother 'incredible uneasiness', bordering sometimes on 'obstreperousness'. She may experience difficulty in passing urine, suffer from constipation, varicose veins and swollen legs. Maubray's advice for an expectant mother was to eat little but often, take moderate exercise, take laxatives and baths to 'moisten the passages', rest well and drink strengthening cordials, although he also advised the eating of raw eggs 'if the stomach can take it'.[8] Writing in 1790, Dr Charles White, in *A Treatise on the Management of Pregnant and Lying-In Women*, recommended women took asses' milk and seltzer water and bathed in cold sea water to prevent miscarriage; 'several have bathed to within a few days of their delivery'. He also criticised the fashion for women lacing the stays tightly on their bodices, in the belief that the child would be carried lower and the 'mother would have better times.' In the later stages of pregnancy, White advised women to lie frequently upon a couch or bed to take the strain of their muscles, preventing the legs from swelling and pain developing in the back and hips.[9]

As her time approached, Charlotte began to plan her lying-in. It is unclear exactly where she chose to give birth, with some sources stating she had selected the Royal Lodge, in Windsor Great Park; others name Cumberland Lodge and

Buckingham House, later Buckingham Palace. Some locate the event at Windsor Castle itself. Wherever the queen did labour, there were certain measures that needed to be taken for her comfort and safety. According to Maubray the room should be a 'convenient temperature' not too hot, not too cold, as one condition could constrict and close the womb, while the other 'dissipates and debilitates' the spirits.[10] The investigations of Dr Bland at Westminster Infirmary led him to conclude that aristocratic mothers did not benefit from their superior diets and methods of heating, as 'the lower sort of people recover more certainly after parturition than persons in higher stations of life'. He noted that puerperal fever was 'nourished' and its 'malignancy increased' by fires, closed rooms and 'septic' diets, but when the poor were unable to 'keep great fires or indulge themselves with animal food', their suffering was less.[11] White urged the labouring mother to enjoy fresh air and not crowd her chamber with friends. In the summer, she should keep the door and windows open and not allow the air to be 'rendered foul', nor herself to become overheated. She should not allow her pores to become clogged with sweat and revive herself with cordials if she felt cold. In cases of muscle spasms, she should be relieved by taking an opiate. The seventeenth-century doctor Thomas Sydenham had recommended opium, or laudanum, for sleeplessness and as a pain reliever; by the eighteenth, it was widely used for nervous disorders. The old Biblical taboo about the necessity of female suffering during delivery was finally changing.

One of the most influential midwives of the period was Margaret Stephen. She had thirty years of training other women in the profession by the time she wrote her 1795 manual *The Domestic Midwife, or The Best Means of Preventing Danger in Childbirth, Considered.* Its lessons include the anatomy of the pelvis and foetal skull as well as the use of forceps and other obstetrical instruments. Margaret had been trained by a pupil of William Smellie and was herself a mother of nine. At about seventeen centimetres long, the book was designed to be small enough for a woman to carry it in her pocket as she went about visiting and attending on her patients. Stephen rejected the notion that men could perform the role of midwife, claiming they were jealous and competitive over their positions and tried to take advantage of the profession for financial and social gain. In her eyes, there were three main reasons to reject male midwives: men did not have superior knowledge in this field, their employment made women redundant and the close contact with labouring and assisting women could lead to 'improper conduct'. In the case studies she outlines, Stephen describes the occasions when difficulties led her to summon a surgeon, only for the mother to insist she retain overall charge.[12]

Like Margaret Stephen, Queen Charlotte rejected the notion of a male accoucher. She had her royal midwife at her side when she went into labour, a Mrs Johnson, who had attended the arrival of all her other children. On 7 August 1783, she bore a daughter, who was laid in a cradle of ivory satin, under a coverlet embroidered with garden flowers. Charlotte was well looked after, in keeping with the advice of Dr James Maubray, who compared the recently delivered mother to a ship returning to port after a dangerous voyage, 'not well armoured against sudden winds and storms'. It was imperative to protect her from cold air, so she was wrapped in warm cloths, with all the windows and doors closed, and fed a little chicken broth. 'Strong' meat, as well as 'hot and strong' liquor, were forbidden. After resting, her limbs were washed with a mixture of warm wine and almond oil, although barley, linseed, chervil, violet leaves or marsh mallow, mixed with a few drops of honey and roses, would do equally well as a cleanser. Her breasts were to be covered with warm, soft cloths so the milk would not curdle; they would also benefit from a mixture of the leaves of mint, dill and parsley. All noise and loud chatter was forbidden in her presence, as it would disturb her rest and stop the 'natural course' of humours. She was to be fed over the coming days, as if she was a fever patient, with broth, jellies, ale soup with butter and fresh-laid eggs, gradually introducing small portions of chicken, veal or mutton. After twenty days, she was permitted more 'stringent' medicines and stronger food.[13] Under a careful regime, the child grew strong and healthy and the queen made a 'perfect recovery'.[14] On 17 September, Charlotte was well enough to be up out of bed and travel to St James's Palace. There, in the chapel royal, her daughter was given the name Amelia.

Less than a month after her birth, on 3 September, the Treaty of Paris was signed, ending the War of Independence. America's population was, by then, around a third of Britain's and many of them considered George to be a tyrant. A satirical cartoon of 1782 represented America as a semi-clad Native woman, celebrating her territories at the expense of other European powers, while George states, 'I gave them independence.' In reality, he had not wished to give them anything. The loss was considered a humiliation for George and his nation; the artist Benjamin West began a painting of the delegates gathered to sign the treaty, but with the British representative, David Hartley, refusing to pose, the work was never completed. It was also a cause of resentment against George at home, with one extreme cartoon, *The Allies*, depicting the king in league with, if not orchestrating, acts of barbarism by Native Americans, including the butchering and consumption of babies. Ironically, Amelia Island, a British-held territory north of Jacksonville, was returned to the Spanish in the treaty, so in naming the baby, George may have lost America but he gained a daughter. Amelia, or Emily, as her father often called her, became his new favourite and comfort in his advancing age. When she died of tuberculosis at the age of twenty-seven, in 1810, a contemporary memoir recorded, 'The venerable Father of his people bends his sacred head in grief over the cold remains of her, so lately the delight and comfort of his age.'[15]

It has been suggested that her death precipitated George III's final illness. Towards the end of his life, suffering from cataracts and rheumatism, he would have imagined conversations with his two dead sons, Octavius and Alfred. In 1811, it was apparent that he could no longer rule and his eldest son, George IV, became regent months before the old king's descent into complete madness. He died at Windsor Castle in 1820, unaware that his wife Charlotte had predeceased him in 1818.

19

George, 1817

Napoleon called him 'the handsomest young man I ever saw at the Tuileries'.[1] When he appeared on his London balcony, in May 1816, the assembled crowd cheered to see him in his blue coat with its star. Prince Leopold was twenty-six, an impoverished younger son of the German house of Saxe-Coburg-Saalfeld, who had campaigned against Napoleon in the Russian cavalry. He was a romantic, dashing figure, dark and handsome, who was about to become the husband of the twenty-year-old Princess of Wales, second in line to the English throne. It was a love match and the English people loved a romance. Princess Charlotte was reputed to have identified strongly with Jane Austen's creation Marianne Dashwood, of the 1811 novel *Sense and Sensibility*, a spirited and idealistic young woman who falls readily in love and initially rejects convention and 'sense' as portrayed by her elder sister. Coupled with her youth, beauty and romantic sentiments, the marriage made the young Charlotte popular with a general public who had become increasingly disillusioned with the extra-marital exploits and scandals of her parents' generation. It was heralded as an idyll of domestic harmony, an ideal of the quiet family life, on which the Victorians would place such high value.

The throng of people assembled in the Park to see

them arrive at Carlton House exceeded all expectation. Attempting to enter his carriage, Leopold was 'assailed by a number of females, patting him on the back and giving him good wishes' while the crowd shouted, 'Huzzah!'[2] The wedding was conducted in the Great Crimson Room, where a temporary altar was set up, covered in crimson velvet and adorned with the great mahogany candlesticks from Whitehall Chapel. The bride was dressed in a spangled lace gown, with short sleeves and long, rounded train, which cost £10,000 and glittered in the flickering light. After they had spoken their vows, Charlotte and Leopold stood arm in arm to receive the congratulations of their friends, before a salute was fired from St James's Palace and the bells of London pealed out the news.

Princess Charlotte was beloved by the people of England. She had been raised strictly by her father, although her childhood had been complicated by the scandals and quarrels between her estranged parents. At the age of seventeen, her marriage had become a controversial issue, as, young and passionate, she developed a number of passions for unsuitable men, including her illegitimate cousin, George FitzClarence, the son of William IV and the actress Dorothy Jordan. This led to conflicts with her father, who kept her on a tight rein. His preferred candidate for her hand was William, Prince of Orange. The match was negotiated for months but Charlotte was reluctant to leave England and her mother behind; although she had actually signed a contract with William, her insistence that her mother be welcomed in their marital home led to the alliance being dissolved. Her father also believed her to be infatuated, at different times, with the Duke of Gloucester and a Prussian prince, but Charlotte had other ideas. At a party at the Pulteney Hotel in London, she had met Prince Leopold and fallen in love. The pair had secret meetings and when she broke off the engagement with William, her father forbade her from leaving the house; her response was to run away to her mother. There was no love lost between her parents, the future George IV and Princess Caroline of Wales.

The marriage of Charlotte's parents had been a publicly enacted disaster. George IV's wife was his first cousin, Princess Caroline of Brunswick, whom he had chosen on the recommendation of his mistress, Lady Jersey. *The Lover's Dream*, a satirical cartoon by Gillray, depicts George dreaming about the beautiful princess who would endow him with her riches, to the exclusion of all his other mistresses. However, it proved to be a mésalliance on the scale of Henry VIII and Anne of Cleves, when Charles objected to her appearance, manners and personal hygiene. Caroline was equally disappointed by the looks of her future spouse and his marked preference for certain of her female attendants. The pair were married soon after in England, on 8 April 1795. George was drunk on the wedding night; apparently he only slept with the 'monster' on three occasions, although this was sufficient to leave Caroline pregnant. She gave birth to Princess Charlotte on 7 January 1796, although she was to have little influence over her daughter's life beyond pushing her out into the world; George's mother, Queen Charlotte, would choose even the bed linen and cradle for the occasion. The baby's parents separated three months later, with George returning to his morganatic wife, Maria FitzHerbert, while Charlotte was raised by a governess. Her father's Will, written around this time, specified that Caroline, with her 'improper and bad' influence, was to have no role in the education or rearing of her own child. She went on to adopt more children, although this provoked an investigation into the rumours that at least one of them was her illegitimate offspring. Their daughter later stated that her 'mother was bad, but she would not have been so bad if my father had not been much worse still'.[3]

Charlotte's marriage promised to be more successful. A few months after the ceremony, she suffered a miscarriage but conceived again in January 1817. One account of Charlotte's pregnancy recorded the public interest in her condition as soon as the news was announced: 'the greatest interest was excited through the nation' and her 'every step' was watched with 'anxious attention'. It recorded the gratitude Charlotte was reputed to have expressed to one of the ladies of her court, in making an 'addition' to her 'excess of happiness'.[4] The English people were 'elated' that they were to have an heir to the throne and hoped Charlotte's 'progeny would prove more worthy of a crown than some of the sons of the austere grandmother', George III's wife, Charlotte of Mecklenburg-Strelitz. Betting shops even opened book on the baby's gender, giving rise to national speculation and anticipation on the identity and nature of this future monarch.[5]

Charlotte chose as her obstetrician one Sir Richard Croft, 6th Baronet Croft, an accoucher, or fashionable male midwife. He was considered the most able of his profession and all her ladies-in-waiting were 'unfit to render advice or assistance upon any emergency' as none of them had been through the experience themselves. The queen, Charlotte's grandmother, asked Croft to move into Claremont in the final stages of the pregnancy in order to be on hand and employed a nurse, Mrs Griffiths, a woman of 'experience and repute in that capacity'.[6] It was fashionable at the time, in courtly circles, to employ a male-midwife, although this was still being criticised among the women working in the profession, such as Sarah Stone and Margaret Stephen.

Elizabeth Nihill had identified the difference between the approaches taken by male and female midwives back in 1709. With hindsight her words seem particularly pertinent to Charlotte's case. In *A Treatise on the Art of Midwifery*, she wrote that in uncomplicated cases, attending males would 'pass off tolerably well' but as soon as the labour pains began, she defied him 'with all his learning, to equal the female skill and cleverness, not only for lessening the suffering of the patient but for facilitating the happy issue of her burden'. Worse still, when complications did arise, 'trusting to these men-dabblers in midwifery is a folly that may be fatal to both mother and child'.[7] In the coming years, some powerful male voices had joined the cause of the women midwives. In 1827, Sir Henry Halford would write that 'midwifery was an act foreign to the habits of a gentleman' while Sir Anthony Carlisle added, in 1834, that it was an 'imposture to pretend that a medical man was required in labour'.[8]

Some of the decisions that were made regarding the princess's antenatal care seem unwise by today's standards. Croft put Charlotte on a strict diet, which weakened her considerably; she was 'scarcely allowed any animal food or wine, to both of which she had previously been accustomed'.[9] This may have been a measure to prevent the child from growing too large, as Croft also bled Charlotte frequently in her middle trimester, which was considered a factor in foetal growth and the prevention of haemorrhaging. *The Lady's Own Book* of 1847 was critical of the practise of bleeding as a means of controlling 'nervous irritability' or 'unusual feeling'. Bleeding could 'agitate the system and increase irritability', which led the doctor to bleed his patient more, in order to quieten her.[10] The doctor's report on Charlotte's labour, included by Coote at the end of his text, includes the comment that the princess's 'high state of health' and 'morbid excess of animal spirits' led to concerns.[11] This helps explain why she was so frequently bled. However, combined with the 'low diet' Charlotte was fed, this only 'enfeebles the mother and robs the child' and could lead to miscarriage or premature labour. Interestingly, the author of *The Lady's Own Book* comments that the theoretical practitioner, whom is referred to throughout as male, would weaken the woman so much as to need 'as much of his bodily strength as may become necessary to drag the child into the world'[12] and in 1790, Charles White had written that bloodletting was 'too indiscriminately used and too often repeated'. The pregnancy appeared to be straightforward, although there were concerns about the weight of mother and child. The princess took regular exercise, continuing to walk and ride with her husband around their home, Claremont House, up until the end.

Calculations made in July estimated that Charlotte's second baby was due in mid-October. The date arrived and passed; when she was three weeks overdue, on 3 November 1817, her waters broke and she took to her bed in expectation. It was announced that she had gone into labour at three in the morning but she did not progress and had remained in a similar condition by the following morning. Dr Croft suspected she may be carrying twins or there was some 'irregular action of the uterus' and summoned two other doctors, Baillie and Sims, to witness proceedings.[13] On the morning of 4 November, the three doctors issued a statement that 'the labour of her Royal Highness, the Princess Charlotte, is going on very slowly but, we trust, favourably'. The same statement was made at four that afternoon. An hour and a half later, a further statement that she had 'considerably advanced, and will, it is hoped, within a few hours be happily concluded'.[14] Croft's opinion was that they should let nature take its course and not intervene, to which Sims acquiesced. Sims also declined to enter the room in case he should distress the princess, so he did not get to examine her.

This decision contradicts the advice offered in a 1724 midwifery text, *The Female Physician*, which, in cases where a woman is 'debilitated' and unable to expel a child from her womb, 'it depends chiefly upon the subtile [*sic*] hand of the midwife to assist the womb in its function'. *The Female Physician* devotes a chapter to 'touching and handling the woman', which was so important 'as life itself depends upon it'. It was 'requisite' that a labouring woman be touched, before and after her waters had broken. Only through touch could a midwife reliably establish whether the birth would be 'easy and speedy or difficult and lingering'. This could assist particularly in the case of 'difficult births' and in certain cases, if the midwife 'understands her business', she 'must resolve to sweat at her work'.[15] This advocates the direct physical intervention that Croft and his fellow doctors decided against. With the earlier advice aimed at women assistants being explicit and detailed in the handling of the female body, the question arises over whether there was a degree of protocol or squeamishness which cause the male doctors to refrain from intervening. Nineteenth-century portrayals of ailing or deceased females increasingly tended towards the ideal, with queens and princesses semi-deified in popular culture, to the extent that pregnancy and birth became a social taboo. Where the 1724 text encourages the midwife to 'introduce her fingers into the orifice, dilating it cautiously with one or two until she can enter them all' and open the womb, it is difficult to imagine Charlotte's doctors willingly being so invasive.[16] There was no attempt to use the forceps, which, according to historian Alison Plowden, might have saved her life.[17]

Charlotte's labour did not progress. Due to her restricted diet and frequent bleeding, she was debilitated by the time her contractions began and spent over fifty hours attempting to expel her child without success. Finally, on the evening of 5 November, a stillborn boy was delivered, although Charlotte was considered to be doing 'extremely well'. The little prince was rushed into a side room but all attempts to revive him failed. Attention then turned to the princess. Initially, as Charlotte gave birth 'no great discharge issued' but Croft observed that her uterus was acting irregularly and it was anticipated that there would follow an 'unfavourable separation of the placenta'.[18] Half an hour later, she experienced a huge issue of blood but then seemed to rally. Leopold fed her chicken broth and gruel before retiring for the night at about 11 p.m. Charlotte fell ill at about midnight, vomiting and suffering from breathing difficulties, convulsed with spasms and developing the ominous coldness of extremities. In the early hours of the following morning, the princess died in the arms of her nurse. She was twenty-one. Sir Richard Croft announced the news to Leopold and messages were sent to other members of the royal family. Charlotte's father would soon send a letter to Dr Croft, expressing his gratitude for the doctor's assistance and assuring him he was 'satisfied with his skill and superior merit', concluding that her death had been 'the will of divine providence'.[19]

There was a widespread public reaction to the deaths of Charlotte and her son. Lady Anne Hamilton recorded 'the heavy tolling bell, the silence of the streets and the mute astonishment of all [with] unfeigned sorrow'. The death of England's 'star of promise', the 'beacon' which would 'light the traveller to escape the quicksand', brought 'the hopes of this great nation' to 'nought'.[20] Her demise was represented in the popular mass media of the time. Poems and essays were written in celebration of her blend of domestic and regal goodness and expressing dismay and injustice over her unexpected loss; in one *Sacred Memorial* she was the 'epitome of all the virtues that could adorn the woman'.[21] Richard Courbold's 1817 engraving of Britannia weeping over the princess's tomb bore the legend, 'She was a nation's hope, a nation's pride; with her that pride has fled, those hopes have died.'[22]

Charlotte's image was depicted on accessible memorial items such as printed scarves, commemorative coins, ribbons and transfer-printed china, affordable to many of her subjects in one form or another and giving them a sense of ownership of her and outlet for grief.[23] In popular memory, she became an increasingly romanticised figure, as a domestic idyll, typifying the emerging values of a quiet family life, which would prove so central to Victorian life. The marriage had presented 'so uninterrupted a scene of British comfort' and 'such a home of happiness' with 'so large a promise'.[24] One poem, 'Sincere Burst of Feeling', published in John Gwilliam's anthology *A Cypress Wreath*, stressed the connection between her sexuality and her death: 'Hath hymen dug, alas, thy tomb and widow'd Coburg's Princely bed?'[25] Shelley also wrote 'Address to the People on the Death of Princess Charlotte', casting her in the role of Liberty and, with so many others, lamenting the lost opportunity she represented. Interestingly, the emphasis in most of the mourning literature was on the princess, as a future queen, rather than her son.

It was not until 1837, with the Registration of Deaths Act, that national statistics for maternal mortality were recorded and collated. Initially, this was done on a voluntary basis and it was not until 1870, that the cause of death needed to be specified. These showed that death rates rose steadily over the next century, but by the 1930s, the more widespread use of birth control and antibiotics meant that the numbers fell.[26] At the end of the eighteenth century, Dr Alexander Gordon recognised the role that birth assistants played in cases of puerperal fever, stating, 'It is a disagreeable fact that I, myself, was the means of carrying the infection to a number of women.'[27] He advised that all clothing and bed linen be burned after delivery, with doctors and nurses fumigated. Tests in the Vienna Maternity hospital also proved that lives were saved when staff washed their hands with carbolic soap after attending deliveries. Joseph Lister introduced carbolic sprays and the work of Louis Pasteur initiated a search for the antiseptics that would kill bacteria.[28] In cases like Charlotte's though, when labour would not progress, the only option to save mother and child was active intervention. By the 1850s, for every 200 live births, one mother and twenty babies were lost. Many wrote letters of farewell and prepared their shrouds before they went into labour.[29]

The funeral procession to Windsor consisted of three carriages; one for the stillborn son, George, one containing Charlotte's coffin and a third, in which Leopold rode. Even the weather echoed the dismal scene, as it was a 'fine night' with the moon shining brightly until they reached the castle, where, 'in remarkable manner', the sky suddenly became overcast 'and darkness ensued'. This 'visibly affected' the mourners who had turned out to witness their arrival, behaving with the 'utmost decorum'. The intention had been to admit the public into the room draped with black cloth on walls, ceiling and floor but Leopold's grief, as he sat with the coffins, meant the decision was taken to exclude the majority. The few who were admitted saw her coffin covered with a pall of black velvet, with a border of white, to symbolise the means of her death, and were 'highly wrought' in remembrance of her 'ardour of youth' and 'glow of health', now exchanged for 'the paleness of the cold cold corse [*sic*]' and the 'still sleep of death'.[30]

The funeral took place in St George's Chapel on Wednesday 19 November 1817. Coote recorded how it was the last sight of 'her whom, from a child, we have watched with increasing sentiments of respect, admiration and affection'.[31] Business was suspended throughout the city and all the churches in England and throughout the empire 'were opened for humiliation and prayer', with 'the most humble individual' claiming a 'right to lament the common affliction' alongside the 'loftiest'. A 'whole people' were 'prostrate before God' at a spectacle 'at once holy, majestic and edifying'.[32] The coffin of her stillborn son, George, was made of mahogany, covered with crimson velvet and lined with white satin.[33]

Despite messages of support from the royal family, Croft was deeply depressed by the princess's death and never managed to recover. Three months later, he committed suicide. His death, along with that of the mother and child, led to the episode being referred to as the 'triple obstetrical tragedy'. The political implications of Charlotte's death were huge, opening up the line of succession. Her uncles now rapidly cast off their mistresses and made legitimate marriages, one of which resulted in the birth in 1819 of the future Queen Victoria.

20

Victoria, 1840

Despite her reputation for demure staidness and her famous refusal to be amused, Queen Victoria was a passionate woman. Her name has become something of a byword for sexual repression but her love life with adored husband, Albert, was far from the prudery that her era has been assumed to typify. The day after her wedding, the twenty-year-old queen wrote to her confidant and Prime Minister, Lord Melbourne, that 'it was a gratifying and bewildering experience ... his excessive love and affection gave me feelings of heavenly love and happiness. He clasped me in his arms and we kissed each other again and again.'[1] Her three-day honeymoon at Windsor Castle left her the 'happiest, happiest being that ever existed'[2] and she had Albert design and install a bedside switch to activate mechanical locks on the bedroom door, so that their impromptu love-making sessions would not be interrupted. However, when it came to the consequences, or what she called the 'shadow side'[3] of love, pregnancy and birth, Victoria was less enthusiastic.

Victoria married her cousin, Albert of Saxe-Coburg, on 11 February 1840. After an unsuccessful first meeting in 1837, when the teenager had made little impact on the new queen, he returned two years later. Then, she fell passionately in love and proposed. He accepted. Many members of her cabinet were opposed to a German bridegroom so Victoria retaliated by only inviting five of them to the ceremony, saying that 'it is my marriage ... and I will only have those who can sympathise with me'.[4] The wedding dress, designed by her seamstress, Mrs Bettans, was fairly unostentatious white satin trimmed with lace and frilled sleeves but it set the trend for white dresses that has persisted ever since. The ceremony took place in the royal chapel at St George's Chapel, Windsor, but with photography in its infancy, no images were captured. However, the devoted couple would re-enact their vows fourteen years later, specifically for the newly developed cameras.

Victoria conceived within days of her wedding. It seems likely that neither she nor Albert had any idea about how this could have been prevented.[5] There was a certain amount of material published on birth control by the time of their marriage, such as Richard Carlile's 1828 *Every Woman's Book*, which recommended coitus interruptus as well as the sponges that French and Italian women were reputed to wear on their wrists, so as to literally have them to hand. It was possible to purchase sponges and 'gentleman's nightcaps' (condoms), cervical caps and an early American form of the femidom, or female condom, made from eel skin. Some upper-class women also practised 'irrigation', which involved the rinsing out of the vagina using a syringe, although the instructions, given in *Every Woman's Book*, made the process seem arduous and cumbersome. Social activist Annie Besant worked to raise public knowledge about the various options available to married couples, publishing the instructive *The Fruits of Philosphy*. This led to Besant's arrest and trial for obscenity. Initially convicted, the verdict was overturned on appeal and huge numbers of the book were sold.[6]

Victoria would not have begun to suspect her pregnancy until certain physical signs began to appear and, even then, she would have been cautious about diagnosis. An episode that occurred early in her reign had taught her a bitter lesson about the treatment incurred by women who were perceived to be pregnant, albeit unmarried ones. Two years after Victoria had become queen, her popularity suffered as a result of her role in the Flora Hastings scandal. Flora had been lady-in-waiting to the queen mother, the Duchess of Kent, and was reputed to be having an affair with the duchess's own favourite, John Conroy. In 1839, when Flora experienced pain and swelling in her lower abdomen, she visited Victoria's own doctor, Sir James Clark, who was unable to diagnose her without the physical examination she refused to grant him. Suspecting an illegitimate pregnancy, Clark remained discreet but Flora's appearance gave rise to court gossip, which reached the ears of the queen. Loathing Conroy, the inexperienced Victoria criticised him and Flora for immorality, but the lady's worsening condition finally led to the diagnosis of a cancerous liver tumour, giving her only months to live. Following her death that July, Conroy and Lord Hastings mounted an attack in the *Morning Post* on Victoria and Dr Clark for spreading false rumours. It affected the reputation of both, although the queen's popularity was to recover following her marriage and the birth of her first child. Dr Clark, who had treated Keats before his death in Rome, remained as physician-in-ordinary to Victoria and Albert, assisting with her subsequent deliveries.

The first signs of pregnancy were outlined by Dr Chavasse in his 1861 *Advice to a Mother on the Management of her Offspring*, in predictably euphemistic terms. First, a woman would 'cease to be unwell', referring to the cessation of the menstrual cycle and its associations with sickness, rather than as a natural healthy function. There was little difference from the advice given by medieval medical texts, which had listed the enlargement of the breasts, nausea and quickening at the fifth month that Chavasse now cited.[7] Victoria's reign saw the publication of a number of new manuals giving advice on pregnancy and childbirth. *The Lady's Own Book* of 1847, *Hints to Husbands* of 1857 as well as the 1863 *Observations in Midwifery*, and *A Few Suggestions to Mothers on the Management of their Children*, made contemporary knowledge and a range of cures accessible to a wider, increasingly literate public. The authors' views of motherhood as a skill to be acquired led them to denounce women who thought they could act 'without instruction', whom they blamed for the loss of young lives.[8]

The late summer and autumn of 1840, spent waiting in seclusion, proved frustrating for Victoria. As she later wrote to her daughter, it had all happened too quickly and denied her the opportunity to enjoy being married: 'What made me so miserable was ... to have the first two years of my married life utterly spoiled by this occupation.'[9] She felt as if motherhood had 'tried [her] sorely; one feels so pinned down, one's wings clipped, only half oneself'.[10] In September, when she was seven months pregnant, she made Albert a member of the Privy Council and issued him with a set of duplicate keys to her official boxes, so he could take over when she was incapacitated. It was a symbolic act, recognising her inability to act as queen during her numerous pregnancies and the tension of power this created between husband and wife. Victoria would have sought advice from her doctors as soon as she suspected her condition but physical examinations of any sort were shunned. Even the placing of a stethoscope on a woman's belly to monitor the foetal heartbeat was considered indecent.[11] As a result, many nineteenth-century women suffered 'the extremity of danger and pain rather than waive those scruples of delicacy which prevent their maladies from being fully exposed'.[12]

It has been estimated that in the 1870s, married women spent an average of twelve years pregnant and breastfeeding, having borne around five live children, although many had suffered miscarriages and stillbirths. Like Victoria, 80 per cent delivered within twelve months of the wedding ceremony, while only 12 in 1,000 gave birth in less than seven months, having been pregnant at the altar.[13] Many endured multiple pregnancies, equalling the queen in having nine children under the age of fifteen, which made her feel 'more like a rabbit or a guinea pig than anything else'. Labour conditions improved for Victoria for the delivery of her son Leopold in 1853, when she was administered with chloroform for the first time, inhaling every ten minutes from a cloth soaked in the liquid. After her experience, this form of pain relief became widely used among her subjects.

Still, Victoria disliked the process of bearing children, writing retrospectively about the 'humiliation to the delicate feelings of a poor woman, above all a young one ... especially with those nasty doctors'.[14] She also found the condition 'quite disgusting' in others, particularly 'those ladies who are always enceinte' and responded to the impending birth of her grandchild by claiming 'the horrid news has upset us dreadfully'.[15] It may also have been the case, with her aunt Charlotte in mind, that Victoria feared her coming ordeal; Mrs Panton certainly believed that 'these times are looked forward to with dread by all young wives'.[16] This attitude, coupled with her dislike of breastfeeding and small children, has led some historians to conclude that she suffered from prenatal and postnatal depression[17] although this is underpinned by the assumption that all women must enjoy motherhood and any deviation from this model requires a medical explanation. Perhaps readers should take Victoria at her word, as her view remained unchanging, that the 'shadow side' of love had got in the way of her marriage.

Victoria was not alone. The fear of birth was common to many women of the time, victims of a social prudery that denied them the opportunity for proper examination, control over and knowledge about their condition. This led to an understandable dislike of pregnancy, even a sense of morbidity, and a rejection of the act which could result in conception. Of course, this was only possible when women were able to say no. Mary Timms wrote, in 1833, 'Sometimes I think I shall never again enter this house, death may have marked me for his prey ... the hour of trial is approaching,'[18] while Mary Walker admitted she 'began to feel discouraged, felt as if I almost wished I had never been married'.[19]

Just over nine months after her wedding, Victoria went into labour. On the evening of 20 November 1840, she summoned her doctors and Albert, who remained at her side throughout. Soon after this, fashions changed again and it became less common for husbands to attend deliveries; in fact, they would not begin to return to the labour room until the 1960s. A daughter was born just after midday on 21 November, with Victoria announcing, 'Never mind, the next will be a prince.'[20] In keeping with tradition, the queen would have remained in bed, on her back, for a couple of weeks, possibly with the windows closed, sandbags lain in place and cobbles covered with sand to minimise external noise. Victoria had been lucky: from 1847 to 1876, 5 women in every 1,000 died as a result of childbirth, many from puerperal fever, for which there was no cure.[21] *The Lancet* argued that these deaths were the result of women living 'unnatural lives', plus the 'mental emotion' and 'overexcitement' of giving birth. Others suggested it was due to post-partum mothers eating 'fanciful trash', which echoed the descriptions of Jane

Seymour's end over three centuries earlier.[22] The March 1844 issue of *The Magazine of Domestic Economy* stated that the annual maternal death rate of 3,000, followed by the loss of 13,350 boys and 9,740 girls in the first month after delivery, was 'natural and inevitable'.[23] More babies than mothers were lost but the new princess was strong and healthy. The little girl was referred to as 'the child' until her christening, when she became Princess Victoria, or Vicky.

The queen was equally disgusted by breastfeeding. Her own daughters concealed from her the fact that they were suckling their own babies, but she found out and called them 'cows'.[24] Mrs Beeton thought breastfeeding 'a period of privation and penance' and tried to discourage mothers from sharing a room with their child, as it might continue to feed while she slept, 'to imbibe to distension a fluid sluggishly secreted and deficient in those vital principles', causing the mother to wake 'languid and unrefreshed ... caused by her baby vampire'.[25] Early Victorian newspapers were full of advertisements offering 'good breast milk' in comparison with the often diluted milk that could be bought, in unwashed churns, warmed in the sun and whitened with chalk. The *English Woman's Domestic Magazine* confirmed the queen's dislike by asserting that 'nature never ordained a child to live on suction after having endowed it with teeth'. Victoria advised her daughters that breastfeeding 'is the ruin of many a refined and intellectual young lady'.[26]

By the middle of the nineteenth century, the production of cheaper glass feeding bottles and prepared foods allowed some mothers greater choice. Mrs Beeton considered bottle-feeding to be more nutritious and rendered the child less prone to disease and better able to fight it if they did become infected. Before the introduction of rubber teats and sterilisation in 1890, calf's teat nipples were tied onto the glass bottle and replaced every couple of weeks.[27] When babies were weaned, they had traditionally been fed on a mixture of bread and water, sweetened with sugar, but this took time and could not guarantee that the child received sufficient nourishment. Mrs Beeton recommended arrowroot and baked flour, although diets varied and must have caused considerable discomfort to those infants that survived the process, such as the baby suffering from terrible diarrhoea after being fed oatmeal in 1857.[28] In the same year, the journal *British Pharmacopoeia* suggested a weaning mixture of boiled vineyard snails and pearl barley. Powdered milk and prepared foods became increasingly popular towards the end of the century, although they were initially expensive. The contraceptive benefits of weaning were not widely appreciated, so many a Victorian mother's disgust of breastfeeding caused her to conceive more rapidly and begin the whole dangerous process again.

Victoria's daughter, known as Princess Vicky, was the first of nine born to the queen. Naturally, she had hoped for a boy to inherit her empire but the value of a daughter lay in her potential to forge foreign alliances. Vicky married Frederick III, heir to the Prussian throne, and bore him eight children, of whom one was the future Kaiser Wilhelm II. Her mother later wrote to inform her that 'I never cared for you near as much as you seem to about the baby. I cared much more for the younger ones,' and that she had 'no adoration for very little babies … an ugly baby is a very nasty object'. Victoria bore her last child, Beatrice, in 1857, after which the doctors informed her it should be her last. Four years later, in December 1861, Prince Albert died from typhoid fever, leaving her a widow at the age of forty-two. Victoria always blamed her eldest son Bertie, Prince of Wales, for his death, as Albert's last weeks were spent intervening to extract the young man from a sexual scandal, which took a severe toll on Albert's health. After his death, she continued to order his shaving mug to be filled with warm water every morning and slept with a plaster cast of his hand in her bed.[29] She continued to reign until 1901, after which Bertie became Edward VII.

21

Edward, 1894

By the end of the nineteenth century, the profession of midwifery was changing again. In 1869, a committee of the London Obstetrical Society had been set up to investigate rates of infant mortality and the percentages of births with midwives in attendance. It was found that, while most women were assisted by a medical professional when in labour, the standard of training those midwives had received was inadequate. In 1871, Florence Nightingale published *Introductory Notes on Lying-In Hospitals* and a subsequent fund raised to commemorate her work helped establish a training college for midwives at King's College, London. The Midwives' Institute, founded by women working in the profession, was established in 1881, in order to improve their status and petition Parliament for recognition but, despite a number of bills being proposed in Parliament, they were blocked or withdrawn. The situation had not improved by 1892, when a House of Commons Select Committee reported that there was still 'serious and unnecessary loss of life and health and permanent injury to both mother and child in the treatment of childbirth'. It recommended that some 'legislative provision for improvement and regulation is desirable'.[1] It would not be until 1902 that the Midwives' Act would become law. Against the backdrop of this struggle to improve conditions for the average mother and her child, another royal wife was preparing to deliver.

It had all begun with a royal wedding; actually, two royal weddings. In 1891 Princess Mary of Teck, known as May, became engaged to Prince Albert, Duke of Clarence, otherwise known as 'Eddy'. He was the elder son of Edward VII and the grandson of Queen Victoria. The initial plans for a gown featuring a lily of the valley design for their nuptials had been discussed with Arthur Silver of Silver Studio House, one of the most fashionable art nouveau design studios of the day. Silver had established his business in 1880, since when it had supplied wallpaper, textiles, metalwork and other items to Liberty of London. He drew inspiration from Celtic imagery, Arts and Crafts and Charles Rennie Mackintosh's Glasgow studio and employed the skills of leading designers such as Archibald Knox. By 1893, their direction was increasingly influenced by the influx of Japanese art into the European market. Silver would have started picturing a wedding dress that would have been a spectacular fusion of Eastern and Parisian influences, with gentle, perfumed late Victorian flowers.[2] Some truly stunning bridal gowns survive from this time. One beautiful ensemble from the same year, held in the Los Angeles County Museum of Art, follows traditional lines with its huge leg-of-mutton sleeves, bodice and jacket with a full skirt, made in cream silk lined with cambric. The gauzy train is gathered on the bride's head, from where it cascades down to the ground. Another more exotic creation of 1890 has layers of ecru silk chiffon over a taffeta gown, trimmed with gold point de Venise lace and boughs of wax lilacs. A third dazzling dress of golden silk, with a pearl-trimmed bodice, has a neckline of wax orange blossom garlands over a high chiffon collar.

However, the wedding gown was never made. Mary and

Albert's engagement was announced at the end of 1891, when telegrams of congratulations flooded in from every corner of the empire. *The Times* column 'Court Circular' stated that 'it is understood the engagement will not be of long duration' and speculated that the young couple might use St James's Palace as their first marital home.[3] Yet, within weeks, all the plans had come to nothing. 'Eddy' died in a flu epidemic on 14 January, a week after his twenty-eighth birthday. Mary attended his funeral and laid her wreath of orange blossom on his coffin. Yet she was not to remain single for long. During the period of mourning she grew close to Albert's younger brother, George, Duke of York, who was now next in line to the throne. In May 1893, he proposed and was accepted. The media hinted at the opposition of George's mother, the Princess of Wales, to the match, although Mary was a favourite of Queen Victoria herself. Even if the princess had disliked Mary's moving on from one of her sons to the next, her wedding gift of jewels worth £250,000 seemed to signal a final acceptance.

A second dress was planned, only this time it became a reality. On 7 July 1893, the wedding took place in the Chapel Royal at St James's Palace. Never, wrote *The Times*, 'had an English sun ... poured its rays upon a more imposing spectacle' of a thirteen-carriage procession passing along a route of 6 or 7 miles, where onlookers climbed up into the trees to get a better view. At the end of Pall Mall, two columns were made to look like marble, topped with floral decorations while garlands, flags and streamers abounded. Opposite the palace entrance hung a banner saying 'all happiness be yours for ever more'.[4] Mary was married in a satin gown with ivory and silver brocade, designed by Linton and Curtis of Albemarle Street. Art Nouveau roses, shamrocks and thistles, trimmed with orange blossom, were included in the design, which was a very English creation, in contrast to the plans for her first, unmade gown. Mary's mother, the Duchess of Teck, was president of the Ladies' National Silk Association and had wanted to patronise the English industry. The appreciative *Philadelphia Evening News* wrote that 'the terrible depression of trade ... [has] made this wise consideration very welcome in England'.[5] Princess Mary and her mother had been to visit the silk weavers in Spitalfields, in London's East End, from where they had ordered the required silks, silver laces and brocades.

Mary's dress also featured diamond pins from Queen Victoria, a long train and her future husband's gift, a brooch in the shape of an open-petalled rose, made from pearls and diamonds. The fascinated American press reported that 'orange blossoms [were] tucked in among the coils and curls of Princess May's [*sic*] bonny brown hair'.[6] A studio photograph shows Mary in profile, wearing the tiny S-shaped bodice of the time, with her bosom covered in lace and her arms bare. Her skirts are pinned up at the sides, exposing the layers of lace beneath and a huge bustle cascades down her legs and onto the floor, quite eclipsing the diaphanous veil attached to her head with blooms and feathers. She is wearing her trademark choker, her curls severely dressed high on her head, where she retained them through later life. Queen Victoria, aged seventy-four, attended the ceremony in a carriage drawn by cream-coloured horses, allowing the crowd a glimpse of her small coronet of diamonds and shoulders draped in lace. The Bridal March from *Lohengrin* was played as Mary entered the chapel.

After their honeymoon, the couple set up home in York Cottage, on the Sandringham Estate in Norfolk. Two months later, Mary conceived her first child. The communication of this fact, and the interaction of expectant mothers within polite circles, posed considerable difficulties at the time. Pregnancy during Victorian times was a social and domestic taboo. As a reminder of female sexuality and bodily functions, it was concealed to the extent that even the words were unacceptable in common usage. Mrs Panton, in her 1888 *From Kitchen to Garret: Hints for Young Householders*, titled her chapter on childbirth 'In Retirement' and wrote that she could 'only touch lightly on these matters' as she did not know into whose hands her book might fall.[7] Images of women in the fine and applied arts were sanitised, clean, perfect and hairless; how else could the art critic John Ruskin have been horrified to discover the realities of his new wife's body in 1848? An expectant mother's condition would have necessitated her being discreet, if not secretive, and can only have created, for some, a sense of confusion regarding their own bodies. In 1875, American author Elizabeth Edson Evans, author of *The Abuse of Maternity*, described how women often 'avoided speaking of their situation' even to their closest friends and relatives. Some continued to lace themselves tightly into corsets, causing damage to themselves and their developing foetus and few specific maternity garments were developed. However, among those that were, a maternity corset had been developed to minimise the appearance of the condition, featuring whalebone stays instead of steel and having expandable bandages over the abdomen and bosom.[8] Long shawls were another favourite method of concealing the growing belly, until a woman retired completely from sight, often fairly early in her final trimester.[9]

Mary also had to be careful of what she ate during this period. The lavish banquets of late Victorian England, with their penchant for heavy meat and rich creamy sauces would have been considered damaging to her constitution;

instead she would have been advised to eat lightly, favouring fruit and vegetables and plain, wholesome fare. With the greenhouses of the home counties supplying London's markets all year round, forcing and grafting buds out of season, the royal family would have had little difficulty in ensuring Mary had a constant selection of exotic delicacies such as strawberries, pineapples and asparagus. Alcohol was frowned upon, as was the consumption of tea and coffee. Not too dissimilar to medieval advice, the 1910 *Every Woman's Encyclopaedia* urged expectant mothers to think pure, wholesome thoughts, in good surroundings, with plenty of fresh air.

Mary had planned for her first child to be born at Buckingham Palace, but a heatwave made the city unbearable and, instead, she prepared to deliver her first son at her parental home, White Lodge, in the middle of Richmond Park. Now part of the Royal School of Ballet, White Lodge is a solid Georgian building in the Palladian style, set amid extensive grounds. Quite literally, there was no one to overhear Mary's screams. It was still common for babies of all classes to be delivered at home, although this was particularly important for the protection of the royal family. It would not be until well into the twentieth century that women increasingly sought the pain relief and safer surroundings that the best hospitals could offer, especially when complications arose. Mary's chamber would have been prepared and equipped and nurses were hired in readiness.

One innovation made the Lodge more accessible in case of emergency. A telephone line had been recently installed, but instead of being used to call for assistance, it enabled the spread of the good news that, at around 10 p.m. on 23 June 1894, Queen Victoria's first great-grandson had arrived, weighing 8 lbs. The boy's father, the Duke of York, had waited in the library during the labour, pretending to read *Pilgrim's Progress*. Mary recovered well from the ordeal, of which the last two and a half hours had been fraught with danger.[10] A book was set up in a marquee the following day, in which over 1,500 people wrote messages of congratulations. The queen drove over to the Lodge to inspect the 'fine, strong-looking child' and had been pleased with what she saw. Mary's sister, the Grand Duchess of Mecklenberg-Strelitz, wrote that she had visited 'mentally – on my knees, tears of gratitude and happiness flowing, streaming.'

The boy was baptised in the Green Drawing Room at White Lodge on 16 July by Edward Benson, Archbishop of Canterbury. There were twelve godparents and a cake 5 feet wide and 30 inches high. After some discussion with the queen, the baby was given the full name of Edward Albert Christian George Andrew Patrick David. This selection included the four patron saints of the British Isles as well as paying homage to his late uncle Eddy, his great-grandfather Albert and his grandfather Christian, King of Denmark. It was a weighty mantle of responsibility for the child, full of expectation that, in time, he would feel unable to fulfil. Amid all the celebrations, one sour note sounded. The first socialist Member of Parliament, Keir Hardie, pronounced that

> this boy will be surrounded by sycophants and flatterers ... a line will be drawn between him and the people he is one day to be called upon to reign over. In due course ... he will be sent on a tour round the world, and probably rumours of a morganatic alliance will follow, and the end of it will be the country will be called upon to pay the bill.

It would prove to be a startlingly accurate prediction for the life of the future Edward VIII.

22

Albert, 1895

Although Mary and George now had the much-desired heir, the future inheritor of Victoria's throne, their family was not complete. Infant mortality, accident and childhood illnesses still proved to be the unpredictable threats that affected all classes, even though conditions in general were beginning to improve. By 1880, the average family size had fallen from four or five, to three surviving children per couple, but the royal family did not conform to the concept of 'average' in any sense. Remembering the fate of his own elder brother, Mary's former fiancé, the pair was keen to ensure that they produced a spare heir to the throne.

Nine months later, in the spring of 1895, Mary fell pregnant again. Her son Edward, always known to the family as David, was nursed and raised by a nanny at the various royal properties, in the usual way. By the end of the year, Mary was at their Sandringham home of York Cottage, in Norfolk, in anticipation of her second delivery. A pretty house, with picturesque views over the estate, it had been built by George's father and given to the couple as a wedding present. There, Mary was attended by Sir John Williams, who was Queen Victoria's doctor and later accused by one of his twenty-first-century descendants of being Jack the Ripper.[1] The second doctor was obstetrician Sir Alan Manby, a Norfolk man who had been surgeon-apothecary to the Prince of Wales at Sandringham since 1885. The Duke of York wrote in his diary that 'a little boy was born, weighing nearly 8 pounds at 3.40 a.m. Everything most satisfactory, both doing well.'[2] *The London Gazette* recorded that 'her Royal Highness and the infant prince are both doing perfectly well' and that the city had been alerted to the news by the firing of gun salutes. Sir Matthew White Ridley, Home Secretary, wrote to the Lord Mayor to break the news and a copy of his letter was put up on the outside of Mansion House for the public to read.[3]

However, the baby's birthdate of 14 December was significant for another reason, being the anniversary of the death of Queen Victoria's husband, Prince Albert, in 1861. As such, it had long been considered the 'blackest day in the calendar of the royal family' but there were hopes that this new happy event would finally rid it of its negative associations.[4] *The Globe* anticipated that the 'august lady' might find a 'solace for [her] mournful memories', while the *Standard* foresaw that the day's sorrow, which it believed 'incompatible with the healthy activities either of individual or national life', would no longer be 'devoted exclusively to mourning and regret'.[5] Victoria herself was 'rather distressed' and 'regretted' that he had been born on the anniversary but was pleased that the child was going to be named Albert after his great-grandfather. She wrote to the Duke of York to express her 'joy at dear May's (sic) doing so well and recovering so quickly. She is ... very strong. She gets through these affairs like nothing.' She was 'all impatience to see the new one', the 'dear little boy', and would have liked to attend the christening in person, at her residence of Osborne House. However, the baby was baptised at the Sandringham church of St Mary's on 17 February; his given name was Albert Frederick Arthur George, but he was always known to his family as Bertie.[6] Victoria wrote in her diary, 'I have a feeling [the birthdate] may be a blessing for the poor little boy, and may be looked upon as a gift from God.'[7] The young Edward was present, and was encouraged to hold his brother, until the point when the baby began to scream, when the elder boy, aged eighteen months, decided to outdo him by screaming even louder!

The boys were raised by a nanny, along with their siblings: Mary who arrived in April 1897, Henry in March 1900, George in December 1902 and John in July 1905. At the age of two, Bertie was given the title of His Royal Highness Prince Albert of York. The children were given lessons by tutors, Helen Bricka, Henry Hansard and Frederick Finch, and often stayed with their grandparents, the king and queen, during the absence of their own parents on official duties. They also had specific tutors for German and French until such time as they were sent away to school, Edward in 1907 and Bertie in 1909, to the Royal Naval College at Osborne, on the Isle of Wight. While Edward was a confident boy, Bertie suffered from an extreme stammer, as well as knees that turned inward, which were corrected by wearing splints. Their youngest brother, John, was soon established in his own home, with his own nurse, due to the severe epilepsy that would kill him at the age of thirteen.

The coming years brought the brothers even closer to the throne. Queen Victoria had died in 1901 and her son and successor, Edward VII, had died in 1910. Edward's son George inherited the throne as George V, which made his sons, Edward and Albert, next in line to the throne, with Edward invested as Prince of Wales in 1911. Yet, as the boys grew up, their father had a clear preference when it came to his successor. George always hoped that his second son, Albert, would become king, reputedly saying he wished

Edward would not marry and that nothing would 'come between Bertie ... and the throne'. Increasingly, he felt uncertain of Edward's ability to provide stable rule, disliking his womanising and affairs, especially the reckless behaviour he exhibited in the 1920s, and looking instead to the quiet dignity of his second son. Bertie had married in 1923 and fathered two daughters, preferring a quiet life to that in the public eye. He was certain that Edward would ruin himself within twelve months of his succession. However, on the death of King George in January 1936, the title passed to the dashing Prince of Wales, who became Edward VIII.

Edward, though, had his own doubts. After a string of relationships, he had fallen in love with the American beauty Wallis Simpson who was then married to her second husband. The pair became close, to the extent that they were followed by the Police Special Branch, in an attempt to establish the nature of their relationship. Edward continued to insist to his father that they were not lovers, although the testimonies of his staff said otherwise, and the king and queen refused to receive Wallis. The pair's relationship caused considerable concern and, from 1935, when they holidayed together, the prince's infatuation began to interfere with his royal duties.

Even before his coronation, Edward understood that he would be unlikely to retain the throne and marry the woman of his choice. That October, Wallis was divorced from her second husband on the grounds of his adultery, making her available to marry Edward, but was considered deeply unsuitable to become a queen consort at the time. The following month, Edward entered into talks with Parliament to try and find a way that would allow him to combine marriage and kingship, but his suggestion of a morganatic marriage was rejected. With the scandal breaking to the public, Wallis fled to France. Edward signed a declaration of abdication on 10 December. It made his younger brother, Bertie, into a reluctant king. To emphasise continuity with his father, he chose to adopt the name by which he is known to history: George VI.

23

Elizabeth, 1926

Britain was on the verge of a general strike. Despite the popular image of 'bright young things' dancing away the roaring twenties, many people were finding times hard following the First World War. Around two-thirds of the population saw their annual incomes falling although prices were on the rise.[1] Recent economists have suggested that, as the country's output was continually falling through the twenties, with low industrial output and high exchange rates, Britain actually suffered a twenty-year depression from 1918 onwards.[2] By the mid-1920s, conflicts between mine owners and their employees was reaching a critical situation. The nation's rich seams of coal had been heavily dug during the war and now, as a result of falling prices on the international market, miners' wages were drastically cut, forcing many of their already over-stretched families into poverty. Miners were forced to accept the pay cuts or else be locked out of their pits. With union backing, they chose to make a stand and, in early May 1926, around 1.5 million workers went on strike, bringing the national transport network to a standstill.

Amid this national chaos, a future queen was born. One newspaper headline read, 'Birth brings joy, strike brings fear.' Even then, when little Princess Elizabeth was only third in line to the throne, the *Toledo Blade* described her arrival as bringing 'a little brightness into the drab lives of people torn by the impending general strike and the miseries of mass unemployment'. The choice of name was significant, according to the paper: 'Elizabeth makes a strong appeal to the popular imagination because of the possibility of the little newcomer one day ascending to the throne' and bringing 'another Elizabethan era'.[3] Twenty-five years later, after the disruptions of the 1920s gave way to the Great Depression and the Second World War, the baby Elizabeth did indeed inherit the English throne to become one of the country's longest-reigning monarchs.

The baby's mother was the Honourable Elizabeth Bowes-Lyon, a beautiful young aristocrat who had nursed wounded soldiers at her Scottish home, Glamis Castle, during the First World War. She and her future husband, Albert, Duke of York, had met as children at a party when, as a five-year-old, she had given him the cherries from the top of her cake.[4] By the early 1920s, her slim figure, dark hair and twinkling blue-violet eyes had already attracted many suitors. When the shy Prince Albert noticed her again at a society ball, he could not take his eyes from her. That summer, while staying at Balmoral, he visited her at Glamis and wrote to his mother, Mary of Teck, that 'the more I see of her, the more I like her'.[5] Elizabeth was a commoner, so the marriage would not follow the traditional lines of a dynastic alliance but, at this point, Albert's elder brother was heir to the throne and there appeared to be little chance that he would ever become king. In choosing her, rather than a foreign princess, the duke was considered to be taking a step towards the modernisation of the monarchy. If there were fears about the young woman's suitability, they soon evaporated. Lady Airlie, who had known Elizabeth since her birth, endorsed her as a future bride in glowing terms: 'She was a girl who would find real happiness only in marriage and motherhood. A born homemaker.'[6] Albert's father, the king, told him, 'You will be a lucky fellow if she accepts you.'[7]

At first, Elizabeth did not accept Bertie. She turned down his proposal of 1921, citing that she was concerned about the limitations on her life that a royal role would bring. The next day she wrote to the duke, saying 'how dreadfully sorry [she was] about yesterday' and hoping they could still be good friends.[8] On hearing of the rejection, Queen Mary herself accompanied her son to Glamis, where Elizabeth acted as hostess, due to her own mother's illness. Mary was quickly convinced that the young lady was 'the one girl who could make Bertie happy', but refrained from attempting to influence either, as 'mothers should never interfere in their children's love affairs'. Early in 1922, Elizabeth acted as a bridesmaid to Bertie's sister, Mary, after which he made a second unsuccessful proposal. Sometime after that, Elizabeth changed her mind. Finally, during a walk through the woods, she accepted his third appeal, on 23 January the following year.

With only three months between her acceptance and the wedding day, there appeared to be little time for public excitement to develop, yet, at once, the media began to record a growing interest in the forthcoming nuptials. Stories were written about the pair's background, their suitability and courtship. The day quickly arrived. Elizabeth was photographed leaving her parents' Bruton Street home on the morning of 26 April 1923, on her way to Westminster Abbey. Her dress had been designed by Madame Handley Seymour, with ivory chiffon, pearl beading, silver thread and sprigs of green tulle hanging from the girdle, in defiance of traditions that claimed that colour brought bad luck. One old rhyme claimed 'married in green, ashamed to be seen' but Elizabeth and Bertie were proudly and publicly married in Westminster Abbey. The wedding ring was made of Welsh gold, establishing a tradition that would be continued by the next three generations. Six bridesmaids were in attendance as the bride spoke her vows before leaving her bouquet on the Tomb of the Unknown Soldier; a gesture of remembrance to her brother, who had been killed during the First World War. The BBC, a relatively new institution, had requested permission to broadcast the event on the radio but this was considered inappropriate and consent was denied. The couple went on to honeymoon at Polesden Lacey, a secluded Regency house on the North Downs in Surrey.

Elizabeth was not to fall pregnant for another two years. This may purely have been down to nature, or it may imply that some form of birth control was being used. At this time, commensurate with the rise of the women's movement, Elizabeth's peers were increasingly taking greater control over their own fertility, but the question of birth control was proving controversial. Margaret Sanger opened a Planned Parenting Clinic in America at a time when purchasing a single condom was a criminal activity in thirty states. Working with poor women on the Lower East Side in Manhattan, her promotion of contraception in her magazine, *The Woman Rebel*, led to her indictment on counts of obscenity and inciting murder. She fled to England. A talk she gave to the Fabian Society on birth control, in 1915, was attended by a newly divorced Marie Stopes, whose marriage had been annulled on the basis on non-consummation. Stopes was still a virgin when she wrote and published the explicit *Married Love*, in 1918, followed by *Wise Parenting: A Book for Married People*, which prompted a flood of letters asking for her advice.

However, Stopes's own experience of birth was not a happy one. At the age of thirty-eight, she was denied the opportunity to deliver in the position of her choice and her child was stillborn. The first reliable pregnancy tests were also being developed. Around 1900, scientists had discovered that the presence in a woman's body of a hormone called hGC could be reliably used to diagnose whether conception had taken place. In early laboratory-based tests, scientists injected samples of women's urine into mice, rats or rabbits, which would then show responses which could establish the condition. However, decades would pass before this process was perfected into the hand-held devices that would allow women the freedom to perform easy, fast tests in their own homes.

The early decades of the twentieth century also saw advances in pain relief, which was no longer considered taboo during childbirth, and other methods designed to alleviate maternal suffering. Ether and chloroform had previously been used as anaesthetics but, in Germany, in 1914, a mixture of morphine and scopolamine was developed, called 'Twilight Sleep'. As well as numbing the pain, it removed the memory of it, so women simply went to sleep and woke up having given birth. Initially, it was welcomed by upper-class women but studies showed that it had an impact upon the baby's nervous system, causing breathing difficulties. Then, in 1915, American Dr Joseph DeLee described childbirth in the first edition of the *American Journal of Obstetrics and Gynaecology* as a 'destructive pathology' and outlined steps that could be taken to lessen the 'evils natural to labour', which shifted the emphasis from cure to prevention. Elizabeth's baby was born by caesarean section, which was a procedure still in its infancy and mostly used as a last resort. In 1874, the mortality rate from the operation was as high as 75 per cent and often accompanied by hysterectomy.[9] Until this time, doctors had believed the uterine wall would repair itself, with the result that many women bled to death, but in the 1870s, they discovered it could be stitched, rapidly improving their patients' chances of survival. Initially, the operation was carried out by making a vertical incision in the top of the uterus but, by 1906, this changed to the lower part of the abdomen, with a decreased risk of subsequent rupture. It was unusual for a woman to choose the operation though and still carried a mortality risk of up to 30 per cent. Rapid improvements made it more widespread by the 1920s, by which time the risks were considered 'little more than normal labour'.[10] Survival rates for mothers in general were increasing drastically. Statistics collected by the *Journal of the Royal Society of Medicine* show that rates of maternal mortality fell from 2 in 1,000 in 1934 to 0.5 by 1940.[11]

Elizabeth would have suspected she had conceived in the late summer of 1925; the precise date would have been somewhere in July. Still considered an indelicate topic, the pregnancy was 'discretely' handled by the press[12] but another member of the royal family grew increasingly excited about the impending arrival. Soon to be a grandmother, Queen Mary spent weeks before the birth buying baby clothes, powder boxes, toiletries and coverlets for the crib. Others brought Elizabeth flowers, including dozens of bunches of daffodils, then in bloom.[13] The operation was carried out by Australian surgeon Sir Henry Simpson Newland, a safe pair of hands, who had been the first recipient of the University of Adelaide's Master of Surgery degree. A baby girl was delivered, feet first, in the early hours of the morning on 21 April 1926, at the home of her maternal grandfather, the Earl of Strathmore, at 17 Bruton Street. One of her first visitors, Queen Mary, reputedly leant over the cot and said, 'I wish you were more like your mother.' Another visitor,

Home Secretary William Joynson-Smith, described how the baby had yawned in his face, while the *Toronto Daily Star* followed the British press in reporting that the Duchess of York 'had always loved children'. The baby was christened Elizabeth Alexandra Mary on 29 May in the private chapel at Buckingham Palace; it had been built in 1840, for Queen Victoria, with a copper ceiling supported by sixteen white columns. In a tradition reputed to date back to the Crusades, the baby was christened with water from the River Jordan. It was held in a 'gold lily' font designed for the christenings of Victoria's children; Princess Vicky had been the first one to be baptised there in 1840, when plate and furniture had been transferred from the chapel at St James's Palace. That spring, the perfume company Floris released a scent called Royal Arms to celebrate the birth. The blend of rose, violet and ylang-ylang was recreated in 2012 to celebrate her Diamond Jubilee.

Princess Elizabeth, whose later inability to pronounce her own name led her to be called Lilibet among the family, arrived amid turbulent times. The general strike ended after nine days but many miners did not return to the pits for months and the industry was profoundly in decline when the country slipped into depression. When Elizabeth was ten years old, her world changed entirely. On the abdication of her uncle, Edward VIII, her father ascended the throne as George VI and she became Princess of Wales, next in line to inherit. She was thirteen at the outbreak of the Second World War. The royal family chose to stay in London, visiting bomb-damaged sites and boosting morale, and the princess made a radio broadcast to speak to evacuated children across the country. Later, she learned to drive and to understand mechanics. She joined the Women's Auxiliary Service and, after a change in the law, acted as a Counsellor of State as her father's deputy. Adolf Hitler referred to her mother, Elizabeth, now queen, as the most dangerous woman in Britain, for her ability to rally the nation's spirits. Her elder daughter was also a significant opponent. In 1947, the princess married Prince Philip of Greece and Denmark and, on the death of her father in 1952, ascended the throne as Elizabeth II. Her mother died at the age of 101 in 2002.

24

William, 1982

It promised to be a fairytale wedding. Across the world, 750 million people tuned in to watch it on television, with radio figures reaching almost 1 billion. According to national statistics, that was almost eighteen times the population of the UK that year. Thousands more took to the streets to line the route that the royal couple would take from St Paul's Cathedral, along the Mall to Buckingham Palace, with some camping out on the pavements for forty-eight hours in order to secure a good view in the morning. The nation was draped in red, white and blue bunting as streets up and down the land hosted parties. The thirty-two-year-old Prince Charles, eldest son of Queen Elizabeth and Prince Philip, was to marry Lady Diana Spencer, after a courtship of only six months. Over a dinner for two at Buckingham Palace, he had asked her if she would become his wife. The nineteen-year-old playgroup assistant accepted.

Diana had been born on the Park Estate at Sandringham on 1 July 1961. Her education had taken her from the traditional all-girls' boarding school to a Swiss boarding school by the time she arrived in London as a shy teenager. She fitted the ideal image of a princess, being beautiful, modest, young, with no serious relationship in the past; it was hoped she would prove fertile and provide male heirs to the English throne. While Charles had been linked to other women during his bachelor days, Diana was quite inexperienced, probably remaining virginal until her wedding day. During the courtship, she addressed him as 'Sir'.[1]

The engagement was officially announced by Buckingham Palace at 11 a.m. on 24 February, when the press photographed the couple, with Diana wearing her new ring, an oval Ceylon sapphire set amid fourteen diamonds, which had cost £30,000. An interview with the pair was broadcast on ITN the same evening, when Diana explained, 'It wasn't a difficult decision in the end. This is what I wanted, what I want.'[2] According to *The Times*, she described herself as 'delighted, thrilled, blissfully happy'. Charles, by contrast, acquiesced that he was in love, 'whatever that was'. At once speculation was rife over the details of the coming day, with the media making predictions about the choice of venue, dress designer and cake. Schoolchildren were issued with commemorative spoons and medals, while the shops filled with cups and saucers, books, flags, key fobs, badges and similar souvenir items. The date was set for 29 July. Yet Diana was having doubts, concerned about Charles's friendship with his former flame Camilla Parker-Bowles. According to the biography written by Andrew Morton, she even considered cancelling the wedding two days before but Charles sent her the gift of a signet ring and a card saying, 'I'm so proud of you and when you come up, I'll be there at the altar waiting for you.'[3] The very next day, Diana gave another interview to ITN, when she stated she was 'looking forward to being a good wife'[4] but she was unprepared for being suddenly catapulted into the public glare and found all the attention quite difficult.

On the morning of the big day, there was no escape. London was heaving and *The Times* reported that by eight in the morning it was impossible to move in Trafalgar Square. The eyes of the world were on Diana as she arrived in the famous 'glass coach', which had been used for most royal weddings since it had been built in 1910. Charles travelled to the cathedral in the 1902 state postilion landau built for Edward VII. *The Times* reported that her composure was 'entirely regained after the strain of recent days'. The wedding dress had been designed by Elizabeth and David Emanuel and exceeded even press speculation, with its 10,000 pearls, hand-embroidered lace, silk taffeta, frilled neckline and huge puffed sleeves. The 25-foot train was carried by five bridesmaids, with two page boys in attendance. Shoemaker Clive Shilton made her 'Cinderella slippers' in Covent Garden, with the heart-shaped tabs Diana chose personally, edged with gold piping and Queen Mary's lace sent from Buckingham Palace. On her head, the princess-to-be wore the tiara that had been in the Spencer family for generations. Her ring was made of gold dug from the mine at Clogau in Wales, smelted in Birmingham and made by the London jeweller Garrard's. The 42-inch bridal bouquet, made by florist Doris Welham, included white orchids, gardenias, freesia, lilies of the valley, yellow 'Mountbatten' roses and myrtle.

The couple were married by Robert Runcie, Archbishop of Canterbury, in a traditional Church of England service beginning at 11.20 in the morning. The congregation rose to sing the national anthem and Diana's favourite hymn, 'I Vow to Thee, My Country', before departing for Buckingham Palace. There, on the balcony, they exchanged the famous kiss that became the subject of so many photographs. The cake, a fantasia of sugar icing, marzipan and fruit sponge, was made in the royal naval college kitchens at Chatham and stood five tiers high. It had taken three and a half days to make, with half an hour alone needed in order to break all the eggs. A replica was also prepared, in case of damage, while twenty-six other cakes graced the table at the wedding breakfast. On the menu were brill in lobster sauce, chicken breasts stuffed with lamb mousse and strawberries with Cornish cream. The following day, *The Times* headline read, 'Day of romance in a grey world.'

There were three phases to the honeymoon. The first was spent on the beautiful Broadlands estate in Hampshire, following the tradition set by the Queen and Prince Philip in 1947. Then the newly-weds set off on the Royal Yacht *Britannia* for a two-week Mediterranean cruise before flying up to the Balmoral estate for September. There had been considerable pressure on Charles, Elizabeth II's eldest son and now aged thirty-two, to marry and father an heir. Diana fell pregnant around the middle of September, while still on honeymoon at Balmoral, before the marriage was two months old. On returning to London, she carried out her first official duties that October but was already suffering from morning sickness and had lost weight. Her condition was officially announced on 5 November to great public interest but she continued to be unwell and her engagements were restricted to ensure she did not become overtired. Two weeks later, she cancelled a trip to Bristol, leading the medical advisor at *The Times* to reassure their readers that 'rest and dietary treatment is usually all that is needed'. The Queen's obstetrician, Sir George Pinker, oversaw her care, having already delivered seven royal babies, including Charles's niece and nephew, Zara and Peter Phillips. Breaking with the tradition of delivering the family's children at home, he established a new location at St Mary's Hospital, Paddington, which has been used ever since. From the moment the news was made public, Diana found it difficult to adjust to her new royal role and the frenzy of attention it brought.

In December, the Palace issued a plea to the press to keep their distance, for the sake of the princess's health. According to *The Times*, Diana was feeling 'totally beleaguered' although she had made no complaint herself and had 'coped splendidly with her public duties'. Now, though, she was becoming 'increasingly despondent at the idea that she could not go outside her own front door without being photographed' and that 'stress was being created by the constant surveillance of her private life by the press'. Considerable concern was expressed about 'a girl of twenty, expecting her first child, who had not been subject to the same public exposure since early childhood as the rest of the royal family'.[5]

Although Diana was ill, all appeared to be progressing well. Then, twelve weeks into the pregnancy, exhausted and ill, in the middle of a quarrel with a husband she perceived to be unsympathetic, she threatened to take her own life. Charles dismissed this but she then threw herself downstairs at Sandringham in January 1982.[6] It was more the act of a desperate woman than a serious attempt but gave rise to fears about the viability of her condition. After examining her, Pinker was able to reassure the anxious parents that the baby was unharmed despite her bruising. The remainder of the pregnancy advanced with success although Diana continued to feel under pressure from the press. An article published in *The Times* on 8 June explored her choice of made-to-measure maternity clothes, arguing that manufacturers had failed 'to take in the sociological changes of our times' and citing the average age of first-time mothers as having recently risen to over twenty-five. The baby's due date had been estimated at 1 July, which was also

Diana's twenty-first birthday. She was unprepared when her labour pains began in the morning of 21 June at 4.30 a.m. and travelled to St Mary's Hospital in the back of a police Land Rover, with only the green polka dot maternity dress in which she was later photographed. Diana was shown into a private room on the fourth floor of the Lindo Wing, where she ate a light breakfast of toast and marmalade, coffee and orange juice in order to keep up her strength.[7] As her labour progressed, her temperature rose so high that a caesarean section was considered but Diana refused it, along with the drugs that could have made the labour faster, wanting to deliver her child naturally. By the afternoon, the baby still had not arrived and Geoffrey Chamberlain, Professor of Obstetrics at London's St George's Hospital, told BBC News that, while most first babies arrived within twelve hours, it was not uncommon for a labour to last for twenty-four hours.[8] At least Diana knew she was in safe hands with Dr Pinker overseeing the entire proceedings. Eventually, biting her lips in pain, she agreed to an epidural injection to lessen the pain after such a lengthy ordeal.

Crowds gathered outside the hospital, awaiting news, and deliveries of flowers arrived throughout the day. After sixteen hours of labour, a baby boy arrived at just after 9 p.m. that evening, weighing 7 lbs and 1.5 ounces. When the news spread, a forty-one gun salute was fired in Hyde Park and at the Tower of London. Reporters asked Charles whether the baby looked like him and he replied, 'Fortunately not,' describing his new-born son as having 'a wisp of fair hair, blondish, with blue eyes'.[9] The label around his tiny wrist read 'baby Wales'. Diana was delighted with her baby and claimed that she couldn't wait to have more. She insisted on being discharged from hospital the following evening, being photographed leaving with a tiny white bundle in her arms.

The baby was christened William Arthur Philip Louis on 4 August in the music room at Buckingham Palace. According to genealogists, he was born the most British heir to the throne since James I.[10] To assist her in the early weeks at their Kensington Palace home, Diana employed paediatric nurse Anna Wallace for a month, before the arrival of a permanent nanny, Barbara Barnes.

Months later, the birth was still the topic of discussion, even when Diana lent her support to charities sponsoring research into the needs of premature babies and the diagnosis of handicapping conditions. That November she attended a fashion show at the Guildhall, in aid of the Birthright charity, on whose council George Pinker sat. In the media the following day, it was stated that 'all the women' involved in the charity had hoped 'that the new princess would choose to give birth at Buckingham Palace ... rather than in hospital'. According to *The Times*, 'such a decision was claimed by some to be the wish of her royal highness but overruled by Mr Pinker'. Apparently her decision to breastfeed William had pleased her critics but the circumstances of his arrival had 'prevented the young royal mother being taken as a figurehead for the new movements' but, as *The Times* concluded, 'it is hard to believe that her doctors would ever allow her precious cargo to be discharged into the world without their active help'.[11] In September 1984, Diana's second son, Prince Harry, was also born at St Mary's Hospital.

William's parents' marriage did not turn out to be that of a fairytale. The very public nature of their separation in 1992 and the subsequent divorce, with the publication of biographies, interviews and accounts sensationalised in the media, made the details of their intimate lives public in way that was unprecedented among royal couples. Only a year after they legally parted in August 1996, Diana and her companion, Dodi Al Fayed, were killed in a car crash in a Paris underpass, attempting to escape from the press. Her death provoked national hysteria. Masses of flowers and flickering candles piled up outside Buckingham Palace in advance of her funeral, on 6 September 1997, which was one of the most watched events in history. Prince William, then aged fifteen, and his younger brother, Prince Harry, walked with their father and uncle in a solemn procession behind her cortège. The ceremony at Westminster Abbey was attended by members of the royal family, politicians and celebrities. She was laid to rest privately on an island in the Althorp estate.

Prince George of Cambridge, 2013

Since before his birth, the cameras had been expecting him. No prince has ever attracted so much media attention as William, Duke of Cambridge, elder son of Charles and Diana. This is partly due to the explosion of the late twentieth-century press, as well as his position in the British line of succession, his career in the Royal Air Force, modesty and blonde good looks. From the moment Diana's pregnancy was first announced, in the autumn of 1981, the cameras followed her movements and audiences around the world waited to hear the news of his arrival. His first steps, anecdotes about his infant years, his preferences, private life and hobbies have all fuelled an increasing public appetite for their future king and speculation as to what sort of ruler he would make. His courtship and marriage to Catherine Middleton, earlier known as Kate, has been hailed as a modern romance, with a Valentine's Day poll naming the couple the most inspiring romantic pair, 'capturing the nation's hearts' with the relationship we most 'aspire' to. Their wedding, on 29 April 2011, which attracted the inevitable 'fairytale' comparison with that of William's parents, is a contemporary, companionate union that has done much to redefine the image of the royal family for the twenty-first century. Eighteen months after the ceremony, it was announced that Catherine, Duchess of Cambridge, was expecting a baby.

William's future wife was the eldest of three children raised in Berkshire. As a schoolgirl, she put up a poster of William on the wall of her dormitory at Marlborough, little knowing what the future would bring. After enrolling on a degree course in the History of Art at the University of St Andrews, she discovered that the prince was her fellow undergraduate and had also been housed in the same college. William noticed the willowy brunette after attending a charity fashion show in which she was appearing and the couple soon began dating. They went on to share lodgings in the city and their relationship continued after graduation, when they attended the celebrations for the Queen's eightieth birthday together in 2006. Described by the *Daily Mail* as looking 'demure in a low-cut sundress and ... simple jewellery', Kate and her prince were 'affectionate, at ease and – in a heart-stirring way – familiar'. Her 'quiet poise and solidity', making her seem as if she was 'wrapped in privacy even in the midst of intense public interest', were already being juxtaposed with the way Diana had looked 'thin, tense and lost' as if she, like her clothes, did not 'fit'. Alexandra Shulman, editor of *Vogue*, said, 'I think Kate is a contemporary version of Diana. She has the same mainstream style and will go on, like Diana, to get more glamorous.' Geordie Greig, editor of *Tatler* and a friend of Princess Diana, says, 'Kate has not put a foot wrong. She appears modest and beautiful, and is liked by the press. There is a breezy unpretentiousness about how she looks and what she wears. The perfect princess-in-waiting.'[1] Then, in 2007, what had seemed like an ideal pairing crumbled and the pair split. Fortunately, the breach was only temporary and the following year, William was reunited with the woman whom the press had dubbed 'waity

Katie'. Her patience paid off, as on 16 November 2010, the Palace announced that the couple had become engaged on a trip to Kenya. The engagement photographs showed off the beautiful sapphire and diamond ring on Kate's finger, which had once belonged to William's mother.

Around 25 million people in the UK tuned in to watch the wedding live on television. Kate, to be known as Catherine from that point onwards, arrived for the 11 a.m. service in Westminster Abbey in a vintage Rolls-Royce Phantom, as photographers and members of the public lining the route tried to catch a glimpse of her dress inside. When she alighted before the abbey steps, they were not disappointed. Sarah Burton, a designer from the Alexander McQueen fashion house, had united symbolic imagery and historical fabrics to follow the notion of royal wedding dresses using the best of British materials to promote national skills. The stunning bodice was overlaid with appliquéd nineteenth-century Irish lace roses, thistles, daffodils and shamrocks on a background of ivory silk netting. Reported in *The Daily Telegraph* on the morning of the wedding, Burton said, 'It has been the experience of a lifetime to work with Catherine Middleton, to create her wedding dress, and I have enjoyed every minute of it.' The paper went on to describe the dress, which was inspired by those worn by Princess Margaret and Grace Kelly, as 'a very sensitive and fitting homage to Diana', who had an 'instant rapport' with Grace, her style icon. It had a 'sumptuous simplicity perfectly suited to the sweet and serene style of the woman ... destined to be the future Queen of England.'[2] The bride wore her long dark hair in loose curls, with her veil held in place by a diamond tiara lent to her by the Queen. Her wedding ring was made from Welsh gold, continuing the tradition established by William's great-grandmother Elizabeth in 1923.

Catherine's bouquet was heavy in symbolism. Designed by Shane Connolly, it featured lily of the valley, meaning the 'return of happiness', hyacinth for constancy, ivy for fidelity and friendship, myrtle for marriage and sweet william for gallantry and its obvious personal significance. The myrtle leaves were taken from a shrub planted at Osborne House in 1845 by Queen Victoria, which had also contributed to the bouquet of Queen Elizabeth in 1947. The couple chose their brother and sister to fill the roles of best man and maid of honour. Dressed in his military uniform, Prince Harry kept the wedding rings safe inside special pockets that had been added for the occasion, while Pippa Middleton attracted admiration in her Sarah Burton ivory satin-based crêpe dress with a cowl front. The bridesmaids wore full, long ballerina skirts decorated with English Cluny lace and shoes with crystal buckles. The wedding cake comprised eight tiers adorned with 900 sugar paste flowers. After the ceremony, back at Buckingham Palace, the couple appeared on the balcony for the traditional kiss.

The day was designated a bank holiday. It was a Friday, the second most popular day of the week to be married, with statistics from 1994 showing that 14 per cent of people were wed on that day as opposed to 68 per cent on a Saturday.[3] Thousands of street parties were held across Britain. Magazines featured glossy photographs of the courtship alongside the bride and groom's family pedigrees and the outline of the big day. Millions of items of merchandise were produced, with William and Catherine personally approving a range of ceramics. Pill boxes, biscuit tins, badges, dolls, coins, postage stamps and cardboard masks went on sale, and although Buckingham Palace refused to sanction the production of cushions and t-shirts, a compromise was reached over the production of tea towels.

Rumours about a royal pregnancy began at once. In fact, one online parenting site, *Parentdish*, published an article repeating claims made by an unspecified US magazine that the couple would announce Catherine's condition once they had returned from their honeymoon. Time proved this to be incorrect, with the pair confirming to the British media that they intended to wait at least a year before trying to have a child. According to the *Daily Mail*, one source stated that Catherine had conceived almost as soon as they started trying, soon after their return from a South Pacific tour, in the autumn of 2012. Their sources claimed she was not 'actively trying for a baby during the two-week trip due to the anti-malaria medication that she was taking, drugs that she would needed for a further week after returning home on 20 September'. She conceived in October, soon after finishing this course of pills.

As with many couples, William and Catherine had intended to keep this news secret until the confirmation of the baby's health in the twelve week scan. Not even their families had been informed. However, it soon became apparent that the duchess's morning sickness was so severe as to warrant hospital treatment, so the pregnancy was announced early in December, midway through Catherine's first trimester. She had fallen ill early in the month, with vomiting and nausea leading to severe dehydration, and was admitted to the King Edward VII Hospital in Marylebone. Doctors diagnosed her with hyperemesis gravidarum, an acute form of pregnancy-related sickness, and required her to remain there for three days. It was during her stay that two Australian radio DJs rang the hospital impersonating members of the royal family and asking to be put through to the duchess's ward. After a flurry of intense media activity, the nurse involved in the case took her own life, to the deep sorrow and regret of her colleagues and the royal family. It was another terrible example of the effects that media pressure can produce on those unused to such attention. While the DJs were roundly condemned, the duke and duchess praised the entire hospital staff for the discretion, care and attention they had received during Catherine's stay.

The new year, 2013, started on a brighter note, with the announcement that the baby was due to arrive in July, but it was not long before the expectant mother was to experience more media intrusion. While holidaying on the Caribbean island of Mustique, photographs of Catherine in her bikini were taken by the Italian magazine *Chi*. The previous year, the same publication had featured images of her sunbathing topless on holiday in France, and, in spite of the editors not seeing 'what all the fuss was about', an injunction successfully prevented the images being used. The duchess then began to prepare herself for the arrival of her 'little grape', reading parental manuals, ensuring she slept well, playing music to her 'bump' and hiring a yoga instructor to teach her at home. She stopped running, which she had previously enjoyed as a means of keeping fit, and just took gentle walks with her dog. However, she did develop a sweet tooth, craving chocolate, biscuits and cake, as reported by one Palace insider.

Early in March, Catherine reputedly let slip the child's gender when accepting a gift offered by a member of the public while visiting Grimsby, leading the betting chain Ladbrokes to offer odds of 1/3 a girl and a 5/2 for a boy. These were slashed in April from 10/1 to 2/1 that the child would be female and be given the name Alexandra. Through the years, the most popular name given to British princesses by birth has been Mary, followed by Louise and then Victoria, with Alexandra appearing as a middle name of Queen Elizabeth.

More online speculation arose regarding the baby's name, with Diana topping polls as the people's favourite, as voted by 29,000 Yahoo readers. George was initially given as the favoured boys' name, though by the end of April this was outstripped by James and Louis. The *Inquisitr* stated with confidence that the future potential queen would be called Elizabeth Diana Carole Mountbatten-Windsor, in honour of the Queen and the two grandmothers; if this was the case, a daughter of William and Catherine, if she ascended the throne, would be crowned Elizabeth III.[4] On the verge of her final trimester, the expectant mother was planning her movements before and after the birth. In keeping with recent royal tradition, she would deliver her child in the Lindo Wing of St Mary's Hospital, Paddington, where William had been born. A new apartment was being prepared for them in Kensington Palace, to be ready in time for the early summer. Then, in late April, the *Daily Mail* reported that asbestos had been uncovered during building works, so an alternative home would need to be found. Unwilling to travel back to their Anglesey home, Kate planned to reject the usual practice of hiring a monthly nurse after the birth of her baby, but was instead planning to move in with her parents for at least six weeks. The headline played on her non-royal background, stating that the 'future monarch [was] to start life in commoner's home in Berkshire'.

As the duchess's due date approached, intense media speculation focused on the importance of this child as a symbol of hope for the modern monarchy and a mark of how the new generation of royals were redefining their roles. The duke and duchess's intentions to raise their baby themselves, as well as their more 'hands-on' and equal approach to the process of pregnancy and birth, struck a chord with many of their contemporaries. From the end of

June, rumours began to flood the internet that the duchess had given birth, but it was not until the fourth week of July 2013 that she was admitted to the Lindo Wing of St Mary's Hospital, Paddington, the same location that Princess Diana had chosen in the 1980s. At 4.24 on the afternoon of the same day, 22 July, following a straight-forward labour, Catherine delivered a baby boy weighing 8 lb 6 oz. William was at her side throughout.

The press were camped out on the pavements outside Buckingham Palace, in anticipation of the traditional method of royal declaration, which would see the announcement posted on an easel on the Palace gates. However, in this age of the internet and mobile phone technology, a more immediate method was required. The news was broken first by press release, followed soon after by the usual golden easel, informing the world that the duchess had been safely delivered of a baby boy. He was named George Alexander Louis. Commemorative coins and other memorabilia were issued, the perfume company Floris created a new scent called 'Cambridge', Westminster Abbey's bells were rung and the soprano Hayley Westenra recorded a version of Paul Mealor's lullaby 'Sleep On'.

The duchess recovered well after the delivery. The following afternoon, she was well enough to leave hospital and return home with her husband and son. The pair emerged to a vast crowd, appearing relaxed and happy, with Catherine dressed in blue and white, holding little George wrapped in a blanket. After posing briefly for photographs, Prince William drove his family home, beginning two weeks of paternity leave. The christening took place that October, in the Victorian chapel at St James' Palace, conducted by the Archbishop of Canterbury. Formal photographs were taken of the Queen, Prince Charles, Prince William and George, to mark the second occasion in which four generations of heirs to the throne were alive.

Prince George was not the first royal baby to arrive in the twenty-first century. He will not be the last. His cousins, Louise and James, the children of Prince Edward and Sophie, Countess of Wessex, had been born in 2003 and 2007 respectively. The Queen's grandson, Peter Philips, son of Princess Anne, had become a father when his wife, Autumn Kelly, gave birth to Savannah in 2010, who was the Queen's first great grandchild. She was followed by a sister, Isla, in 2012, and two years later, Philip's sister, Zara, also gave birth to a daughter named Mia Grace Tindall at the Gloucestershire Royal Hospital. However, George's significance as a future monarch marks a milestone in royal history. He and his royal peers, including his anticipated royal sibling, due to arrive in April 2015, will define a new era of monarchy.

Notes

1 Matilda, 1102

1. Hilton, Lisa, *Queens Consort: England's Medieval Queens* (Phoenix, 2008).
2. Green, Judith A., *Henry I: King of England and Duke of Normandy* (Cambridge University Press, 2009).
3. Farrer, W. (ed.), 'An Outline Itinerary of Henry I', *English History Review*, 34 (Oxford: F. Hall, 1920).
4. Blois, Peter of, *Ingulf's Chronicle of the Abbey of Croyland*.
5. McGurk, P. (ed.), *The Chronicle of John of Worcester: The Annals from 1067–1140* (Oxford University Press, 1998).
6. Green.
7. Farrar.
8. Lawrence-Mathers, Anne, *The True History of Merlin the Magician* (Yale University Press, 2012).
9. Huneycutt, Lois L., *Matilda of Scotland: A Study in Medieval Queenship* (Boydell Press, 2003).
10. Green, Monica Helen, *The Trotula: An English Translation of the Compendium of Women's Medicine* (University of Pennsylvania Press, 2002).
11. Name given by its nineteenth-century editor, based on the Anglo-Saxon word for 'remedies'.
12. Rohde, Eleanour Sinclair, *The Old English Herbals* (Longmans, Green & Co., 1922) [Project Gutenberg: http://www.gutenberg.org/files/33654/33654-h/33654-h.htm].
13. Cockayne, Oswald (ed.), *Leechdoms, wortcunning, and starcraft of early England : being a collection of documents ... illustrating the*

history of science in this country before the Norman conquest, Vol. 2 (HMSO, 1866).

14. Skemer, Don C., *Binding Words: Textual Amulets in the Middle Ages* (Pennsylvania State University, 2006).
15. Lawrence-Mathers.
16. Abernethy, Susan, *Matilda of Scotland, Queen of England* (2013) [Medievalists.net].
17. *Chronicle of Henry of Huntingdon* (Britannica).

2   William, 1153

1. Weir, Alison, *Eleanor of Aquitaine, by the Wrath of God, Queen of England* (Random House, 2011).
2. Hall, Hubert, *Court Life Under the Plantagenets* (Macmillan, 1890).
3. Green.
4. *Ibid.*
5. *Ibid.*
6. *Ibid.*
7. *Ibid.*
8. *Ibid.*
9. Fishwick, Duncan, 'An Early Christian Cryptogram?', *CCHA*, 26 (1959), pp. 29–41.
10. Turner, Ralph V., *Eleanor of Aquitaine: Queen of France, Queen of England* (Yale University Press, 2009).
11. Thorley, Virginia, 'Mothers' Experiences of Sharing Breastfeeding or Breastmilk, Part II', *Nursing Reports*, 2 (1), (2012).
12. Henry of Huntingdon.
13. *Ibid.*
14. Hall.
15. Ditchfield, P. H. and W. Page, 'Windsor Castle: History', *A History of the County of Berkshire*, 3 (1923).

3   Eleanor, 1215

1. Lancelott, Francis, *The Queens of England and their Times* (New York: D. Appleton & Co., 1858).
2. Church, S. D., *King John: New Interpretations* (Boydell & Brewer, 1999).
3. Rohde.
4. Coulton, G. G., *Social Life in Britain from the Conquest to the Reformation* (Cambridge University Press, 1918).
5. BL MS Royal 14 C VII.

4 Edward, 1284

1. Nichols, John Gough, *London Pageants* (J. B. Nichols, 1831).
2. O'Boyle, Cornelius, *The Art of Medicine: Medical Teaching at the University of Paris 1250–1400* (Brill, 1998).
3. Lemay, Helen Rodnite, *Women's Secrets: A Translation of Pseudo-Albertus Magnus's* De Secretis Mulierum (State University of New York Press, 1992).
4. *Ibid.*
5. *Ibid.*
6. Lyte, Maxwell (ed.), H. C. *Calendar of the Charter Rolls of Henry III and Edward I. 1257–1300* (1906).
7. Warner, Katheryn, 'Caernarfon Castle and the Birth of Edward II' (2009) [http://edwardthesecond.blogspot.co.uk/2009/10/caernarfon-castle-and-birth-of-edward.html].
8. *Ibid.*
9. Tout, T. F., *Edward the First* (Macmillan & Co., 1920).
10. Warner.
11. *Ibid.*
12. Peele, George, *The Famous Chronicle of Edward I* (1593).

5 Edward, 1330

1. http://www.canterbury-archaeology.org.uk/#/bp tomb/4567153894.
2. Ormrod, W. Mark, *Edward III* (Yale University Press, 2012).
3. Mortimer, Ian, *The Perfect King: The Life of Edward III, Father of the English Nation* (Vintage, 2008).
4. Ormrod.
5. BNF Fr. 187, fol. 14V.
6. BNF Fr. Latin 18014, fol. 32V.
7. http://mentalfloss.com/article/31877/12-terrible-pieces-advice-pregnant-women.
8. Rohde.
9. BNF Fr. 241, fol. 98.
10. British Library Royal 6 E VI, fol. 296.

6 Henry, 1386

1. Chaucer, G., *The Canterbury Tales* (*c.* 1386).
2. Thornbury, Walter, *Old and New London, Volume 3* (1878).

3. Froissart, Jean, *Chronicles* (ed. Geoffrey Brereton) (Penguin 1978).
4. Brown, Petrina, *Eve: Sex, Childbirth and Marriage Through the Ages* (Summersdale, 2004).
5. Mortimer, Ian, *The Time Traveller's Guide to Medieval England* (Vintage, 2009).
6. Kunz, George Frederick, *Magic of Jewels and Charms 1915* (Kessinger Publishing, 2003).
7. *Ibid.*
8. Maitre, François, *Birth of Esau and Jacob* (*c.* 1475–80). Miniature at the Museum Meermanno Westreenianum, The Hague, from Augustine's *La Cité de Dieu* books I–X.

7 Edward, 1453

1. Erasmus, Desiderius, *Pilgrimages to St Mary of Walsingham and St Thomas of Canterbury* (1512).
2. *Ibid.*
3. Licence, Amy, *In Bed with the Tudors* (Amberley, 2012).
4. Kendall, P., *Richard III* (Norton & Co., 2002).
5. *Ibid.*
6. Gristwood, Sarah, *Blood Sisters: The Women Behind the Wars of the Roses* (Harper Collins, 2013).
7. Licence.
8. Gristwood.
9. Licence.
10. Ditchfield, P. H. and W. Page, 'Windsor Castle: History', *A History of the County of Berkshire*, 3 (1923).

8 Edward, 1470

1. Falkus, Gila, *The Life and Times of Edward IV* (Weidenfeld & Nicolson, 1981).
2. More, T., *The History of King Richard III* (ed. J. Rawson Lumby) (Cambridge University Press, 1883).
3. Mancini, *The Occupation of the Throne by Richard III* (1483).
4. Loades, D. M., *The Tudor Queens of England* (Continuum International Publishing Group, 2009).
5. More.
6. Mancini.
7. Cited in Loades.
8. Ellis, Henry (ed.), *Three Books of Polydore Vergil's English History,*

comprising the reigns of Henry VI, Edward IV and Richard III (Camden Society, 1844).

9. *Ibid.*
10. Holinshed, Raphael, *Chronicles of England, Scotland and Ireland* (London: J. Johnson, 1807).
11. Anon., *Celsus De Medicina* (Heinemann, 1935).
12. *A Collection of Ordinances and Regulations for the Governance of the Royal Household, made in divers reigns from King Edward III to King William and Queen Mary* (London: Society of Antiquities, 1790).
13. *Ibid.*
14. Bruce, J. (ed.), *Historie of the Arrivall of Edward IV in England and Finall Recouerye of his Kingdomes from Henry VI* (Nichols, B., 1838).
15. Metlinger, Bartholomeus, *Children's Book* (1473).

9 Arthur, 1486

1. Hall, Edward, *Hall's Chronicle* (London: J. Johnson, 1809).
2. Simpson, Jacqueline and Steve Roud, *A Dictionary of English Folklore* (Oxford, 2000).
3. Doubleday, H. A. and W. Page (eds), 'St Swithin's Priory, Winchester', *Victoria County History: Hampshire* (1973).
4. *A Collection of Ordinances and Regulations for the Governance of the Royal Household, made in divers reigns from King Edward III to King William and Queen Mary* (London: Society of Antiquities, 1790).
5. Licence.
6. Gunn, Stephen and Linda Monckton, *Arthur Tudor, Prince of Wales: Life, Death and Commemoration* (Boydell Press, 2009).

10 Henry, 1511

1. Fraser, Antonia, *The Six Wives of Henry VIII* (Phoenix, 1992).
2. Withington, Robert, *English Pageantry: An Historical Outline* (Cambridge: Harvard University Press, 1918).
3. Rosslin, Eucharius, *Rose Garden for Pregnant Women and Midwives* (1513).
4. *Ibid.*
5. Fraser.
6. SLP Henry VIII Jan 1510.
7. Fraser.
8. *Ibid.*

9. *Ibid.*
10. Hall.

11 Elizabeth, 1533

1. Zupanec, Sylwia S., *The Daring Truth About Anne Boleyn* (Create Space, 2012).
2. Norton, Elizabeth, *Anne Boleyn in her Own Words and the Words of Those Who Knew Her* (Amberley, 2011).
3. *Ibid.*
4. *Ibid.*
5. *Ibid.*
6. For more on pregnancy customs see Licence, Amy, *In Bed With the Tudors* (Amberley, 2012).
7. Norton.
8. *Ibid.*
9. *Ibid.*
10. *Ibid.*
11. Brown.
12. *Ibid.*
13. Fraser.
14. Licence.
15. *Ibid.*
16. Clifford, Henry, *The Life of Jane Dormer, Duchess of Feria* (Burns & Oates, 1887).
17. Norton.

12 Edward, 1537

1. Chalmers, C. R. and E. J. Chaloner, '500 Years Later: Henry VIII, Leg Ulcers and the Course of History', *Journal of the Royal Society of Medicine*, 102 (2009) pp. 513–7.
2. Licence.
3. SLP Henry VIII July 1536.
4. SLP Henry VIII October 1538.
5. SLP Henry VIII April 1537.
6. *Ibid.*
7. Licence.
8. *Ibid.*
9. Skidmore, Chris, *Edward VI: Lost King of England* (Phoenix, 2008).
10. Licence.

11. Weir, Alison, *Henry VIII: King and Court* (Random House, 2011).
12. *Ibid.*
13. *Ibid.*
14. Pruhlen, Sunje, 'What was the Best for an Infant from the Middle Ages to Early Modern Times in Europe? The Discussion Concerning Wet Nurses' (Helmut Schmidt University, Hamburg: unpub.).
15. Weir.

13 James, 1566

1. Strickland, Agnes, *Letters of Mary Queen of Scots* (H. Colburn, 1845).
2. Harris, William, *An Historical and Critical Account of the Life and Writings of James I, King of Great Britain* (James Waugh, 1753).
3. Knox, John, *The First Blast of the Trumpet Against the Monstrous Regiment of Women* (1558).
4. Strickland.
5. *Ibid.*
6. Fraser, Antonia, *Mary, Queen of Scots* (Weidenfeld & Nicolson, 1969).
7. 'From Piss-Prophets to Rabbits; A History of the Pregnancy Test (Random History, 2007) [http://www.randomhistory.com/1-50/018pregnancy.html].
8. Fraser.
9. *Ibid.*
10. Cassidy, Tina, *Birth, A History* (Chatto & Windus, 2006).
11. Fraser.
12. *Ibid.*
13. *Ibid.*
14. *Ibid.*

14 Henry, 1594

1. Scott, George (ed.), *The Memoirs of Sir James of Melvil of Hal-Hill* (1683).
2. Bruce, John (ed.), *Letters of Queen Elizabeth and King James VI of Scotland* (Camden Society, 1849).
3. Harris.
4. Daybell, James, *Women and Politics in Early Modern England 1450–1700* (Ashgate Publishing Ltd, 2004).
5. Willughby, Percivall, *Observations in Midwifery* (Warwick: H. T. Cooke & Son, 1873).

Notes

6. Cassidy.
7. ancestry.com.
8. Harris.
9. *A Collection of Ordinances and Regulations for the Governance of the Royal Household, made in divers reigns from King Edward III to King William and Queen Mary* (London: Society of Antiquities, 1790).
10. Harris.
11. D'Ewes, Simmonds, *The Autobiography and Correspondence of Simmonds d'Ewes.*
12. *Ibid.*

15 Henrietta, 1644

1. Marshall, Rosalind K., *Henrietta Maria: The Intrepid Queen* (1991).
2. SLP Charles I June 1625.
3. *Ibid.*
4. *Ibid.*
5. Marshall.
6. SLP June 1625.
7. Marshall.
8. Brown.
9. *Munk's Roll*, 1878, p. 165.
10. Marshall.
11. Markham, Gervase, *The English Hus-Wife* (1615).
12. Culpeper, Nicholas, *The English Physician* (1652).
13. Maubray, John, *The Female Physician* (London: James Holland, 1724).
14. Marshall.
15. *Ibid.*
16. Simpson, Jacqueline and Steve Roud, *A Dictionary of English Folklore* (Oxford, 2000).
17. Marshall.
18. Sharp.

16 James, 1688

1. Sharp, Jane, *The Midwives' Book or, the Whole art of Midwifry Discovered* (1671, reprinted Oxford University Press, 1999).
2. Haile, Martin, *Queen Mary of Modena: Her Life and Letters* (Dent, 1905).

237

3. *Ibid.*
4. *Ibid.*
5. Dalrymple, John, *Memoirs of Great Britain and Ireland, Volume II* (Strachan & Caddell, 1773).
6. Haile.
7. Known as the 'warming pan bed', this is usually kept at Kensington Palace.
8. Haile.
9. 'America and West Indies: June 1688', Calendar of State Papers Colonial, America and West Indies, Volume 12: 1685–1688.
10. Speck, William Arthur, *James II* (2002).
11. EBBA 20865 Pepys 2.251.
12. EBBA 22371 Pepys 5.109.
13. EBBA 22394 Pepys 5.128.
14. Haile.
15. *Ibid.*
16. *Ibid.*
17. Cassidy, Tina, *Birth, A History* (Chatto & Windus, 2006).
18. Haile.

17   George, 1738

1. Huish, Robert, *The Public and Private Life of His Late Excellent and Gracious Majesty George the Third* (London: Thomas Kelly, 1821).
2. Baker, Kenneth, *George III: A Life in Caricature* (Thames & Hudson, 2007).
3. Maubray, John, *The Female Physician* (London: James Holland, 1724).
4. *Ibid.*
5. http://eclipse.gsfc.nasa.gov/phase/phases1701.html.
6. Maubray.
7. Jeffries, F., *The Gentleman's Magazine* (London, 1732).
8. Nihill, Elizabeth, *A Treatise on the Art of Midwifery* (1709).
9. Jeffries, F., *The Gentleman's Magazine* (London, 1732).
10. *The Lady's Decoy: Or, the Man-Midwife's Defence: Occasion'd by the Revival of a Bill of Indictment Against the Famous Doctor D—* (London 1738).
11. Brown.
12. Maubray.

18 Amelia, 1783

1. Trager, James, *The New York Chronology* (Harper Collins, 2003).
2. Monod, Paul Kleber, *Imperial Island: A History of Britain and its Empire 1660–1837* (Wiley Blackwell, 2009).
3. http://www.tea.co.uk/page.php?id=98.
4. Churchill, F., *Manual for Midwives and Monthly Nurses* (Dublin: Fannin & Co., 1867).
5. Masset, Claire, *Tea and Tea Drinking* (Shire Album 2010).
6. Bland, R., *Some Calculations of the Number of Accidents or Deaths Which Happen in Consequence of Parturition; And the Proportion of Male to Female Children, as well as the Number of Twins, Monstrous Productions and Children That are Dead-Born, Taken from the Midwifery Reports of the Westminster General Infirmary...* (Royal Society of London, 1871).
7. *Ibid.*
8. Maubray.
9. White.
10. Maubray.
11. Bland.
12. Stephen, Margaret, *The Domestic Midwife, or The Best Means of Preventing Danger in Childbirth, Considered.* (Piccadilly: S. W. Fowes, 1795).
13. Maubray.
14. Huish.
15. Scott, Honoria, *Sketch of the Life and Character of her Royal Highness, the Princess Amelia* (D. N. Shury, 1810).

19 George, 1817

1. Packard.
2. Coote, J., *A Biographical Memoir of the Public and Private Life of the Princess Charlotte Augusta, Princess of Great Britain* (1817).
3. Packard.
4. Coote.
5. Behrendt, Stephen C., 'Mourning, Myth and Merchandising: The Public Death of Princess Charlotte' in Riegel, Christian, *Response to Death: The Literary Work of Mourning* (University of Alberta, 2005).
6. Coote.
7. Nihill.

8. Van Blarcom, Caroline Conant, *The Midwife in England, Being a Study in England of the Working of the English Midwives Act of 1902* (New York, 1913).
9. *Ibid.*
10. Brown, Z. J., *The Lady's Own Book* (Marshall, 1847).
11. Coote.
12. Brown.
13. Coote.
14. *Ibid.*
15. Maubray.
16. *Ibid.*
17. Plowden, Alison, *Caroline and Charlotte: The Regent's Wife and Daughter* (Sidgwick and Jackson, 1989).
18. Coote.
19. Hamilton, Lady Anne, *Secret History of the Court of England, From the Accession of George III to the Death of George IV* (London: Stevenson, 1832).
20. *Ibid.*
21. Behrendt.
22. *Ibid.*
23. Coote.
24. Behrendt.
25. Coote.
26. Chamberlain, Geoffrey, 'British Maternal Mortality in the C19th and C20th', *Journal of the Royal Society of Medicine*, 99 (11) (November 2006), pp. 559–63.
27. *Ibid.*
28. *Ibid.*
29. http://www.papapetros.com.au/History_Childbirth.pdf.
30. Coote.
31. *Ibid.*
32. *Ibid.*
33. *Ibid.*

20 Victoria, 1840

1. www.victoriana.com.
2. *Ibid.*
3. *Ibid.*
4. *Ibid.*
5. Packard, Jerrold M., *Victoria's Daughters* (Sutton, 1998).
6. Brown.

7. Chavasse, Dr Pye Henry, *Advice to a Mother on the Management of her Offspring* (John Churchill, 1861).
8. Brown.
9. www.victoriana.com.
10. *The Daily Beast*, 13 January 2010.
11. Brown.
12. Meigs, Charles D., *Females and their Diseases* (1848).
13. Flanders, Judith, *The Victorian House* (Harper Collins, 2003).
14. www.victoriana.com.
15. *Ibid.*
16. Panton, Mrs Jane Ellen, *From Kitchen to Garret: Hints for Young Householders* (Ward & Downey, 1888).
17. Rappaport, Helen, *Magnificent Obsession* (Windmill Books, 2012).
18. Gristwood.
19. *Ibid.*
20. Packard.
21. Flanders.
22. *Ibid.*
23. Brown.
24. www.victoriana.com.
25. Flanders.
26. Brown.
27. Flanders.
28. *Ibid.*
29. Packard.

21 Edward, 1894

1. Van Blarcom, Caroline Conant, *The Midwife in England, Being a Study in England of the Working of the English Midwives Act of 1902* (New York, 1913).
2. Jackson, Lesley, *Twentieth-Century Pattern Design* (Princeton University Press, 2007).
3. *The Times* online archive.
4. *Ibid.*
5. *Philadelphia Evening Telegraph*, 9 July 1893.
6. *Ibid.*
7. Panton.
8. Flanders, Judith, *The Victorian House* (Harper Collins, 2003).
9. Summers, Leigh, *Bound to Please: A History of the Victorian Corset* (Berg, 2001).
10. Ziegler, Philip, *King Edward VIII* (Harper Collins, 2012).

22 Albert, 1895

1. Williams, Tony and Humphrey Price, *Uncle Jack* (Orion, 2005).
2. *Ibid.*
3. *The Times* online archive.
4. Ziegler.
5. *Ibid.*
6. Judd, Denis, *George VI* (I. B. Tauris, 2012).
7. Bolitho, Hector, *George VI* (New York: J. B. Lippincott Company, 1938).

23 Elizabeth, 1926

1. Taylor, D. J., *Bright Young Things: The Rise and Fall of a Generation 1918–1940* (Vintage, 2008).
2. Economist Lee Ohanain.
3. *Toledo Blade*, 25 May 1953.
4. Judd.
5. *Ibid.*
6. *Ibid.*
7. *Ibid.*
8. Binney, Ruth, *Amazing and Extraordinary Facts: Royal Family Life* (David & Charles, 2012).
9. http://www.papapetros.com.au/History_Childbirth.pdf.
10. *Ibid.*
11. Chamberlain, Geoffrey, 'British Maternal Mortality in the C19th and C20th', *Journal of the Royal Society of Medicine*, 99 (11) (November 2006), pp. 559–63.
12. Judd.
13. Bousfield, Arthur and Garry Toffoli, *Fifty Years the Queen: A Tribute to Her Majesty Queen Elizabeth II on her Golden Jubilee* (Dundern, 2002).

24 William, 1982

1. Binney, Ruth, *Amazing and Extraordinary Facts: Royal Family Life* (David & Charles, 2012).
2. www.dianaforever.com.
3. Binney.
4. www.dianaforever.com.
5. *The Times* online archive, December 1981.

6. Graham, Tim and Peter Archer, *William: HRH Prince William of Wales* (Simon and Schuster, 2012).
7. www.dianaforever.com.
8. http://news.bbc.co.uk/onthisday/hi/dates/stories/june/21/newsid_2518000/2518435.stm.
9. Graham and Archer.
10. *Ibid.*
11. *The Times*, 9 November 1982.

25 Prince George of Cambridge, 2013

1. Sarah Sands, *Daily Mail*, 2006.
2. *The Daily Telegraph*, 29 April 2011.
3. Simpson, Jacqueline and Steve Roud, *A Dictionary of English Folklore* (Oxford, 2000).
4. http://www.inquisitr.com/572176/prince-william-and-kate-middletons-daughter-gets-a-name/#GtUs8GWEkBi6Y8zK.99.

Bibliography

Primary Sources

Anon., *Celsus De Medicina* (1475, reprinted Heinemann, 1935).

Bland, R., *Some Calculations of the Number of Accidents or Deaths Which Happen in Consequence of Parturition; And the Proportion of Male to Female Children, as well as the Number of Twins, Monstrous Productions and Children That are Dead-Born, Taken from the Midwifery Reports of the Westminster General Infirmary...* (Royal Society of London, 1871).

Blois, Peter of, *Ingulf's Chronicle of the Abbey of Croyland.*

A Collection of Ordinances and Regulations for the Governance of the Royal Household, made in divers reigns from King Edward III to King William and Queen Mary (London: Society of Antiquities, 1790).

Brown, Z. J., *The Lady's Own Book* (Marshall, 1847).

Bruce, J. (ed.), *Historie of the Arrivall of Edward IV in England and Finall Recouerye of his Kingdomes from Henry VI* (Nichols, B., 1838).

Bruce, John (ed.), *Letters of Queen Elizabeth and King James VI of Scotland* (Camden Society, 1849).

Chavasse, Dr Pye Henry, *Advice to a Mother on the Management of her Offspring* (John Churchill, 1861).

Chronicle of Henry of Huntingdon (Britannica).

Churchill, F., *Manual for Midwives and Monthly Nurses* (Dublin: Fannin & Co., 1867).

Cockayne, Oswald (ed.), *Leechdoms, wortcunning, and starcraft of early England : being a collection of documents ... illustrating the history of science in this country before the Norman conquest, Vol. 2* (HMSO, 1866).

Coote, J., *A Biographical Memoir of the Public and Private Life of the Princess Charlotte Augusta, Princess of Great Britain* (1817).

Culpeper, Nicholas, *The English Physician* (1652).

Ditchfield, P. H. and W. Page, 'Windsor Castle: History', *A History of the County of Berkshire*, 3 (1923).

Ellis, Henry (ed.), *Three Books of Polydore Vergil's English History, comprising the reigns of Henry VI, Edward IV and Richard III* (Camden Society, 1844).

Erasmus, Desiderius, *Pilgrimages to St Mary of Walsingham and St Thomas of Canterbury* (1512).

Farrer, W. (ed.), 'An Outline Itinerary of Henry I', *English History Review*, 34 (Oxford: F. Hall, 1920).

Froissart, Jean, *Chronicles* (ed. Geoffrey Brereton) (Penguin 1978).

Haile, Martin, *Queen Mary of Modena: Her Life and Letters* (Dent, 1905).

Hall, Edward, *Hall's Chronicle* (London: J. Johnson, 1809).

Hamilton, Lady Anne, *Secret History of the Court of England, From the Accession of George III to the Death of George IV* (London: Stevenson, 1832).

Holinshed, Raphael, *Chronicles of England, Scotland and Ireland* (London: J. Johnson, 1807).

Jeffries, F., *The Gentleman's Magazine*, Vol. 2(London, 1732).

Knox, John, *The First Blast of the Trumpet Against the Monstrous Regiment of Women* (1558).

Lyte, Maxwell (ed.), H. C. *Calendar of the Charter Rolls of Henry III and Edward I. 1257–1300* (1906).

McGurk, P. (ed.), *The Chronicle of John of Worcester: The Annals from 1067–1140* (Oxford University Press, 1998).

Mancini, *The Occupation of the Throne by Richard III* (1483).

Markham, Gervase, *The English Hus-Wife* (1615).

Maubray, John, *The Female Physician* (London: James Holland, 1724).

Meigs, Charles D., *Females and their Diseases* (1848).

More, T., *The History of King Richard III* (ed. J. Rawson Lumby) (Cambridge University Press, 1883).

Nihill, Elizabeth, *A Treatise on the Art of Midwifery* (London, 1709).

Panton, Mrs Jane Ellen, *From Kitchen to Garret: Hints for Young Householders* (Ward & Downey, 1888).

Rosslin, Eucharius, *Rose Garden for Pregnant Women and Midwives* (1513).

Scott, George (ed.), *The Memoirs of Sir James of Melvil of Hal-Hill* (1683).

Scott, Honoria, *Sketch of the Life and Character of her Royal Highness, the Princess Amelia* (D. N. Shury, 1810).

Sharp, Jane, *The Midwives' Book or, the Whole art of Midwifry Discovered* (1671, reprinted Oxford University Press, 1999).

Stephen, Margaret, *The Domestic Midwife, or The Best Means of Preventing Danger in Childbirth, Considered* (Piccadilly: S. W. Fowes, 1795).

Strickland, Agnes, *Letters of Mary Queen of Scots* (H. Colburn, 1845).

The Times online archives.

Van Blarcom, Caroline Conant, *The Midwife in England, Being a Study in England of the Working of the English Midwives Act of 1902* (New York, 1913).

William of Malmesbury, *Gesta Pontificum Anglorum* (trans. David Preest) (Boydell Press, 2002).

Willughby, Percivall, *Observations in Midwifery* (Warwick: H. T. Cooke & Son, 1873).

Other Sources

Abernethy, Susan, *Matilda of Scotland, Queen of England* (2013) [Medievalists.net].

Baker, Kenneth, *George III: A Life in Caricature* (Thames and Hudson, 2007).

Behrendt, Stephen C., 'Mourning, Myth and Merchandising: The Public Death of Princess Charlotte' in Riegel, Christian, *Response to Death: The Literary Work of Mourning* (University of Alberta, 2005).

Binney, Ruth, *Amazing and Extraordinary Facts: Royal Family Life* (David & Charles, 2012).

Bolitho, Hector, *George VI* (New York: J. B. Lippincott Company, 1938).

Bousfield, Arthur and Garry Toffoli, *Fifty Years the Queen: A Tribute to Her Majesty Queen Elizabeth II on her Golden Jubilee* (Dundern, 2002).

Brown, Petrina, *Eve: Sex, Childbirth and Marriage Through the Ages* (Summersdale, 2004).

Cassidy, Tina, *Birth, A History* (Chatto & Windus, 2006).

Castor, Helen, *She-Wolves: The Women Who Ruled England before Elizabeth* (Faber & Faber 2010).

Chalmers, C. R. and E. J. Chaloner, '500 Years Later: Henry VIII, Leg Ulcers and the Course of History', *Journal of the Royal Society of Medicine*, 102 (2009) pp. 513–7.

Chamberlain, Geoffrey, 'British Maternal Mortality in the C19th and C20th', *Journal of the Royal Society of Medicine*, 99 (11) (November 2006), pp. 559–63.

Church, S. D., *King John: New Interpretations* (Boydell & Brewer, 1999).

Clifford, Henry, *The Life of Jane Dormer, Duchess of Feria* (Burns & Oates, 1887).

Coulton, G. G., *Social Life in Britain from the Conquest to the Reformation* (Cambridge University Press, 1918).

Dalrymple, John, *Memoirs of Great Britain and Ireland, Volume II* (Strachan & Caddell, 1773).

Daybell, James, *Women and Politics in Early Modern England 1450–1700* (Ashgate Publishing Ltd, 2004).

Falkus, Gila, *The Life and Times of Edward IV* (Weidenfeld & Nicolson, 1981).

Fishwick, Duncan, 'An Early Christian Cryptogram?', *CCHA*, 26 (1959), pp. 29–41.

Flanders, Judith, *The Victorian House* (Harper Collins, 2003).

Fraser, Antonia, *Mary: Queen of Scots* (Weidenfeld & Nicolson, 1969).

Fraser, Antonia, *The Six Wives of Henry VIII* (Phoenix, 1992).

Graham, Tim and Peter Archer, *William: HRH Prince William of Wales* (Simon & Schuster, 2012).

Green, Judith A., *Henry I: King of England and Duke of Normandy* (Cambridge University Press, 2009).

Green, Monica Helen, *The Trotula: An English Translation of the Compendium of Women's Medicine* (University of Pennsylvania Press, 2002).

Gristwood, Sarah, *Blood Sisters: The Women Behind the Wars of the Roses* (Harper Collins, 2013).

Gristwood, Sarah, *Recording Angels: The Secret World of Women's Diaries* (Harrap, 1998).

Gunn, Stephen and Linda Monckton, *Arthur Tudor, Prince of Wales: Life, Death and Commemoration* (Boydell Press, 2009).

Hall, Hubert, *Court Life Under the Plantagenets* (Macmillan, 1890).

Harris, William, *An Historical and Critical Account of the Life and Writings of James I, King of Great Britain* (James Waugh, 1753).

Hilton, Lisa, *Queens Consort: England's Medieval Queens* (Phoenix, 2008).

Huish, Robert, *The Public and Private Life of His Late Excellent and Gracious Majesty George the Third* (London: Thomas Kelly, 1821).

Huneycutt, Lois L., *Matilda of Scotland: A Study in Medieval Queenship* (Boydell Press, 2003).

Jackson, Lesley, *Twentieth-Century Pattern Design* (Princeton University Press, 2007).

Judd, Denis, *George VI* (I. B. Tauris, 2012).

Kendall, P., *Richard III* (Norton & Co., 2002).

Kunz, George Frederick, *Magic of Jewels and Charms 1915* (Kessinger Publishing, 2003).

Lancelott, Francis, *The Queens of England and their Times* (New York: D. Appleton & Co., 1858).

Lawrence-Mathers, Anne, *The True History of Merlin the Magician* (Yale University Press, 2012).

Lemay, Helen Rodnite, *Women's Secrets: A Translation of Pseudo-Albertus Magnus's* De Secretis Mulierum (State University of New York Press, 1992).

Licence, Amy, *Elizabeth of York: The Forgotten Tudor Queen* (Amberley, 2013).

Licence, Amy, *In Bed with the Tudors* (Amberley, 2012).

Loades, D. M., *The Tudor Queens of England* (Continuum International Publishing Group, 2009).

Mahood, Linda, *The Magdalenes: Prostitution in the Nineteenth Century* (Taylor & Francis, 1990).

Masset, Claire, *Tea and Tea Drinking* (Shire Album, 2010).

Monod, Paul Kleber, *Imperial Island: A History of Britain and its Empire 1660–1837* (Wiley Blackwell, 2009).

Mortimer, Ian, *The Perfect King: The Life of Edward III, Father of the English Nation* (Vintage 2008).

Mortimer, Ian, *The Time Traveller's Guide to Medieval England* (Vintage 2009).

Nichols, John Gough, *London Pageants* (J. B. Nichols, 1831).

Norton, Elizabeth, *Anne Boleyn in her Own Words and the Words of Those Who Knew Her* (Amberley, 2011).

O'Boyle, Cornelius, *The Art of Medicine: Medical Teaching at the University of Paris 1250–1400* (Brill, 1998).

Ormrod, W. Mark, *Edward III* (Yale University Press, 2012).

Packard, Jerrold M., *Victoria's Daughters* (Sutton, 1998).

Peele, George, *The Famous Chronicle of Edward I* (1593).

Plowden, Alison, *Caroline and Charlotte: The Regent's Wife and Daughter* (Sidgwick & Jackson, 1989).

Pruhlen, Sunje, 'What was the Best for an Infant from the Middle Ages to Early Modern Times in Europe? The Discussion Concerning Wet Nurses' (Helmut Schmidt University, Hamburg: unpub.).

Rappaport, Helen, *Magnificent Obsession* (Windmill Books, 2012).

Rohde, Eleanour Sinclair, *The Old English Herbals* (Longmans, Green & Co., 1922) [Project Gutenberg: http://www.gutenberg.org/files/33654/33654-h/33654-h.htm].

Simpson, Jacqueline and Steve Roud, *A Dictionary of English Folklore* (Oxford, 2000).

Skemer, Don C., *Binding Words: Textual Amulets in the Middle Ages* (Pennsylvania State University, 2006).

Skidmore, Chris, *Edward VI: Lost King of England* (Phoenix, 2008).

Summers, Leigh, *Bound to Please: A History of the Victorian Corset* (Berg, 2001).

Taylor, D. J., *Bright Young Things: The Rise and Fall of a Generation 1918–1940* (Vintage, 2008).

Thorley, Virginia, 'Mothers' Experiences of Sharing Breastfeeding or Breastmilk, Part II', *Nursing Reports*, 2 (1), (2012).

Thornbury, Walter, *Old and New London, Volume 3* (1878).

Tout, T. F., *Edward the First* (Macmillan & Co., 1920).

Trager, James, *The New York Chronology* (Harper Collins, 2003).

Turner, Ralph V., *Eleanor of Aquitaine: Queen of France, Queen of England* (Yale University Press, 2009).

Warner, Katheryn, 'Caernarfon Castle and the Birth of Edward II' (2009) [http://edwardthesecond.blogspot.co.uk/2009/10/caernarfon-castle-and-birth-of-edward.html].

Weir, Alison, *Eleanor of Aquitaine, by the Wrath of God, Queen of England* (Random House, 2011).

Weir, Alison, *Henry VIII: King and Court* (Random House, 2011).

Weir, Alison, *Mary Queen of Scots and the Murder of Lord Darnley* (Vintage, 2008).

Withington, Robert, *English Pageantry: An Historical Outline* (Cambridge: Harvard University Press, 1918).

Ziegler, Philip, *King Edward VIII* (Harper Collins, 2012).

Zupanec, Sylwia S., *The Daring Truth About Anne Boleyn* (Create Space, 2012).

Acknowledgements

Thanks go to the team at Amberley; Jonathan, for suggesting this book and Nicola and the publicity department for their continuing support and promotion. Thanks also to all my family, in particular to Tom for his love and support; also the Hunts, for Sue's generosity and John's local knowledge and continual supply of interesting and unusual books. Most of all, thanks to my mother for her invaluable proofreading skills and to my father for his enthusiasm. This is the result of the books they read me, the museums they took me to as a child and the love and imagination with which they encouraged me.

Index

Also available from Amberley Publishing

The tragic love affair that changed English history forever

'Meticulously researched and a great read' *THEANNEBOLEYNFILES.COM*

Anne Boleyn was the most controversial and scandalous woman ever to sit on the throne of England. From her early days at the imposing Hever Castle in Kent, to the glittering courts of Paris and London, Anne caused a stir wherever she went. Alluring but not beautiful, Anne's wit and poise won her numerous admirers at the English court, and caught the roving eye of King Henry.

Their love affair was as extreme as it was deadly, from Henry's 'mine own sweetheart' to 'cursed and poisoning whore' her fall from grace was total.

£9.99 Paperback
47 illustrations (26 colour)
264 pages
978-1-84868-514-7

Available from all good bookshops or to order direct
Please call **01453-847-800**
www.amberleybooks.com

Also available from Amberley Publishing